off center

barbara grizzuti harrison

PLAYBOY
PAPERBACKS

" 'Write the Truth,' My Son Said. 'Write About Me,' " "Growing Up Apocalyptic," "Consciousness-Raising: Truth and Consequences," "Moral Ambiguity: *The Ambivalence of Abortion* by Linda Bird Francke," "A Troubled Peace: *What the Woman Lived* by Louise Bogan," "Dorothy Sayers: Feminism and Individuality," and "The Profound Hypochondriac" first appeared in *Ms.;* "Oh, How We Worshiped the Gods of the Fifties!", "Dick Cavett: 'You Can Tell I'm Not a Wisecracker, Can't You, Honey?' ", and "est: The Invasion of the Mind-Stealers" in *Viva;* "The Other Hustle: *Breaktime: Living Without Work in a Nine-to-Five World* by Bernard Lefkowitz" and "The Facts of Life and Death: *The View in Winter: Reflections on Old Age* by Ronald Blythe" in *The New York Times Book Review* (© 1979 by The New York Times Company); "The Helanders and the Moonies: A Family Story" in *McCall's;* "Imagination and Ideology: *On Lies, Secrets and Silence* by Adrienne Rich" and " 'Jesus Wept': *Billy Graham: A Parable of the American Righteousness* by Marshall Frady" in *The New Republic;* "Going Home: Brooklyn Revisited" and "The Subject Is Roseland" in *The Village Voice* (Copyright © The Village Voice, Inc., 1974, 1977); "Joan Didion: Only Disconnect" in *The Nation;* and "Jane Fonda: Everywoman with a Difference" in *Ladies' Home Journal.* Titles and text in certain cases have been altered since the original publication.

Lyrics from "The House I Live In" by Lewis Allan & Earl Robinson: Copyright © 1942 by Chappell & Co., Inc. Copyright Renewed. International Copyright Secured. All Rights Reserved. Used by permission.

OFF CENTER

Copyright © 1980 by Barbara Grizzuti Harrison

Published simultaneously in the United States and Canada by Playboy Paperbacks, New York, New York. Printed in the United States of America. Library of Congress Catalog Card Number: 81-80030. Reprinted by arrangement with The Dial Press.

Books are available at quantity discounts for promotional and industrial use. For further information, write to Premium Sales, Playboy Paperbacks, 1633 Broadway, New York, New York 10019.

ISBN: 0-872-16870-0

First Playboy Paperbacks printing June 1981.

off center

"Her clear-eyed gaze is right on center as she examines the ambivalences and confusions of modern America ...Harrison's ability to focus on what's going on in contemporary America and see through pretense makes her essays particularly perceptive, sane and enjoyable."
United Press International

"...a good writer...filled with moral indignation."
The New York Times

"...a straight-shooter, a writer who, with compassion, insight and wit slices through multiple layers of subterfuge and disguise to the heart of matters."
Cleveland Plain Dealer

"**off center** contains a certain sanity and truth.... It is a stunning commentary on life, teaching us to laugh, cry and reflect."
Dallas Morning News

For Joyce

CONTENTS

III. CULTURE HEROES

IV. PANACEAS

V. FINAL THINGS

I.

Self
and
Others

"WRITE THE TRUTH,"
MY SON SAID.
"WRITE ABOUT ME."
(1978)

"A child is a guest in the house," says the Bhagavad-Gita, "to be loved and respected, but never possessed." Like all mystical imperatives, easier said than felt. From the moment my firstborn child reluctantly exited from my womb—leaving me scooped out, tearful, afraid of new mysteries—my propensity has been to clutch, to hold on, not to let go. I remember—it seems another life ago—the first time he wore shoes (his fat little peasant's feet, chunky toes I nibbled at, toes that were like little animals . . . *one little piggy* . . . each a separate personality that I loved). "Soon he'll be dating," I said, "and then he'll be married. And she isn't good enough for him." Josh was nine months old, and I was already steeling myself against his eventual flight, defending myself against the rival that would someday take my place. Silly. And dangerous. A mother's pathology? The inexorable jealousy of the protector? The dark side of the coin of supportive love?

The part of me that wants to be privy to Joshua's revelations, that wishes him to give me free and ready access to his heart, that nudges and prods and heaves martyred sighs when he wraps himself in privacy, is alive and twitchingly well: *But I saw you through malaria and amebic dysentery,* it says; *I held your body, broken on a football field, safe in my arms; my will supported your will through months of hospital horrors till you were whole again; I was always there for you—there when our*

3

family broke up and your daddy moved to another country, there when your friendships fractured, there when the going was rough. You belong to me.

But Josh has never allowed himself to be consumed. He has always gently pushed the self-pitying, harassing blackmailer in me away: "Get out of my head, Mom, please." And again, "Mom, I want you to know that I have a bad problem . . . I want you to know that I have it, but I don't want you to ask what it is, I want to solve it myself." "Please tell," I begged, my mother's heart in my overactive mouth. "No," he said, "it's mine . . . I love you," he added. And that—Josh being stoic and generous Josh—was that. Three weeks later, "Mom, you know that problem I had? It's gone." He'd wanted me to know he was involved in struggle but not to ask what it was he was wrestling with. He asked for a patient love that demands nothing, not even the right to act on the loved one's behalf.

How odd: so much love and joy and ease in our relationship —and I begin with self-flagellation, reproaching myself for needing him to need me. Why? Because guilt is the emotion mothers are on most intimate terms with? That guilt is poison. All the mad, bad mother-speeches come from it. I hate it. Josh hates it too. (The hardest words I could ever hear are, "You are not a good mother." I do not allow anyone else to accuse me of what I ritually accuse myself of.) I said once, in despair —over love, work, the kitty litter, whatever—"I'm not a good mother"; and Josh said balefully, "Oh, stop it. Of course you are." And then he glared at me all day long, till bedtime, when he said, "I've been thinking. You do bad things sometimes. But you're not a bad person. Don't you know the difference?" Everybody (me!) needs somebody who loves her better than she loves herself.

It isn't entirely guilt that makes me question my ability to let Joshua go: he has just turned thirteen. What a mysterious difference that one year creates! From twelve to thirteen seems a quantum leap; it is almost as great as the difference between one and none. He is leaving behind the childhood I will remember more perfectly than he will. He is an explorer, now. STOP/GO: I cannot follow and hold his hand at the crossings.

He enters the thirteenth year of his life continents away. He has been in my care for six years since my divorce; he has now gone to live in India with his father for a year. I feel his absence most strongly at night—the quality of silence is different; it is an empty silence. My inner ear is no longer attuned to his body turning restlessly in his bed; his nightmares no longer color my own. Though sometimes he appears in my dreams—his wide, blue-eyed gaze, his husky voice, his sweet, high laugh. It is his voice I miss the most. Hungry for my children's voices, I called them recently in Bombay, where their father lives with his second wife and their four-year-old son. The transcontinental cable transformed my daughter's exuberant outpourings into a series of nearly incomprehensible squeaks, and my son's monosyllabic responses—he hates the telephone—into hollow echo-chamber crypticisms.

I was reduced, in my loneliness, to playing an old tape cassette that the children, pretending to be TV announcers, made one rainy afternoon. Ten minutes into the tape, they began to slang each other: *Give me the mike, dummy! . . . Stupid! That's not the way Walter Cronkite does it! . . . You can't say, "It'll rain or snow depending on the weather." . . . That was a joke. . . . It was a dumb joke . . . Ma! He says I'm dumb!* (I hear my own crisp *Goddamn it!*) I find myself in the ridiculous position of growing moist-eyed and nostalgic over a recorded bit of sibling rivalry.

Before he left for Bombay, Josh said, "For my birthday present, write something for me." I was more gratified by his request than I had ever been by the blandishments of editors. And extremely apprehensive. How does one write in public for a private person? It seemed out of character for a child who insists on decorum and conventional public manners—a child who regards any manifestation of flamboyance or eccentricity on my part as an invasion of *his* privacy—to ask me to make public even so slight a detail as the color of his bedroom walls. "But you know I can't write make-believe stories," I protested. "Write the truth," he said. "Write about me."

I took that as a gesture of trust; and as a seal of approval. For I've sometimes thought that Josh, who loves and demands order, would find it a lot easier if I had a tidier, more structured, contained job—nine to five, dinner at eight, and wholly American, holy-family weekends. We are both moody; he wishes (it would make him feel safe) that I were not. I am always exhilarated when writing a story, and always depressed afterward. I stun myself into insensibility with food and cigarettes until an editor calls to tell me the story is good; then my inertia leaves; and then I feel celebratory and good. Then I cook and sweep and clean and buy presents for the children. "Don't you know what you do is good until somebody tells you it is?" Josh asks me. "Not really," I say. "But you know you take good care of us. Doesn't that make you feel good?"

Josh enjoys, on the one hand, the pleasure of knowing that I am always available to him (physically, at least, though often reluctantly: if there is a way of writing a sentence when a child yells "MA!" from another room, I haven't found it). It disturbs him profoundly, on the other hand, that I should need validation from outside sources—and that his love and approbation, and my own self-love, are not wholly enough. That the approval of strangers should weigh so heavily with me is a bewilderment to him.

I also understood Josh's request to write something for him to be the desire of a child on the edge of puberty to return to the sheltered childhood of bedtime cocoa and fairy stories, when "Tell me a story" marked the beginning of a white magic that eased the way into black sleep. He loved hearing about purple dragons and knights in golden armor, and of his own infancy in North Africa: "Tell me a story about the baby who was born by the sea." We would both pretend that I was telling a fable about somebody else. His delight was fresh each time I told the familiar story (which assumed the power of myth); each time, caught in the spell of a story about the sea and a villa where pomegranate and lemon trees grew, he thrilled to learn that *he* was the protagonist.

And I think he was saying, *I like having a mother who is a writer . . . even though she lives through words, while silence is the climate I am most comfortable in.* I think he was giving *me* a birthday present.

Some people say, "My God, how can you stand their being away? Don't you miss them?" And other people say, "Aren't you lucky! To have a year without children's demands!" I agree with all of them. I miss my children; and I'm glad to have a year without their incessant demands. A year ago I could not have admitted that I could welcome a childless year. My children provided the structure for my life; they framed and claimed my days. I could not conceive of life without them, of starting each day asking, *What do I want?*, of dealing with the onerous responsibilities of freedom. I had a year to prepare myself emotionally for their departure; during part of that year I tried to behave like a madonna—so that they would want to come back to me. (I was frightened.)

Then, somehow, things righted themselves. Children have built-in bullshit detectors: my madonna act didn't pass muster. We began to talk honestly about our anxieties; and we began also to allow ourselves to anticipate the pleasures the year ahead would hold for us. We were cranky one day, overly scrupulous with one another's feelings the next. (Home, as a friend of mine says, is where the heartbreak is.) Out of all this—and I don't pretend to understand the process—came such certainty of our tender regard for one another that parting was divested of its terror, though not of its pain.

The aren't-you-lucky-they're-gone people say, "Now you can work undisturbed." What I'm not sure they understand—what I'm not sure I've always understood—is that I might never have done any good work at all had it not been for the fact of their existence. They are not just devourers of psychic energy and time, and money, not just pains in the ass, though God knows they are frequently that. They are also nourishing. And fun. How can I say it? Even to watch television with a child who is not yet jaded is to convince one that, while pessimism of the intellect may be here to stay, optimism of the spirit is still—gloriously—possible.

Joshua's birthday seems as good an occasion as any for me to celebrate him. His birthday is my birthday, too: a renewal.

Some peculiar, blessed alchemy began to work when Josh was in my womb. I have always felt the physical world to be fraught with menace. (It is still a matter of some amazement to me each time I arrive home safely from the world and an air conditioner hasn't fallen on my head, a mugger hasn't attacked me, an airplane hasn't spiraled down to crash at my feet.) But all the while I was pregnant, I felt invulnerable. I felt as if I could pick my way through minefields unscathed. Hypochondria—the enemy to whom I extend every hospitality—deserted me. I never once entertained the thought that the child stirring in my womb would be less than perfect. I was sublime in my self-confidence. From that sacramental high, of course, there had to be a fall.

My fears are still outrageous and debilitating. But Josh has made me a less fearful person—and largely because he has refused to be contaminated by my fears. He accepts them for what they are, a mild form of craziness. He doesn't enter into them. He reads all the signs: he knows when I'm afraid of stairs or escalators and offers me his hand. He has never made me the object of his scorn. (He was a solemn, kind little boy, and he is a solemn, kind adolescent.) I learned to ride a bike when I was thirty-six—because Josh taught himself to ride a bike, in spite of my anxious, busy clucking; I learned to swim when I was thirty-eight, because Josh (with no help from me) gave himself to the water so trustingly and gracefully.

Josh has helped me to redefine love. Somewhere along the line, I had assumed the belief that love and anger were mutually exclusive. (With that garbage in my head, how could I ever have done honest work?) I learned to receive anger from Josh without interpreting it as contempt and to express anger toward Josh without feeling that I was a killer. Josh taught me that anger heals.

In spite of having, for many years, an almost pathological desire to please people, betraying myself in the process, through Josh I learned that there were more important things than being nice, that being nice is as different from being good as conventional piety is from being saintly. One can't be a "nice girl" and a mother at the same time. The need to wear ingratiating masks pales beside the naked need to protect one's young. Had I been nice to incompetent or uncaring doctors, or sadistic street predators, or bullying, interfering adults, Josh might have been dead. Learning to be fierce on his behalf has helped me to be strong on my own.

He wakes in the night and calls out urgently, "Mom!" I find him pensive in the darkness. "Do you think I'll grow up to be a good person? . . . Do you think the peace marches did any good? . . . There are some good rich people, aren't there? I get mad when you act like you think all rich people are bad. . . . Do you think Julie Nixon should have defended her father? . . . Was Serpico a good man? Did he change anything? If nothing changed, what good did it do for Serpico to be good?

... I've been thinking about dreams and I think they're the thoughts our ancestors had and were too dumb to put in words, so now we dream their thoughts for them. ... Are you happy?"

From a child who keeps his own counsel, these moral and metaphysical outpourings always come to me as a surprise. No wonder he distrusts surfaces: Josh spent the earliest years of his life in poor countries—Libya, India, Guatemala. He played with the children of the poor and the children of the rich. He has seen and experienced both the brutalization and the brutality of the hopeless poor, witnessed at firsthand the civilized pleasures, the careless, casual generosity—and the murderous indifference—of the rich.

When he was five, his golden cocker spaniel was killed by the German shepherd of millionaire neighbors in Guatemala. They sent their maid over with his broken-necked dog wrapped in a towel: "The senora says, please return the towel soon, she needs it," the maid said.

When he was three years old, Josh played daily with the child of a tribal Indian construction worker; one day Josh saw his friend's father fall to his death from the girders of a building that was being constructed ten yards away from his own bright and airy nursery. He heard the widow wail, and the next day the little boy he had played with disappeared forever, no one knew where.

When he was seven, a Guatemalan family who subsisted on rice and beans, to whom Josh had brought firewood and old clothes and an old tricycle as presents, pridefully gave him their only chicken in exchange.

When he was ten, Josh was mugged in Prospect Park by black kids who held a knife to his throat and debated whether to kill him. He came home, snot and tears all over his face, and delivered a sociological lecture: "They're poor and angry," he said, "that's why they did it." (But for weeks afterward, he called black people *niggers*.)

He has eaten from plates of gold and been waited on by gloved and turbaned bearers, surrounded by the Arabian Nights luxury of India's superrich . . . who are very charming (the rich are charming; it costs them very little).

Out of this welter of confused experience, he forges his morality. I am overwhelmed with tenderness and pity as I watch him struggle with the nature of goodness; and I am also thrilled. How nice to be with someone who proceeds directly to the heart of the matter ("What does it mean to be good? Will I be good?"), instead of always squirreling around in the debris of my own mind. How nice to be asked difficult questions by someone for whom the asking is not an exercise but a need to make order of the world.

"You write about Anna a lot," he says. "You almost never write about me." He's right. I have a daughter and a son; I write about my daughter more. *Say you love me better, best. . . . Say you love me more. . . . Let it be our secret that you love me more.* Whose voice said that? Mine? My son's? Anna's? It's what we all say; it's what Auden called the error bred in each man's heart—to wish to be loved alone.

"Well, I don't *love* Anna more," I say. "Hmmm," he says.

I adore her, my fierce, sweet girl, my mirror, my biological twin. When I need to understand my opaque past, I turn to Anna, hoping, in her, to find clarity and clues. She reflects my body's changes; like two sister planets we share the same cycles. She is Anna; she has her own reality; she is also a metaphor for myself. Where Anna goes, I have been. It is familiar territory. I write about the territory I know.

Where Josh goes . . .

Where does Josh go? Into a good and happy manhood, I hope. Gently and high-spiritedly, I hope, into that perilous country of male adulthood, and with the quiet strength I love him for. He will continue, I hope, as he has begun: brave, challenging, loving—a miracle not of my making but of his own creation.

... Oh, and I forgot to say he's funny; he makes me laugh. "That movie stinked," he said once to me. *"Stinked?* That's not English." "It's American," he said. *"Stank* and *stunk* are British. *Stinked* is the American way." And he looked at me and laughed, so pleased. And then he flung himself out of the house to play football. His voice joined with other boys' voices; I heard his rowdy laughter echoing all the way down the street.

GOING HOME:
BROOKLYN REVISITED

(November, 1974)

During World War II my grandfather had a victory garden in Bensonhurst, a small plot of city-owned land on which, as his contribution to the war effort, he planted hot and sweet peppers, zucchini, tomatoes, oregano (without which the Allies must surely lose the war), mint, and sweet basil. To be able, with the blessing and under the patronage of the American government, to do the noble work of farming the good earth made glad his lyrical Italian heart; he sang aloud with happiness. The song he sang aloud (*very* loud), as he harvested and hoed, was the Italian Fascist Youth Anthem. Grandpa was unable to see any irony in this; attempts to persuade him that the work of his hands contradicted the words of his mouth merely reinforced his conviction that all American-Americans were simpletons, *pazzi* (crazy). Wasn't he Italian, after all? And wasn't he American, after all? And weren't all American-Americans perverse—unable and unwilling to understand the first thing about Italian-Americans, who in any case had no wish to be understood by people so *pazzi* that they couldn't even pronounce Il Duce's name correctly? Till the day he died, Grandpa persisted in pronouncing Mussolini *Mussolino*, arguing with awesome circuitous logic that if FDR called him Mussolini, then—since all Americans were *pazzi* and perverse and had never cared enough to get the final vowel of any Italian name right—it must of necessity be Mussolino. Toward the

13

end of his life, Grandpa, as fierce in senility as he had been in
full-blooded vigor, regaled visitors with the story of his flight
across the Atlantic with Charles Lindbergh. He had been denied recognition, he claimed, because *they* wouldn't let it be
known that an Italian had shared the controls with "an American boy." Italians were always deprived of their just rewards.
(My grandfather, a carpenter, had once worked with Bruno
Hauptmann, the kidnapper of the Lindbergh baby; even his
most baroque fictions usually had some remote link to an esoteric truth.)

I grew up in Bensonhurst among people who, if they had
little else, had the courage of their contradictions. I grew up
trying to sort truth from fiction (which was almost always more
picturesque and more compelling than truth) among proud,
stubborn Italian-Americans who were convinced that they
were doomed to be misunderstood . . . a conviction that paradoxically was a source of stoic pride. To compound the paradox, these same people—who were eloquent in their belief that
they would be forever deprived, by the *pazzi* Americans, of
what was rightfully theirs—managed also to believe absolutely
in the American Dream: when Grandpa wasn't singing hymns
to the Brownshirts, he was singing Frank Sinatra's *What Is
America to Me? The house I live in . . . the street, the house,
the road . . . the church, the school, the clubhouse . . . the little
corner newsstand . . . the dream that's been agrowin' for about
two hundred years.*
Bensonhurst is still Sinatra territory. Some say it is Mafia
territory. It is still peopled by proud, stubborn, first-, second-,
and third-generation southern Italians for whom the ownership
of a little bit of land represents not just material success but
the attainment of the highest moral and ethical ideal. The
church, the school, the clubhouse—especially the neighborhood school—are regarded now, as they were then, as theirs to

love and theirs to defend. Now, more than ever, Bensonhurst's Italian-Americans are convinced that *they* are trying to take away the just rewards—especially the neighborhood schoolhouse—that by right should have accrued to decent, hardworking patriots.

What is no longer certain is that anyone in Bensonhurst believes, any more, in the American Dream. The dreams of Bensonhurst's Italian-Americans are blood-colored now; and the stink of fear is in the air.

On Monday, October 7, racial tension exploded into racial violence at New Utrecht High School (*my* old high school).

During the nine-thirty A.M. third period, a white male student jumped a black male student in a hallway. As news of the attack spread, enraged black students, outnumbered at Utrecht four to one, fled from their classrooms and stormed through the lunchroom and out of the school building. Teachers barricaded their classroom doors and locked white students inside. The following day, racial fights on the nearby BMT "el" and outside the school building resulted in several injuries to both white and black students (some serious enough to require hospitalization) and in the suspension of eighteen students and the arrest of six others. On Wednesday, school was shut down. On Thursday, New Utrecht, heavily guarded by police from four precincts, opened only for Regents exams. On Friday, October 11, school reopened. No serious incidents were reported that day to the more than two hundred policemen who were there to be sure that there would be no repetition of bloody Tuesday. On that tense Friday, however, twenty-one blacks, reputed to be carrying meat cleavers, pipes, and chains, were arrested at the BMT station. None of them was a New Utrecht student.

Those are the facts on which everybody—black students and white students, neighborhood hang-out goons, teachers, school administrators, and community people—seem to agree. Those are the *only* facts on which everybody agrees. From there on in, trying to sort truth from fiction is as onerous a proposition as trying to convince Grandpa that the name of the man who made the trains run on time was Mussolini.

There is one other point of consensus; that is the fact that no one from the press cares enough even to try to sort truth from fiction. The population of Bensonhurst and New Utrecht is vociferously contemptuous of media people and, in particular, of television journalists, who are seen as predatory, manipulative trouble-mongers with scant regard for fact or sensibility. I heard from too many sources not to give credence to the story that television cameramen "posed" and instructed kids ("All right, let's have fists up in the air . . . let's hear 'kill the niggers' " . . . or " 'kill whitey' ") for maximum-impact footage. (The first call alerting anybody to the troubles at Utrecht was made [by a student] not to the cops but to Channel 5 TV.)

I returned to Bensonhurst in the aftermath of the riots, and in permawood-paneled, chandeliered, plastic-and-velvet living rooms that I could feel my way blindfolded around, I found myself once again in that familiar territory where cynicism and sanguinity, pragmatism and rococo fantasies, fight for psychic space in the complex personalities of insular, ghettoized Italian-Americans who, like my grandfather, defend the very contradictions that confound them, and who, like him, seldom manage to coordinate their emotional/political reflexes. There was one added ingredient in the familiar volatile brew; it pervades the working- and lower-middle-class community of Bensonhurst as it pervades New Utrecht High School: that ingredient is despair.

One of the more bizarre aspects of that post-riot evening, which I shared with my brother ex-Utrechtites and former schoolmates, is that almost every conversation wrapped itself around a central myth: "The blacks don't want to be here anyway Wouldn't they rather be jiving with their own kind in their own neighborhood the way we did when we were kids?"

It is inconceivable to most Bensonhurst Italians—who, when they get married, usually move "down the stoop" from their mother's house—that anybody would not want to stay "with his own kind." If anyone leaves his own kind to come to New Utrecht, it is (1) because he's looking for trouble; or (2) because there's no discipline in his home; or (3) because "outside agitators," including parents, have put him in Utrecht against his will. The fact is, of course, that under the Board of Education's Open Enrollment Program every one of the 1,100 black students at NUHS has *chosen* to be there. Black kids from East New York, Crown Heights, and Bed-Stuy (all of which areas Bensonhurst residents tend to lump together under one generic name—*Harlem*) travel up to three and a half hours every day on public transportation to get to the school of their choice. You have to be pretty highly motivated to do that for three years when everybody around is cold-nosing you. Nevertheless, almost without exception, the Italian-Americans I spoke to truly believe that "the coloreds don't want to be bussed in from Harlem in the first place so why are *they* taking away our pride by putting them here?" People who point defensively—"Am I a bigot?"—to framed pictures of Hank Aaron on their walls "swear to God" they wouldn't mind if the blacks who went to New Utrecht were neighborhood kids; it's the feeling of being invaded by outsiders and tricked by *them* that they can't tolerate. (But, on the other hand, what would they do if blacks moved into Bensonhurst? "Move.")

I graduated from New Utrecht in January, 1952. The student body then, reflecting the composition of the neighborhood, was fifty percent Jewish and fifty percent Italian. (There were a few exceptions, among whom was Fatima Ouida, a magnificently endowed Egyptian girl who charmed snakes, and nice Jewish boys, in her bedroom, while her father—universally known as "the guy who prays to the West End train"—made his ritual prayers to Mecca facing the window in the living room that was six inches away from the BMT "el.") It was taken for granted by students and teachers alike that Jews were smart (they took academic courses) and Italians were dumb (we took commercial and general courses). I was once asked by a teacher why I had an Italian last name. He wasn't being hostile or precious; he was, quite simply, puzzled: how could an Italian girl be smart? When, miracle of miracles, my friend Angela made Senior Arista and won a scholarship to Radcliffe, her grandmother, draped in funereal black, accompanied her to Cambridge on the bus, making novenas to Saint Jude, patron saint of Lost Causes, all the way. While Angela was at Radcliffe, Harold Brodkey wrote his famous *New Yorker* short story about a love affair between a Harvard boy and a Radcliffe girl. Angela came back to Brooklyn in a very large hurry and assembled all her friends; together we bought every copy of that *New Yorker* we could find from Bay Parkway to Bath Avenue on the off-chance that Angela's grandmother might come across Brodkey's story, realize that college kids actually *did it*, and yank Angela back to Bensonhurst and the safety of her virginal pink-and-white bedroom forever.

Utrecht in the fifties had a reputation for being a school for "gees"—"hard guys," or "hoods." (While nearby Erasmus Hall High School was nurturing Beverly Sills, we were getting ready to give the world John Saxon and Buddy Hackett.) If you didn't bother the gees, they didn't bother you. You minded your business, you stayed out of trouble. Arnold Horowitz, a lovely, nurturing English teacher, was forever sending packages of pepperoni off to Utrecht gees who'd wound up in jail and forever imploring us to believe in the possibility of redemption and the basic goodness of human nature. We believed.

In my senior class at Utrecht there were 468 whites and one

black girl, Joan Smith. No one ever spoke to Joan Smith, and Joan Smith never spoke to anybody. At the end of the senior year, she was voted "Most Friendly."

My brother remembers what it was like to have one black classmate in 1955: "That kid was lucky. He was bright and good-looking. If he was just a regular black kid, he'd have had bad trouble. . . . Every time teachers talked about black history or slavery, my word of honor I felt sorry for the kid. If they'd have talked about Italian history, there'd have been thirty of us Italians, we wouldn't be embarrassed . . . not that they ever talked about Italian history."

When Jimmie D.—an auto mechanic who still lives, with his wife and three kids, in his mother's two-family house in Bensonhurst—went to Utrecht from '58 to '60, there was one black kid, too; he *wasn't* extraordinarily bright and good-looking. "He never opened his mouth; nobody ever bothered with him. If there'd have been twenty of them, though, we'd have killed them just on general principle. . . .

"Remember when Bay Fifteen in Coney Island was ours? We beat the shit out of any black kid who put a foot past Bay Thirteen, even if he was just an eight-year-old snot who got lost from his mother. Once a colored guy came in and stabbed one of ours with an ice pick," Jimmie said. "We smashed his head against a pier and we never saw black skin for the rest of that summer. That was *our* Bop House." "And the younger Italian kids," my brother said. "We taught them respect. They had to call us 'Uncle.' If they didn't behave good, we'd make them shine our shoes with their spit—just on general principle."

I know those stories don't make Jimmie D. or my brother sound altogether lovable. They rehearsed them because they wanted desperately to believe, for one evening at least, that we all still have a chance, that things are better now, not worse. Perhaps we still believe what Arnold Horowitz told us—that human nature is basically good, that redemption is possible.

"My kids want to know why all this is happening. What can I tell them? I know I got some prejudice left. If one of my kids got mugged I'd take it out on the first colored I saw. But I don't want my prejudice to slip out in front of my kids. I want them to be better than me," Jimmie D. said.

But, he also said, "If one of my daughters dated a black guy, it'd be Bay Fifteen all over again."

And: "I tell the guys on the job people ought to live together —I'm not better than him, he's not better than me. And they call me a nigger-lover. I don't want my kids bussed—and they call me a racist. So what am I?"

What am I? And who is my enemy? . . . contradiction and pain. Confusion and alarm. . . . Years ago, I saw *Dr. Strangelove* at the Bensonhurst Eighty-sixth Street Loews. All through the movie the woman behind me kept saying, "But I don't understand. *Who's the enemy?*" . . . Sitting in a Bensonhurst living room, we tried, once again, to identify the enemy:

"It ain't the kids. It's the politicians—the Communists who send their kids to private schools. Democrats and Republicans, all those creeps, those *giabronis* are all the same. . . . Listen, I'd be demonstrating in front of those schools in South Boston with the Irish. I move out of a ghetto to do good for my kids, how can I have any pride if I gotta send my kids back to the jungle for school? I had to sweat to buy my house. Am I a racist?

"Who cares about us? Does the Board of Education care? Three o'clock and the teachers don't want to know nothin'. Nobody cares. The teachers don't get no support, nobody wants to be bothered."

Fifteen years ago, Diane was a Booster and a Twirler at NUHS. "Look," she said, "this is a safe neighborhood. They used to laugh at Bensonhurst, right? You were a cornball if you lived here. Now they're going to have to put a wall around it, it's so safe. . . . My cousin plays *bocci* in a cottage that a colored lady owns in Long Island. Blacks go there. She plays Scrabble with them. We're colorblind if they're our equal. But tough teenagers aren't my equal. It's not like the gees—you could ignore them. I know all teenagers are wild, but if they look familiar, they don't scare me. Blacks scare me because they don't look familiar. I *know* the tough white kids that hang out on the corners drinking. And it's okay because I *know* them. I'm not saying the blacks are wilder. I'm saying they don't look familiar. So why don't they stay in their own schools and in their own neighborhoods where they're familiar? Why are they sending them here to scare us?"

Richy, an ex-Utrechtite who brings secondhand shoes and clothes and used record albums to the poor black kids bussed into the neighborhood junior high school his kids go to: "It's not the Utrecht kids who are making the trouble. It's the dropouts, the big shots, the candy-store hang-out kids, it's them. Their IQ and their foot size is the same number. They could've been somebody—they could've gotten athletic scholarships. But they're twenty and they're still hanging out in the schoolyard. Fifteen years old, and they think it's glamorous to get drunk on boilermakers and get busted for drugs and have flashy cars and hard-looking girls. They're all playing James Caan playing Sonny. When they're twenty-five they'll look up to the decent people, but then it'll be too late."

"It's the Mafia."

"Yeah, but the Mafia keeps the neighborhood safe."

Jimmie D. adds to the Enemy List the "geeps" from the other side: "We got this big influx of Italians from the old country. They're not like us. They got a chip on their shoulder. Mouth-y. They say, Blacks have been here for a hundred years and they couldn't make it; now it's our turn. It was a geep who beat up on a black kid at Utrecht. The geeps are here three years and they got money to buy a four-family house. That's all they think of is money. They never heard of going to the movies. They never heard of anisette. They never even heard of *coffee*. You go to their house, they don't give you anything to eat. What kind of Italian is that? They work two jobs, and they eat macaroni every night—*pasta lenticci, pasta fazool,* that's it. We're here eating pork chops and drinking highballs and we hear them every night cracking macaroni into the pot —unbelievable."

Diane's cousin, who plays *bocci* in the colored lady's house on Long Island, comes in from an evening class at Bernard Baruch College. "As long as there are blacks and whites there's going to be trouble," she says. "We're all victims of the system."

"You know what," my brother says wryly. "It isn't hip to be racist any more. Aside from it isn't decent."

So what's the solution? "Do something in their own neighborhoods?" "Make their local schools better?"

"There is no solution," everybody says.

"*Clockwork Orange* is just around the corner," Richy says. "It's too late."

As we drive away, my brother says, "Most people are decent. And that's the sin. Are those bad people? Did you ever meet more sincere people?"

Most people need to believe they're decent. Italian-Americans are—it is bred in the bone and marrow of a people who for centuries have had to defend themselves against alien invaders—suspicious and insular, guarded and, now, bitter. But their own hatred terrifies them. Lacking any real political analysis, they can't identify the enemy—the *They* who are taking away everything they've fought for. . . . And that's the tragedy.

All I could think of, as I approached New Utrecht High School with its hundreds of cops, were the cupcakes we used to buy for a nickle in the school lunchroom. Confronted with spiritual crises, I make grocery lists and compose menus. Confronted with that prisonlike building in which I learned for the first time to value myself—because Arnold Horowitz valued me; confronted with that bleak edifice in which I first fell in love—with Arnold Horowitz; confronted with that gothic grotesquerie in which Arnold taught me to question and to doubt the fundamentalist religion that had straitjacketed me in a claustrophobic simplicity, I used my press card to get past the police, past the teachers with their newly issued ID tags—and into my old school lunchroom. To think about cupcakes. To try not to think about Arnold, who died before Bensonhurst's world shattered.

I am an imposter: to be the bearer of a press card is—one is given to understand—proof that one is a reporter. I am here to report the facts; but the essential fact is that this fortress was my womb. I grew up in this building; it is not an exaggeration to say I was born here. I love this place. I try, nevertheless, to get the facts. I don't really want the facts; I want a blessing. I want Arnold again—his charity, his clarity, his love. I was born here—Arnold gave birth to me here—and now it smells like death here.

There are no more cupcakes in the school lunchroom. New Utrecht was built to accommodate 2,600 pupils. There are 4,300 students enrolled here now. Cupcakes are a luxury New Utrecht cannot afford. And charity is in short supply.

The air in the lunchroom is thick with rumors. It is rumored that the violence was timed to coincide with the threatened strike of Utrecht's eight security guards, and that everybody knew it was coming. It is rumored that on Halloween trouble will explode again; Nair and eggs and hair spray are being stockpiled as defensive weapons. There is the rumor of the Missing Ear. A white ear, some kids say. A black ear, some kids say. Knifed off, some kids say. Bitten off, some kids say.

"Grossly exaggerated, tragic nonsense," the principal, Michael Russo, says. Handsome, all dapper solicitousness, Russo effusively greets smiling matriarchs from the black community as he nods to the priests who mingle with the cops who mingle with the teachers, many of whom hate Russo's guts—or lack of them. "He doesn't even know our names. All he's got is charm. The first year he was here, the Italian kids loved him. President Ford should have had the honeymoon he had. He was as cute as Anna Maria Alberghetti doing an Italian-salad-dressing commercial. The second year he was here, we never saw his face—except when he came into the auditorium to throw kisses and say a couple of words in Italian. Now he wears his best suit every day for the television cameras. The entire Board and this whole administration care about appearances, period. Russo will tell you we have a wonderful school—he'll tell you all about the Boosters, the football team, the pep rallies, the Twirlers, the Sings. When everybody else knew trouble was coming, he was planning a fiftieth anniversary alumni dance. All the rottenness is kept under covers. Nobody wants to face the fact that the system is failing."

In the teachers' lunchroom, the air is heavy with bitterness: "*The New York Times* said we were 'overrun with three hundred blacks.' We were *not* overrun with blacks. You can expect to hear that version from some of the kids, too—'A coupla kids gave one black kid a hard time, and then the coloreds came in by the busload from Bed-Stuy.' No black kids came *in* from anywhere. Our black students ran through the lunchroom on Monday because they were scared. I don't want to hear that they looked like Amazons—you could practically taste their fear. On Tuesday, the black kids all arranged to meet at the Pacific Street subway station and come to Utrecht in a group, that's your 'three hundred blacks.' Sure, they looked like a terrifying mob. You should have seen what the white kids throwing bottles out of the windows looked like."

Some of the white kids are eager indeed to advance the busload-of-outsiders-from-Bed-Stuy version of the riots: "After the black guy got jumped, the blacks called all their friends in from Lincoln High School and Jefferson High School and FDR High School—troops, man. They had pipes and chains. So naturally we threw bottles. . . . It was like Attica. Exciting."

The official line, as advanced by Herbert Potell, Assistant Principal, is that "black and white students work and play beautifully together. There are undesirable characters, black and white outsiders, who hang around the school and incite trouble. And up till now we have not been too successful in communicating with black parents, because they live out of the community. Eighty percent of the neighborhood people have never even heard of the '54 Supreme Court decision. But this year got off to an unbelievably good start. There was nothing we could have seen below the surface to alert us to trouble. We were taken unaware." He adds, in an unofficial aside, "You know, the black girls are tough, they're harder than the boys . . . they come from a seamier part of life. Don't get me wrong. Some of them are sweet. But the white girls are always scared." (I remember Mr. Potell when he was an English teacher at Utrecht. In my senior yearbook there is a Last-Will-and-Testament inscription to him: "And to Mr. Potell, we leave an Academy Award for the Most Touching Performance of the Year as Lady Macbeth.")

Student leaders, presenting a united front, agree that it was outsiders—white outsiders, the goons who hang out on the street corners, the ones whose IQ and foot size are the same number—who provoked the riots. They are eager to disabuse interrogators of the notion that blacks and whites at Utrecht are perpetually prepped for battle in separate armed camps. But when they discuss among themselves the viability of black-and-white friendships at Utrecht, their bravado rapidly crumbles into ambivalence and pathos.

Cheryl Walker, fifteen, of the Black Student Coalition: "We have friends. When we have games, we're all together, united against other schools. Last year we had a basketball playoff against Charles Evans Hughes, a black high school. Hughes lost, and they started a riot. The black students protected the white students, male and female. . . . We do good at games. We might not get along too good, but we don't fight. Ordinarily. But a white girl who has a black girl to her house is called a nigger-lover. . . . Maybe I don't have friends. It's hard to know any more. . . . It's always been hard." Toni Napoli, secretary of the G.O.: "I have black friends. But they can't come to my house, they live too far away. . . . And what's going to happen to me if I go to them against my side? You feel bad if you talk to another color against your own kind."

Most of the white students I spoke with had rather odd notions of friendship. (Most of the black students slipped home too fast to be interviewed.)

"Sure, I got black friends. I shake their hands on the handball courts. I play track with them. . . . They're my friends till trouble starts. Now I think we ought to kill 'em all."

"I treat the coloreds just like they were as good as whites. But what are they doing in my school?"

"Alone, a colored can be nice. In a group, we're more civilized."

"We have niggers on all the teams—we're friends."

But I am giving these kids less than their due. Taken alone, one by one, they are not unlikable. They want an education, they want security and familiar fun and familiar faces. Taken in a group—and, by and large, that's how I took them on Friday, October 11—they are tribal and defiant and frighteningly silly, drawing courage from one another's hard-ass talk. They are also—I was occasionally, stunningly reminded, by their sudden excursions into giggles or their uncontrolled, breaking voices, or their ridiculous attempts to be grown-up, back-slapping oracles—children, victims, if you will, of manipulation and polarization, of carefully nurtured ignorance and insularity and paranoia. They are victims; but they are also potential murderers.

At New Utrecht High School, the outline of a simple equation begins to present itself. When inflation and the specter of depression—the corrosive fear that *they* are going to take away everything your people have fought for—tear at your guts, you go for the easy and immediate solution: you "rip a nigger's heart out." With your tribal instincts and your adolescent lust for excitement providing the adrenaline, you collectively go for the jugular of the person you suppose to be the enemy—the jugular of a black. ("They'd kill us if we went into their neighborhood. What do they expect in ours?") Your resentments find the nearest target. ("I can't even get a dumb train pass 'cause I live less than two miles away—so how come they can get in?") You don't shout *Kill Rockefeller*—even if you did perceive any connection between Rockefeller and your pain, Rockefeller is too remote. You shout *Kill a nigger*—a nigger is real to you, present, seen, felt . . . and feared.

And you have the outsiders—the white-agitator hang-out "goons" to egg you on.

It ought to be easy to hate and to despise the hang-out goons. They are bigots hot with bloodlust. They are dangerous children on a murderous rampage; and they scared the hell out of me. But I could not hate them. I hated their words, I abominated their deeds . . . and out of some spiritual left field, I felt in myself feelings that, on the face of it, were totally inappropriate to the situation: I felt pity for them. And—it was hard for me to acknowledge that I was feeling this, and it is harder still to write it—I felt protective of them. Mostly I felt impotent rage . . . which is exactly what they were feeling.

Murderers . . . and victims. They are both.

What can you feel about a twenty-three-year-old man-child

who hangs out at Utrecht because "things bother me. I used to drive a car for the *Daily News* and now I only work three days a week because one of them animals got half my job. They're taking my job away. I never had no opportunity; why should they have an opportunity? When my wife got pregnant I was bringing home seventy-four dollars a week. And I asked for Medicaid and they said, Forget it. And you know if I was a nigger or a spic I'd have got it. . . . Things bother me. They take away our jobs from us and now they're taking our school and pretty soon they'll take our neighborhood; and I'm staying here when there's trouble. This is my place. What other place do I got?"

Can you hate him? He can drive you wild with anger—and inspire a lunatic urge to deliver a lecture on political science and economy, or a diatribe against politicians who give their cronies $500,000 handouts while a hang-out/goon/slob can't get his wife adequate medical care (the baby died). But can you hate him?

It is wonderful, though, and terrible, how hate answers hate. On that Friday, I wanted somebody to hate. Not "the system" or Nelson Rockefeller—nothing, nobody remote—somebody present and real I could decently, cathartically hate.

I thought I'd found him in Johnny G. Johnny G., who put a *No Niggers Allowed* sign in the window of the Utrecht Avenue pizzeria. Johnny G., who snapped his fingers and yelled, "Everybody out of the pizza parlor, I'm talking to this here lady reporter." (Everybody cleared out—fast . . . but not before Johnny G. commanded one freshman to buy his cigarettes, another freshman to get some batteries, and a third to wax his red TR 6 sports car.) Johnny G., who said, exposing beautiful muscled arms, "See these scars? I got them from a nigger. But what I done to him, I broke his jaw—it's hard to break African noses—and I broke his jaw, and I gave him six stitches over his eye. Beautiful." Johnny G., Big Man, who says he's been "shit on" all his life. "They kicked me out of school. Why? Because three colored kids jumped a small white kid, so naturally I wiped the schoolyard with one I caught." Johnny G., twenty years old, half-Italian, half-Arab, whose mouth smilingly issues forth venom, whose face is so broodingly beautiful, so sensitive, I see images of Terry Malloy superimposed on it. Johnny G., whose half-sister was knifed. Johnny G., who says, "Sometimes I get so mad I smash walls, I break things." Incongruously he smiles, that dazzling, heartbreaking, unexpected smile. "Arabs aren't Africans," he says. (Is it a non sequitur?) Johnny G., who has a job: "I deliver teeth." *You deliver teeth?* "Yeah, I work for a creative dental caterer, and I deliver false teeth." The Triumph doesn't belong to Johnny G. It belongs to his boss. It doesn't belong to the Big Man who delivers false teeth. "My sister," Johnny G. says, "ain't half-Arab. She's smart. Once she sang Maria in *West Side Story*—you know, one of them spics. I take care of her."

Take care of yourself, I hear myself say. And I mean it. He takes umbrage. I say, stupidly (but because I'm feeling protective—*protective*—of Johnny G., whom I can't hate): "Why don't you take a screen test and do your fighting in the movies?" (Because some day, Johnny G., a victim with a heart full of murder and a face like an angel's, is going to kill or get killed.) His chest swells. "You gotta be crazy. You think I could *be* somebody?"

I go home and read the Principal's Message in my high school senior yearbook, Class of '52 (Arnie Goldfedder and Anne Bosco, Most Likely to Succeed, where are you now?).

". . . in America, the future belongs to you. That is the way it has always been. That is America's promise to you. The dreams you dream, the hopes you have for yourself and for others, will be realized. . . . They will be yours if you want them hard enough and if you think, work, and plan for them. This kind of fulfillment has come to millions of young Americans before you. It will be yours, too."

Tell it to Bensonhurst.

GROWING UP APOCALYPTIC

(1975)

"The trouble with you," Anna said, in a voice in which compassion, disgust, and reproach fought for equal time, "is that you can't remember what it was like to be young. And even if you could remember—well, when you were my age, you were in that crazy Jehovah's Witness religion, and you probably didn't even play spin the bottle."

Anna, my prepubescent eleven-year-old, feels sorry for me because I did not have "a normal childhood." It has never occurred to her to question whether her childhood is "normal" . . . which is to say, she is happy. She cannot conceive of a life in which one is not free to move around, explore, argue, flirt with ideas and dismiss them, form passionate alliances and friendships according to no imperative but one's own nature and volition; she regards love as unconditional, she expects nurturance as her birthright. It fills her with terror and pity that anyone—especially her mother—could have grown up any differently . . . could have grown up in a religion where love was conditional upon rigid adherence to dogma and established practice . . . where approval had to be bought from authoritarian sources . . . where people did not fight openly and love fiercely and forgive generously and make decisions of their own and mistakes of their own and have adventures of their own.

"Poor Mommy," she says. To have spent one's childhood in love with/tyrannized by a vengeful Jehovah is not Anna's idea of a good time—nor is it her idea of goodness. As, in her considered opinion, my having been a proselytizing Jehovah's Witness for thirteen years was about as good a preparation for real life as spending a commensurate amount of time in a Skinner box on the North Pole, she makes allowances for me. And so, when Anna came home recently from a boy-girl party to tell me that she had kissed a boy ("interesting," she pronounced the experiment), and I heard my mouth ask that atavistic mother-question, "And what else did you do?" Anna was inclined to be charitable with me: "Oh, for goodness' sake, what do you think we did, screw? The trouble with you is . . ." And then she explained to me about spin the bottle.

I do worry about Anna. She is, as I once explained drunkenly to someone who thought that she might be the better for a little vigorous repression, a teleological child. She is concerned with final causes, with ends and purposes and means; she would like to see evidence of design and order in the world; and all her adventures are means to that end. That, combined with her love for the music, color, poetry, ritual, and drama of religion, might, I think, if she were at all inclined to bow her back to authority—and if she didn't have my childhood as an example of the perils thereof—have made her ripe for conversion to an apocalyptic, messianic sect.

That fear may be evidence of my special paranoia, but it is not an entirely frivolous conjecture. Ardent preadolescent girls whose temperament tends toward the ecstatic are peculiarly prone to conversion to fancy religions.

I know. My mother and I became Jehovah's Witnesses in 1944, when I was nine years old. I grew up drenched in the dark blood-poetry of a fierce messianic sect. Shortly after my conversion, I got my first period. We used to sing this hymn: "Here is He who comes from Eden/all His raiment stained with blood." My raiments were stained with blood, too. But the blood of the Son of Man was purifying, redemptive, cleansing, sacrificial. Mine was filthy—proof of my having inherited the curse placed upon the seductress Eve. I used to "read" my used Kotexes compulsively, as if the secret of life—or a harbinger of death—were to be found in that dull, mysterious effluence.

My brother, at the time of our conversion, was four. After a few years of listlessly following my mother and me around in our door-to-door and street-corner proselytizing, he allied himself with my father, who had been driven to noisy, militant atheism by the presence of two female religious fanatics in his hitherto patriarchal household. When your wife and daughter are in love with God, it's hard to compete—particularly since God is good enough not to require messy sex as proof or expression of love. As a child, I observed that it was not extraordinary for women who became Jehovah's Witnesses to remove themselves from their husbands' beds as a first step to getting closer to God. For women whose experience had taught them that all human relationships were treacherous and capricious and frighteningly volatile, an escape from the confusions of the world into the certainties of a fundamentalist religion provided the illusion of safety and of rest. It is not too simple to say that the reason many unhappily married and sexually embittered women fell in love with Jehovah was that they didn't have to go to bed with Him.

Apocalyptic religions are, by their nature, antierotic. Jehovah's Witnesses believe that the world—or, as they would have it, "this evil system under Satan the Devil"—will end in our lifetime. After the slaughter Jehovah has arranged for his enemies at Armageddon, say the Witnesses, this quintessentially masculine God—vengeful in battle, benevolent to survivors—will turn the earth into an Edenic paradise for true believers. I grew up under the umbrella of the slogan, "Millions Now Living Will Never Die," convinced that 1914 marked "the beginning of the times of the end." So firmly did Jehovah's

Witnesses believe this to be true that there were those who, in 1944, refused to get their teeth filled, postponing all care of their bodies until God saw to their regeneration in His New World, which was just around the corner.

Some corner.

Despite the fact that their hopes were not immediately rewarded, Jehovah's Witnesses have persevered with increasing fervor and conviction, and their attitude toward the world remains the same: because all their longing is for the future, they are bound to hate the present—the material, the sexual, the flesh. It's impossible, of course, truly to savor and enjoy the present, or to bend one's energies to shape and mold the world into the form of goodness, if you are only waiting for it to be smashed by God. There is a kind of ruthless glee in the way in which Jehovah's Witnesses point to earthquakes, race riots, heroin addiction, the failure of the United Nations, divorce, famine, and liberalized abortion laws as proof of the nearness of Armageddon.

The world will end, according to the Witnesses, in a great shaking and rending and tearing of unbelieving flesh, with unsanctified babies swimming in blood—torrents of blood. They await God's Big Bang—the final orgasmic burst of violence, after which all things will come together in a cosmic orgasm of joy. In the meantime, they have disgust and contempt for the world; and freedom and spontaneity, even playfulness, in sex is explicitly frowned upon.

When I was ten, it would have been more than my life was worth to acknowledge, as Anna does so casually, that I knew what *screwing* was. (Ignorance, however, delivered me from that grave error.) Once, having read somewhere that Hitler had a mistress, I asked my mother what a mistress was. (I had an inkling that it was some kind of sinister superhousekeeper, like Judith Anderson in *Rebecca*.) I knew from my mother's silence, and from her cold, hard, and frightened face, that the question was somehow a grievous offense. I knew that I had done something terribly wrong, but as usual, I didn't know what. The fact was that I never knew how to buy God's—or my mother's—approval. There were sins I consciously and knowingly committed. That was bad, but it was bearable. I could always pray to God to forgive me, say, for reading the Bible for its "dirty parts" (to prefer the Song of Solomon to all the begats of Genesis was proof absolute of the sinfulness of my nature). But the offenses that made me most cringingly guilty were those I had committed unconsciously; as an imperfect human being descended from the wretched Eve, I was bound—so I had been taught—to offend Jehovah seventy-seven times a day without my even knowing what I was doing wrong.

I knew that good Christians didn't commit "unnatural acts"; but I didn't know what "unnatural acts" were. I knew that an increase in the number of rapes was one of the signs heralding the end of the world, but I didn't know what rape was. Consequently, I spent a lot of time praying that I was not committing unnatural acts or rape.

My ignorance of all things sexual was so profound that it frequently led to comedies of error. Nothing I've ever read has inclined me to believe that Jehovah has a sense of humor, and I must say that I consider it a strike against Him that He wouldn't find this story funny: One night shortly after my conversion, a visiting elder of the congregation, as he was avuncularly tucking me in bed, asked me if I were guilty of performing evil practices with my hands under the covers at night. I was puzzled. He was persistent. Finally, I thought I understood. And I burst into wild tears of self-recrimination: What I did under the covers at night was bite my cuticles—a practice which, in fact, did afford me a kind of sensual pleasure. I didn't learn about masturbation—which the Witnesses call "idolatry" because "the masturbator's affection is diverted away from the Creator and is bestowed upon a coveted object . . . his genitals"—until much later. So, having confessed to a sin that I didn't even know existed, I was advised of the necessity of keeping one's body pure from sin; cold baths were recommended. I couldn't see the connection between cold baths and my cuticles, but one never questioned the imperatives of an elder. So I subjected my impure body, in midwinter, to so many icy baths that I began to look like a bleached prune. My mother thought I was demented. But I couldn't tell her that I'd been biting my cuticles, because to have incurred God's wrath—and to see the beady eye of the elder steadfastly upon me at every religious meeting I went to —was torment enough. There was no way to win.

One never questioned the imperatives of an elder. I learned as a very small child that it was my primary duty in life to "make nice." When I was little, I was required to respond to inquiries about my health in this manner: "Fine and dandy, just like sugar candy, thank you." And to curtsy. If that sounds like something from a Shirley Temple movie, it's because it is. Having been brought up to be the Italian working-class Shirley Temple from Bensonhurst, it was not terribly difficult for me to learn to "make nice" for God and the elders. Behaving well was relatively easy. The passionate desire to win approval guaranteed my conforming. But behaving well never made me feel good. I always felt as if I were a bad person.

I ask myself why it was that my brother was not hounded by the obsessive guilt and the desperate desire for approval that informed all my actions. Partly, I suppose, luck, and an accident of temperament, but also because of the peculiarly guilt-inspiring double message girls received. Girls were taught that it was their nature to be spiritual, but paradoxically that they were more prone to absolute depravity than were boys.

In my religion, everything beautiful and noble and spiritual and good was represented by a woman; and everything evil and depraved and monstrous was represented by a woman. I learned that "God's organization," the "bride of Christ," or His 144,000 heavenly co-rulers were represented by a "chaste virgin." I also learned that "Babylon the Great," or "false religion," was "the mother of the abominations or the 'disgusting things of the earth' . . . She likes to get drunk on human blood. . . . Babylon the Great is . . . pictured as a woman, an international harlot."

Young girls were thought not to have the "urges" boys had. They were not only caretakers of their own sleepy sexuality but protectors of boys' vital male animal impulses as well. They were thus doubly responsible, and, if they fell, doubly damned. Girls were taught that, simply by existing, they were provoking male sexuality . . . which it was their job then to subdue.

To be female, I learned, was to be Temptation; nothing short of death—the transformation of your atoms into a lilac bush—could change that. (I used to dream deliciously of dying, of being as inert—and as unaccountable—as the dust I came from.) Inasmuch as males naturally "wanted it" more, when a female "wanted it" she was doubly depraved, unnatural as well as sinful. She was the receptacle for male lust, "the weaker vessel." If the vessel, created by God for the use of males, presumed to have desires of its own, it was perforce consigned to the consuming fires of God's wrath. If, then, a woman were to fall from grace, her fall would be mighty indeed—and her willful nature would lead her into that awful abyss where she would be deprived of the redemptive love of God and the validating love of man. Whereas, were a man to fall, he would be merely stumbling over his own feet of clay.

(Can this be accident? My brother, when he was young, was always falling over his own feet. I, on the other hand, to this day sweat with terror at the prospect of going down escalators or long flights of stairs. I cannot fly; I am afraid of the fall.)

I spent my childhood walking a religious tightrope, maintaining a difficult dizzying balance. I was, for example, expected to perform well at school, so that glory would accrue to Jehovah and "His organization." But I was also made continually aware of the perils of falling prey to "the wisdom of this world which is foolishness to God." I had constantly to defend myself against the danger of trusting my own judgment. To question or to criticize God's "earthly representatives" was a sure sign of "demonic influence"; to express doubt openly was to risk being treated like a spiritual leper. I was always an honor student at school; but this was hardly an occasion for unqualified joy. I felt, rather, as if I were courting spiritual disaster: while I was congratulated for having "given a witness" by virtue of my academic excellence, I was, in the next breath, warned against the danger of supposing that my intelligence could function independently of God's. The effect of all this was to convince me that my intelligence was like some kind of tricky, predatory animal, which, if it were not kept firmly reined, would surely spring on and destroy me.

"Vanity, thy name is woman." I learned very early what happened to women with "independent spirits" who opposed the will and imperatives of male elders. They were disfellowshipped (excommunicated) and thrown into "outer darkness." Held up as an example of such perfidious conduct was Maria Frances Russell, the wife of Charles Taze Russell, charismatic founder of the sect.

Russell charged his wife with "the same malady which has smitten others—*ambition.*" Complaining of a "female conspiracy" against the Lord's organization, he wrote: "The result was a considerable stirring up of slander and misrepresentation, for of course it would not suit [her] purposes to tell the plain unvarnished truth, that Sister Russell was ambitious. . . . When she desired to come back, I totally refused, except upon a promise that she should make reasonable acknowledgment of the wrong course she had been pursuing." Ambition in a woman was, by implication, so reprehensible as to exact from Jehovah the punishment of death.

(What the Witnesses appeared less eager to publicize about the Russells' spiritual-cum-marital problems is that in April, 1906, Mrs. Russell, having filed suit for legal separation, told a jury that her husband had once remarked to a young orphan woman the Russells had reared: "I am like a jellyfish. I float around here and there. I touch this one and that one, and if she responds I take her to me, and if not I float on to others." Mrs. Russell was unable to prove her charge.)

I remember a line in *A Nun's Story:* "Dear God," the disaffected Belgian nun anguished, "forgive me. I will never be able to love a Nazi." I, conversely, prayed tormentedly for many years, "Dear God, forgive me, I am not able to hate what you hate. I love the world." As a Witness I was taught that "friendship with the world" was "spiritual adultery." The world was crawling with Satan's agents. But Satan's agents— evolutionists, "false religionists," and all those who opposed, or were indifferent to, "Jehovah's message"—often seemed like perfectly nice, decent, indeed lovable people to me. (They were certainly interesting.) As I went from door to door, ostensibly to help the Lord divide the "goats" from the "sheep," I found that I was more and more listening to *their* lives; and I became increasingly more tentative about telling them that I had *The* Truth. As I grew older, I found it more and more difficult to eschew their company. I entertained fantasies, at one time or another, about a handsome, ascetic Jesuit priest I had met in my preaching work and about Albert Schweitzer, J. D. Salinger, E.B. White, and Frank Sinatra; in fact, I was committing "spiritual adultery" all over the place. And then, when I was fifteen, I fell in love with an "unbeliever."

If I felt—before having met and loved Arnold Horowitz, English 31, New Utrecht High School—that life was a tightrope, I felt afterward that my life was perpetually being lived on a high wire, with no safety net to catch me. I was obliged, by every tenet of my faith, to despise him: to be "yoked with an unbeliever," an atheist and an intellectual . . . the pain was exquisite.

He was the essential person, the person who taught me how to love, and how to doubt. Arnold became interested in me because I was smart; he loved me because he thought I was good. He nourished me. He nurtured me. He paid me the irresistible compliment of totally comprehending me. He hated my religion. He railed against the sect that would rather see babies die than permit them to have blood transfusions, which were regarded as unscriptural; he had boundless contempt for my overseers, who would not permit me to go to college—the "Devil's playground," which would fill my head with wicked, ungodly nonsense; he protested mightily, with the rage that springs from genuine compassion, against a religion that could tolerate segregation and apartheid, sneer at martyred revolutionaries, dismiss social reform and material charity as "irrelevant," a religion that—waiting for God to cure all human ills—would act by default to maintain the status quo, while regarding human pain and struggle without pity and without generosity. He loathed the world view that had been imposed on me, a black-and-white view that allowed no complexities, no moral dilemmas, that disdained metaphysical or philosophical or psychological inquiry; he loathed the bloated simplicities that held me in thrall. But he loved *me*. I had never before felt loved unconditionally.

This was a measure of his love: Jehovah's Witnesses are not permitted to salute the flag. Arnold came, unbidden, to sit with me at every school assembly, to hold my hand, while everyone else stood at rigid salute. We were very visible; and I was very comforted. And this was during the McCarthy era. Arnold had a great deal to lose, and he risked it all for me. Nobody had ever risked anything for me before. How could I believe that he was wicked?

We drank malteds on his porch and read T. S. Eliot and listened to Mozart. We walked for hours, talking of God and goodness and happiness and death. We met surreptitiously. (My mother so feared and hated the man who was leading me into apostasy that she once threw a loaf of Arnold bread out the window; his very name was loathsome to her.) Arnold treated me with infinite tenderness; he was the least alarming man I had ever known. His fierce concentration on me, his solicitious care uncoupled with sexual aggression, was the gentlest—and most thrilling—love I had ever known. He made me feel what I had never felt before—valuable, and good.

It was very hard. All my dreams centered around Arnold, who was becoming more important, certainly more real to me, than God. All my dreams were blood-colored. I would fantasize about Arnold's being converted and surviving Armageddon and living forever with me in the New World. Or I would fantasize about my dying with Arnold, in fire and flames, at Armageddon. I would try to make bargains with God—my life for his. When I confessed my terrors to the men in charge of my spiritual welfare—when I said that I knew I could not rejoice in the destruction of the "wicked" at Armageddon— I was told that I was presuming to be "more compassionate than Jehovah," the deadliest sin against the holy spirit. I was reminded that, being a woman and therefore weak and sentimental, I would have to go against my sinful nature and listen to their superior wisdom, which consisted of my never seeing Arnold again. I was also reminded of the perils of being over-smart: if I hadn't been such a good student, none of this would have happened to me.

I felt as if I were leading a double life, as indeed I was. I viewed the world as beautifully various, as a blemished but mysteriously wonderful place, as savable by humans, who were neither good nor bad but imperfectly wise; but I *acted* as if the world were fit for nothing but destruction, as if all human efforts to purchase happiness and goodness were doomed to failure and deserving of contempt, as if all people could be categorized as "sheep" or "goats" and herded into their appropriate destinies by a judgmental Jehovah, the all-seeing Father who knew better than His children what was good for them.

As I had when I was a little girl, I "made nice" as best I could. I maintained the appearance of "goodness," that is, of religiosity, although it violated my truest feelings. When I left high school, I went into the full-time preaching work. I spent a minimum of five hours a day ringing doorbells and conducting home Bible studies. I went to three religious meetings a week. I prayed that my outward conformity would lead to inner peace. I met Arnold very occasionally, when my need to see him overcame my elders' imperatives and my own devastating fears. He was always accessible to me. Our meetings partook equally of misery and of joy. I tried, by my busyness, to lock all my doubts into an attic of my mind.

And for a while, and in a way, it "took." I derived sustenance from communal surges of revivalist fervor at religious conventions and from the conviction that I was united, in a common cause, with a tiny minority of persecuted and comradely brothers and sisters whose approval became both my safety net and the Iron Curtain that shut me off from the world. I felt that I had chosen Jehovah, and that my salvation, while not assured, was at least a possibility; perhaps He would choose me. I vowed finally never to see Arnold again, hoping, by this sacrifice, to gain God's approval for him as well as for me.

I began to understand that for anyone so obviously weak and irresponsible as I, only a life of self-sacrifice and abnegation could work. I wanted to be consumed by Jehovah, to be locked so closely into the straitjacket of His embrace that I would be impervious to the devilish temptations my irritable, independent intelligence threw up in my path.

I wished to be eaten up alive; and my wish was granted. When I was nineteen, I was accepted into Bethel, the headquarters organization of Jehovah's Witnesses, where I worked and lived, one of twelve young women among two hundred and fifty men, for three years. "Making nice" had paid off. Every minute of my waking life was accounted for; there was no leisure in which to cultivate vice or reflection. I called myself happy. I worked as a housekeeper for my brothers, making thirty beds a day, sweeping and vacuuming and waxing and washing fifteen rooms a day (in addition to proselytizing in my "free time"); I daily washed the bathtub thirty men had bathed in. In fact, the one demurral I made during those years was to ask—I found it so onerous—if perhaps the brothers, many of whom worked in the Witnesses' factory, could not clean out their own bathtub (thirty layers of grease is a lot of grease). I was told by the male overseer who supervised housekeepers that Jehovah had assigned me this "privilege." And I told myself I was lucky.

I felt myself to be even luckier—indeed, blessed—when, after two years of this servant's work, one of Jehovah's middlemen, the president of the Watch Tower Bible and Tract Society, told me that he was assigning me to proofread Watch Tower publications. He accompanied this benediction with a warning: this new honor, I was told, was to be a test of my integrity—"Remember in all things to defer to the brothers; you will have to guard your spirit against pride and vanity. Satan will try now to tempt you as never before."

And defer I did. There were days when I felt literally as if my eternal destiny hung upon a comma: if the brother with whom I worked decided a comma should go out where I wanted to put one in, I prayed to Jehovah to forgive me for that presumptuous comma. I was perfectly willing to deny the existence of a split infinitive if that would placate my brother. I denied and denied—commas, split infinitives, my sexuality, my intelligence, my femaleness, my yearning to be part of the world—until suddenly with a great silent shifting and shuddering, and with more pain than I had ever experienced or expect to experience again, I broke. I woke up one morning, packed my bags, and walked out of that place. I was twenty-two; and I had to learn how to begin to live. It required a great deal of courage; I do not think I will ever be capable of that much courage again.

The full story of life in that institution and the ramifications of my decision to leave it is too long to tell here; and it will take me the rest of my life to understand fully the ways in which everything I have ever done since has been colored and informed by the guilt that was my daily bread for so many dry years, by the desperate need for approval that allowed me to be swallowed up whole by a devouring religion, by the carefully fostered desire to "make nice" and to be "a good girl," by the conviction that I was nothing and nobody unless I served a cause superior to that of my own necessities.

Arnold, of course, foresaw the difficulty; when I left religion, he said, "Now you will be just like the rest of us." With no guiding passion, he meant; uncertain, he meant, and often muddled and confused, and always struggling. And he wept.

As an infant I was baptized Roman Catholic. In 1977 I received Communion for the first time. I was far from anticipat-

ing this "conversion"—or, more properly, this return—when I wrote Growing Up Apocalyptic *in 1975. (Life astounds.) I talk about my newfound Catholicism—which confounds many of my friends, and, to some degree, continues to surprise me—in my book* Visions of Glory: A History and a Memory of Jehovah's Witnesses *(Simon and Schuster, 1978).*

—B.G.H., 1979

OH, HOW WE WORSHIPED
THE GODS
OF THE FIFTIES!

(July, 1976)

I have a snapshot taken on my sixteenth birthday in 1950: I am wearing black leotards, a flared quilt skirt that ends midcalf in delicious, provocative waves; my feet are shod in Capezio ballet slippers; my mouth is fixed in a Tangee (orange-in-the-tube, pink-on-your-lips) grin; my hair is tortured in an improbable arrangement that has even less to do with art than it has to do with nature; oversized gold hoop five-and-dime earrings graze my neck. It is my Greenwich Village uniform. But I have never been to Greenwich Village, it is still a country of the mind; and my beauty-parlor perm and my Tangee Natural and my screw-on earrings mark me as ineffably *Brooklyn.* Everything, in fact, is hopelessly out of synch. (How Diane Arbus would have loved me!) I have created myself in the image of my fantasies, fantasies drawn from movies, and novels of the Bohemian life; I look like a child's energetic drawing of something he has never seen—crude, imaginative, and unfinished. The look on my face, bewildered but insanely grinning, is the look I have seen on men's faces two seconds before they've fully understood that their flies are open in public.

Everyone who grew up in the fifties will know that something is missing in that picture: as it is my sixteenth birthday, I should be wearing a bouquet of sugar cubes and pink ribbons. But I was brought up in a fancy religion that frowned upon the frivolity of birthday celebrations; and my Sweet Sixteen birthday came and went without sugar cubes, autograph books, sleep-over parties in baby-doll pajamas, and the exchange of virginal girlish confidences over Going All the Way. It wasn't until I was twenty-two that I slipped out of the reins of parental authority and left my constricting religion—and made a bee-line for Greenwich Village, the finishing school for my genera-tion of energetic, imaginative, fantasy-bemused young women.

Now, this is the nice thing: my eccentric upbringing was in many ways a perfect preparation, and a passport, for my being alive-and-aware (we used the world *aware* a lot) in the Green-wich Village of the fifties. I fit as sweetly into that decade as a nut fits in its shell. Because the thing about the fifties was that everybody—everybody being the people one knew or emu-lated or loved—felt out of synch with his time, and glad of it. We all cherished our idiosyncrasies and our neuroses; we would have laughed est, AT, Esalen, and all the sixties/seventies psychic-smoosh therapies to scorn. In spite of the somewhat paradoxical fact that practically everyone one knew spent his or her lunch hour on the analyst's couch, we couldn't imagine where we'd be without our disfiguring—but *interesting*—neu-roses. Narcissists worshiping our own singularity, we seldom thought that there might be public or group solutions to pri-vate problems. We had been teenagers during the McCarthy H.U.A.C. horror; but neither that cruel nightmare, nor the Cold War, nor the Korean War—so unlike the children of the sixties were we—served to "radicalize" or politicize us. Occa-sionally, it's true, we went to meetings of the Young Socialist Party, and we heaved sighs over our country's racism or Amer-ica's intervention in the affairs of the banana republics, but mostly we took refuge in the rich interior lives we all believed we had; we did not know, or think to figure out, how our personal lives could mesh with public concerns. It was In to be an Outsider.

To be an Outsider was to be of the elect. We were generous

enough to accept people at their own evaluation, and when gray-flanneled drones from Madison Avenue invaded our turf and protested that they had poems in their heads and rebellion in their hearts, we believed them: if the Fat Lady could be Jesus Christ, why *couldn't* the man in the gray-flannel suit be a poet? We distrusted surfaces. This was, after all, the decade that had, without a hint of self-mockery, spawned a literary magazine called *The Noble Savage.* In our kindness and our condescension, we chose to believe in the nobility and the savage innocence of nine-to-fivers who paraded their nerves and sensitivity, their satchels full of unpublished manuscripts, in our bars and our coffeehouses. But in our hearts of hearts, we knew that while everybody was "evolving," we were the people our generation really belonged to, we were more sensitive, more vulnerable, more risk-taking, more alive. Everybody was a rebel without a cause, but everybody living in the Village was a rebel where the rebellion was *happening.* I think we thought we were holy. We thought everybody in pain was holy: when I had a love affair (my first) with a black jazz musician, and my best friend had an affair (her first) with an advertising executive, we quarreled over whose pain was greater—the pain of a black musician living on talent and no money and dope, or the pain of a man whose gray flannels covered quiet desperation and a yearning to "become." (Oh, those fifties words! No wonder Nichols and May were able to satirize us so adroitly.) We were really having a quarrel over who was more holy.

Look at our heroes: Sinatra, Salinger, Camus, Brando. They were holy men.

Okay. On the face of it, Frank Sinatra seems an unlikely candidate for any pantheon of gods. But you have to think not of the cold-eyed, paunchy, stale, and bullying Sinatra of the seventies but of that tough-tender, rakish reed from Hoboken, that sweet survivor. That Sinatra could crack your heart. Stubborn, defiant, proud, cocky, willful and winsome and wholly engaging, buffeted and boisterous and boyishly bashful, he did it his way then—and we loved him for it. And lonely. Of course we thought he was lonely, magnificently lonely, a golden-gloves fighter in the ring with the big bad pros, up against great odds, with nothing but his native wit and his brashness to sustain him. He bucked the crowd, as heroes are meant to do. He was the Outsider who fought back and made it. That astonishing comeback: a has-been in the early fifties (he'd fallen so low as to make a record with a Dumb Blond actress called Dagmar, on which he'd barked like a dog), an Academy Award winner in 1954 for his portrayal—drawn from life, we thought—of Maggio, the feisty rebel, friend-of-the-underdog, always-on-the-side-of-the-victim, wisecracking hero of *From Here to Eternity.* He had no ideology, but he was True to Himself. In the fifties, that was good enough; it was, in fact, perceived as goodness. When Prewitt (Montgomery Clift) said epigrammatically in *From Here to Eternity,* "Unless a man goes his own way, he ain't nuthin'," he might have been speaking for the Sinatra we loved, the Sinatra who had been written off in 1950 as a failure. In the fifties, failures, if they were flamboyant enough, endeared themselves to us; it was almost a mark of virtue to fail spectacularly, it meant that all the Insiders were against you. When Sinatra once again achieved success, his past failures lent piquancy to his victory. What we loved was not so much his success but his persistence. What we admired in him was his rash, solitary courage. He had—this was the pre-*Godfather* myth—done it alone. To do it alone was the great thing.

That, surely, was the message we had drawn from Salinger and from Camus—the message that man had to carry the weight of his life alone. On the surface, the French existentialist author of *The Myth of Sisyphus* and *The Rebel* and the reclusive American ecstatic who wrote *Franny and Zooey* and *The Catcher in the Rye* seem to be writers with vastly different sensibilities. Salinger had chosen, as it were, *against* the world: his characters' Christ-Zen-Vedanta, Kingdom-of-God-Is-Within mysticism transformed everyday occurrences into something holy. Camus, believing that death renders life absurd, accepted the world in all its splendor and futility. From both writers we imbibed the romance of the lonely struggle. (We learned to look for the marks of that struggle in our men.) Salinger wrote with an effervescent, painful ecstasy; it often seemed as if he were writing with his eyeballs, certainly with all his nerve endings exposed. It was his genius to appear to write, just as Sinatra appeared to sing, to each of us alone. Camus wrote out of lucid despair. Both, in an ordered delirium, invited us to be both passionate and detached—or to value those qualities in our men. Salinger's poet-suicide hero, Seymour Glass (one of seven Glass siblings, all of whom we invariably preferred to our own prosaic brothers and sisters), said that his favorite word in the Bible was *watch*! Camus said that the hallmark of the absurd man was anguished awareness. It comes to the same thing. Both Camus and Salinger told us to drain life to its bitter end. And both men propelled us to the purest of joys—to feeling as opposed to thinking.

Camus said "a subclerk in the post office is the equal of a conqueror if consciousness is common to them"; Salinger said that the Fat Lady sitting on her porch in the unendurable heat, swatting flies, cancer eating at her insides, was Jesus Christ. Where one registered *God,* the other registered *human;* for both, everything was hallowed by one's awareness of it. They both inclined us to regard pain as a sacrament. (No wonder they used *terrible* and *beautiful* in the same sentence all the time.) Knowing, or feeling, that there were no victorious causes, both loved lost causes, causes that required "uncontaminated souls." Both conveyed the message that the discipline of awareness led, inevitably, to creation: poets and artists were the true see-ers, the only seers. Both seemed to be living on the dangerous edge of the world. . . . And we said, Whoopee! We'll go live there, too.

So we did. We went looking for terrible beauty and beautiful pain, in search of holy fools and noble absurd men.

And if, in our coffeeshops and bars and jazz clubs, we found, not poets and artists, but dilettantes and poseurs, men who managed to be thoroughly absurd in the vulgar sense—that is, silly—without being at all noble, we did find plenty of lost causes. We found men, that is, who spoke the language of despair and the language of ecstasy, and we took them to our bosoms and to our beds.

It is only on rereading Salinger and Camus that I realize how necessary women were to them as foils. Preferably long-legged, cool, innocent young women with undiscriminating hearts. Neither of our literary idols was a macho writer in the way that, say, Mailer is a macho writer; but both insisted upon the unspoiled beauty of women, the untrammeled souls of women, to set off their ideal man's saintliness or heroism. Women were there to mediate between them and the harsh world, to console. Mostly women were just there, like the ocean and the sky, to provide backdrops for their essential deeds. Men were the inspired lunatics, the lovers, the poets, and the anguished seeers. Women held men to the things of this world—that was their value. Adorable in their sweet simplicity, women brought cups of consecrated chicken soup to sufferers.

Salinger, it's true, created one woman with a life and angst of her own: Franny Glass, who says the Jesus Prayer, and has a nervous breakdown because of all the goddamn phonies in the world. But Franny is an exception, a member of the sanctified Glass family, ennobled and purified by her association with her guru brothers. None of her guru brothers has a love affair with a flesh-and-blood woman who is in any way his equal. Seymour Glass, you may remember, puts a bullet through his head while vacationing in Florida with his beauti-

ful wife Muriel—in large part, we're led to suspect, because the
lovely Muriel never really respected or understood the antic
Pilgrim Soul in him. We despised the Muriels of this world.
Poor Muriel, she wanted a nice middle-class husband; even her
undiscriminating heart couldn't quite understand the impulse
that had led Seymour, when he was a child, to throw a rock
at a beautiful young girl precisely because the girl was so beautiful he couldn't stand it, he loved her so much. Our sympathies
were entirely with Seymour. His rock seemed to us to be flung
from the slingshot of a god. Gods frolic and are driven by
ecstasy to do strange and wonderful things. We thought that
girl had earned her scars, like marks from a god. . . . And we
set out to earn ours.

What it amounted to was that we would accept any damned
nonsense from a man, provided that it was haloed by poetic
feeling. If our men were struggling and in pain—not to put too
fine a point on it, if they were losers—we brought them cups
of consecrated chicken soup.

It grieves me, it really does, to understand that what we
extrapolated from both Salinger and Camus was the message
that we were meant to be handmaidens to the gods. To the
god-in-men. Camus regarded Don Juan as a great wise man
who lived bravely without illusions of eternal love, a man for
whom loving and possessing, conquering and consuming, were
ways of knowing, means of provoking, a nonexistent God.
. . . What good and earnest pupils we were! We invested every
fast-talking faithless womanizer we knew with noble qualities.
We lived to be loved, possessed, conquered, and consumed.

Once I sat on Frank Sinatra's lap. It was when I was living
with a jazz musician. We'd left Birdland, it was three o'clock
in the morning, and a voice—The Voice—hailed us from a
cab. We piled in with alacrity. (Sinatra was, by the way, one
of the few white musicians who had a good press among black

musicians, most of whom insisted that white musicians couldn't swing because they didn't have soul—which is to say that they hadn't suffered enough. White musicians were relatively low in the hierarchy of sufferers.) On the way to a Harlem after-hours club, I sat perched on Sinatra's bony knees, occasionally turning, heart in my mouth, to gaze. Though he was holding me, I felt as if I were holding something priceless and fragile, like a Greek urn. A small epiphany.

There were many such epiphanies—life was never boring—not all of them on a man's knees, most of them on a man's coattails. When I look back at my life, and my friends' lives, in the fifties, it seems to me we were always trying lives on. Another man, another life.

A devoted practitioner of serial monogamy, I went from man to man, believing each time, of course, that this was the only man, that all other loves had been delusions. Each time, not only did I take on the man, I acquired a whole new life (his), a new way of being.

When I lived with my musician, I became thoroughly immersed in the jazz world, and had, it must be said, faint scorn for anyone not privileged enough to be joined to that world of sufferers. It has been suggested that we were the first groupies. Naturally, pleading True Love, I shrink from that label; but I see the point. At the time, I shared the musicians' contempt for female hangers-on who would attach themselves to any musician at all (not that their contempt precluded their availing themselves of the girls' services); I was in love with one musician, not the entire genre. Looking back, though, I can't be absolutely sure that I wasn't in love with the whole genre. G., my musician, was wonderfully appealing; he was witty, wry, selfish, bitter, self-mocking, poor, married, a libertine who demanded total commitment from his women, a good and generous lover (when he was there). A perfect person with whom to break all the rules. His world was magic. I was literally transported to a hot, intense world where men took enormous risks, played their hearts out, blew their minds on drugs (at a time when marijuana was still called the Devil's weed), flirted with death, and lived permanently on the razor's edge of poverty. They were the inner circle of the Outsiders. Our proximity to them guaranteed us a place in that privileged circle. Our world was celebrated by Beat poets. Paris had its existential chanteuses; we had the real thing, we lived next to the real cry of the heart. But I'm terribly afraid that while those men used women to sustain them (both sexually and financially), we played our part in this dicey game: we objectified them by loving their suffering better than we loved them. The truth was, most jazz musicians wanted with all their hearts to become safe studio musicians and to live on Park Avenue with German maids. It was we, their romantic camp followers, who thought the secular equivalent of the Holy Grail could be found at the Five Spot or Minton's or Birdland, we who thought their poverty was a mark of their noble not-belonging. Told to drain life to its dregs, where better could we do it than in smoky clubs, illegal after-hours joints, with wounded men who had lovers in other towns? Everything in that world gratified our hunger for experience, it was like being plunged into pure feeling unsullied by thought. We were chained to men we regarded, not without reason, as rebels and martyrs. The fact that these rebels and martyrs burned us up in the furnace of their own needs made everything all the more dangerous, hence all the more exciting.

That world was full of joy—those men were, after all, true creators, and they laughed a lot. But it was never really happy. To live exhilaratingly in and for the moment is deadly serious work, fun of the most exhausting sort. As Dorothy Parker once remarked, you can say *Live and laugh and love and lie . . . for tomorrow you must die* all you want, the sad truth is you don't die, you wake up with a hangover.

So (understand that I am describing not just my own odyssey but the similar voyages of many of the young women of that time), I went from the furnace of the jazz world to the fire of other men's needs. Poets and writers and artists and such. It was the same story all over again. Love was anything but restful. How very foolish we were, and how gallant: we should have hung out shingles—Lost Causes, Come to Us! A lot has been made of women's masochism; the women I knew in the fifties suffered from another disorder: we all had multiple personalities. When I said good-bye to G., I said good-bye to the jazz world. And hello to the Cedar Bar, hangout of Pollock and Franz Kline, home of abstract-expressionists. The next man, you will have guessed, was an Artist. A Poor, Struggling Artist. So I tried that life on. Saturdays outside McSorley's—a Lower East Side bar that did not then admit women to its sacred sawdusty precincts—sitting on a camp chair, knitting argyle socks for the Artist (those *sensitive* watercolors!). And, after that, it was a Writer, A Bold, Uncompromising, Anti-Establishment Writer who hurt a lot. Blood on the page, and *Would you please correct my proofs?* Sundays at literary salons.

And so on. And on. (I'm not saying it was altogether bad, that multiplicity of personalities. It was, if you didn't forget entirely who you were, exciting. If you did forget entirely who you were, you could have a fifties identity crisis . . . after which you usually got married.) Of course there was an occasional doctor or lawyer, even an insurance salesman. But it was hard to think of any of them as needy and needing. Could one be a handmaiden to a successful eye-ear-and-throat surgeon? Hardly. There was not the necessary glamour, the poetry of pain.

We were suckers for saints in the fifties, lovers of unsuccess. But there was one man who was a success, and still—restless and dissatisfied—out of synch with his time, a permanent

Outsider, a man who stuck his tongue out at "them," even though, as Truman Capote said, he was "a young man sitting on a pile of candy."

There is a story that circulated about Marlon Brando: when he was quite little, his pet dog died. A neighbor lady attempted, with treacly sympathy, to console him. Brando looked her in the eye, said, "There's a bee on your nose," and punched her.

Brando despised Hollywood. Or so he said. We believed him. He sneered and sulked, he had all the fifties words. He questioned the point of being an actor if you didn't *evolve;* he wanted a life that *led* somewhere; endlessly introspective, he publicly doubted his ability to *love* or *relate* to anybody. It seems banal now, his Peck's-bad-boy/Yoga routine.

Brando may have invented himself as he went along, to confound journalists, but whether or not he told the strict truth was almost beside the point. There isn't a single story about him written in the fifties that doesn't have the word *vulnerable* in it, and very few that don't speak of his "terrible honesty." He was called the Valentino of the Bop generation. But we loved him because he kept impatiently shaking the stardust off. He was real, like the men we loved in real life, only more so. While his lofty stated aims seemed at times to be at odds with his behavior—he was making *Teahouse of the August Moon* and *Sayonara* while he was decrying Hollywood potboilers—if he didn't exactly bite the commercial hand that fed him, he snarled at it a lot, and that was enough to make us love him. We forgave him anything.

It's odd that, while he never stopped explaining himself, he was a quintessentially private person. You always got the feeling that if you overstepped your bounds, he'd punch you in the nose. He was the Lonely Struggler incarnate. Uncouth and dignified, sensitive and rebellious, he was the poet-buried-in-the-animal. I'm willing to take bets that there isn't one woman in a thousand who saw *Streetcar* who didn't prefer Stanley

Kowalski to Karl Malden's more sympathetic Mitch; there was poetry, as well as method, in his savagery.

Let's face it, there was something more than a little effete about the coffeehouse intellectuals who talked and talked and talked about life and death and God and happiness; they could make you long for a little healthy brutality. And as gorgeous as the physical, nonverbal world of the jazz clubs was, it was also ultimately stifling; in the fifties, we needed words for salvation, and that world had a limited vocabulary. With beautiful, brainy, muscled Brando, you got it all—Zen and Freud, talk and action, sex and sensibility, passion and detachment and romance. He was a tender man with authority, and he was irresistible.

Brando's beauty is ravaged now. And we've all moved on to other things. More or less. Some of us have gone in the direction Camus led us in: we've understood that in a world where there are victims and victimizers we are obliged to take our stand with the victims. We have, that is to say, become political. Others have retreated into a Salingeresque privacy, hoping by that means to wash their hands of nonessentials. The most interesting problem for people of my age—people who grew up in the fifties—remains how to unite the personal and the political, how to be in the world and of it, but not to be bent out of shape by it.

As for the women I grew up with, a lot of them are still, with scant success, looking for the absurd man, the authentic man, the poet-in-the-animal. We're still carrying those invisible cups of chicken soup around.

I'm still a closet Sinatra fan. I still think of Brando as the best actor in the world. Fifties women are incredibly loyal. They don't forget.

Feminism
and
Individuality

CONSCIOUSNESS-RAISING:
TRUTH AND CONSEQUENCES
(1977)

Consciousness-Raising: Truth and Consequences *appeared originally under a pseudonym—to protect the privacy of the members of my C-R group, I said then. I think now that I disguised my identity from motives of cowardice—to protect myself. I have changed names and identifying characteristics of the women in my group; but I am no longer inclined not to take responsibility for the sentiments I expressed.*

One night our consciousness-raising group met in the sixth-floor walk-up of a woman I didn't like. I didn't like her; I was obliged, by the rules of the game and the tenor of the times —it was 1970—to call her "sister." I felt angry, as a consequence, and put-upon, and guilty. I thought it was silly to pretend that it was possible to love all women, and mischievous nonsense to assume that all women were lovable simply by virtue of their being oppressed. I was unhappy.

Six of us arrived together. One woman sprinted up all six flights of stairs. The rest of us labored far behind, our smoke-filled lungs inadequate to the task, our hearts palpitating with exertion. I'll never forget the look on the sprinter's face when the rest of us—a ragged and breathless lot—arrived on the final landing: pure, uncensored pleasure at our discomfort. "I don't know what's wrong with all of you," she gloated. "You'd better take care of your bodies, sisters." Then she sailed into the apartment, all beams and goodwill, having asserted her strength at the expense of our weakness.

That night we discuss our husbands. It is my turn. I am trying to be fair. I married the man, after all, without loving him, and he had bargained on love. So I feel some responsibility for the shambles our marriage has become. I'm trying to sort out who-did-what-to-whom without taking refuge in a pat and bloodless feminist analysis. On the other hand, I would like someone to help me through the labyrinth of my confused experience because I don't fully understand what I'm living through. But the rules of my group are that no one be judgmental—which means, translated, that it's bad to be analytical. So I have the feeling that I'm talking to my own mouth.

Also, my effort to be fair is exhausting me, because it has been undertaken, to tell the truth, not because I'm so morally scrupulous that I'm incapable of fudging the facts to make myself look good, but because one of the women in my group claims to have had an affair with my husband. Every time I talk about him, she cries. I'm about to divorce him because I can't stand the pain of living with him; she weeps.

After five minutes of this futile exercise, my husband's supposed lover noisily leaves the room, overturning a chair, and goes to the bathroom and vomits. Everybody can hear her. Everybody is meant to hear her. Cold-water packs, glasses of wine, offers of sympathy, are brought to the vomiter—who has chosen the most effective way of silencing me that I can think of. I feel like a hard-faced bitch because I don't join the rescue mission. I also feel abandoned. She has turned her weakness to her own advantage; eight or nine competent women are manipulated by her show of weakness.

Weakness! Six months later, she is to announce, as if she had done something very clever, that she never had an affair with my husband—with whom, however, she is passionately in love.

She has been acting out a fantasy. She does not see the injustice of this. We feel corrupted and betrayed.

This is hard to write. I'll get to the good parts. But I've lived with the horror stories so long I have to tell them first.

So much earnestness. When I think of this horror story, I laugh; I see now that it is funny (but how seriously we took it then): "All my life," one woman said, "I've served people and now I'm learning to be selfish. I don't want to serve you coffee or wine when you come to my house because I find it oppressive to serve people. But if you serve food at your houses, I'll feel guilty. So you'll have to stop serving anything so I won't feel guilty." That's what the woman said; and she stood us on our heads. My good friend Bobbie called me: "I'm Jewish, for heaven's sake! All my life I've offered people food. Food is love, right? I just baked a whole damned bread. So what am I supposed to do? Give everybody a glass of water and a carrot stick just to please what's-her-face?"

Nobody ever told what's-her-face we thought she'd behaved like a horse's ass. But we did tell one another. Because it was bullshit, all that stuff about being nonjudgmental. As soon as we returned from meetings, telephone wires began to hum. Direct confrontations were not allowed; but nothing prevented us from rehashing offenses with our intimates. We were all duplicitous.

What's true of marriages is true of consciousness-raising groups. When marriages break up, it's hard not to see them in terms of their ending; one tends to remember the reasons for their dissolution—the bad parts. It's an act of will to remember the good parts (and maybe an act that threatens one's self-preservation). It's hard to be honest about any relationship after it's broken . . . especially if you feel that you've been, to some extent, broken in the process, too. We have to justify endings to ourselves, and that rules out dwelling on the pleasurable high-hopes beginnings.

Was the potential for bitterness and acrimony present from the very beginning of our C-R relationship? I think it was. We were too high on sisterhood to see it. All in all, I think it's a good thing we chose not to see it. If we hadn't plunged in bravely and impetuously, we might never have plunged at all. We damaged one another; we also nourished and sustained one another. And in the end, each of us understood more clearly who she was. In the frequently painful process of consciousness-raising, we became what we really were. I don't know how to express this more clearly: it's as if each of us were both the potter and the clay—and the group was the kiln.

There were thirteen of us: thirteen "sisters." A year and a half later when the group disbanded, I could call only three women friends. I had started out with six women I could call friends. I lost three friends. I also found my voice. I had known I was a writer from the time I was nine years old. The group unleashed creative energy . . . for me, and for others, too. It's odd when honesty obliges you to be grateful to women you feel have betrayed you—or betrayed their own sane, decent principles. And that's the position I find myself in now. I'm grateful to women I don't like.

I'm grateful to them most of all because I told them the truth. I was too naïve not to.

Still, the fact was that sometimes my felt truth was not perceived as objective truth. Women who knew me expressed surprise at my version of things; it was not their version of me. Some of the women accepted my version of my life; others were dismayed because, Rashomon-like, they had their own versions of what my life was like, and they preferred their own. Not surprising, after all: most of us don't accept people at their own evaluation.

I lost one friend as a result of consciousness-raising because, while she believed the facts of my life, she chose not to accept the motives I (falteringly) attributed to them. I knew to expect a phone call after every meeting, in the course of which I would be told why I had done what I had done—and it all sounded like secondhand news from *her* analyst's couch. I don't like psychiatric parlor games. I felt diminished. Of course, my motives are often obscure to me, whose aren't? But, her arrogance! And I was as foolish as she was arrogant. At first I perceived her attention as love and caring, and luxuriated in it; but she was neither attacking nor loving me, she was defending her view of me. What she chose to believe about me was more precious to her than what in fact I was. That is not a flattering form of attention—but the negative tension it produced did, ultimately, force me to assert myself. I gained more, by doing that, than I lost.

What do you suppose happens when people's noses are put out of joint when they are hearing things they would rather not know because it refutes what they think they already know? One night I was describing a love affair I'd had with a generous lover, a man who'd known not only how to touch the clitoris, but how to touch the heart. (I was tired then, and I'm tired now, of talking about sex as if it were all plumbing and mechanics.) I guess I got carried away. One woman wanted to gag me. She distrusted my extravagance, and she objected to the idea that any man—any heterosexual love affair—could satisfy heart and body and mind. The rules didn't allow her verbally to tell me that I was full of shit, so she rolled her eyes, cracked her knuckles, flung herself around in her chair. I was conscious of her every moment I spoke.

I was conscious of the fact that she was one of the three bisexual members of our group, with an avowed preference for women. The week before, when we were speaking of our relationships with women, I'd said I didn't think I could possibly, et cetera, and I'd given all the reasons why I couldn't possibly. . . . I felt as if I were being punished.

I'm not suggesting that only bisexuals or lesbians threatened the composure of the group. Many of the heterosexual women in my group were, at that time, more negative about committed relationships with men than were homosexual women, for whom the problem(s) didn't arise. It was the heterosexual women—most of whom were breaking out of marriages—who reacted most violently when one woman announced her intention to remarry. It scared them. They got mad at her. They perceived what she was doing as a negative comment on what they were doing. (I don't know why I'm saying *they;* I got mad at her, too. . . . I could remember being loved by a man and loving a man. I couldn't imagine that it would ever happen again. I was wrong, of course. I made the mistake of thinking that if you add up the past, you sum up the future; I forgot how frequently life astonishes us.)

Sometimes, early on, we went on picnics or country weekends together. We swam, we cooked together, we shopped for antiques. We avoided talking about anything important. We felt sisterly then, safe with one another.

My friend Leah says: "Those women should have known more about me than anybody in the world. Yet when I met one of them on the street, we'd greet each other nervously, have nothing to say, not even small talk. Has it occurred to you that we had very little in common?"

We had our femaleness in common. We thought that would be enough. "We have more in common with one another— for that matter, with Clare Boothe Luce—than we have with any man in the world," one woman said at our first meeting. She was wrong. When we were talking about "safe" subjects (the safe subjects tended to be "body" ones, like menstruation and orgasm), we had a great deal in common; we reassured one another, as we did, though to a lesser extent, when we talked about male psychological domination. No one, then, felt herself to be a freak.

We played it safe too often. . . . And playing it safe, I've begun to think, was part of our undoing.

There were subjects no one could talk about without alienating half of the women in the room.

Politics. We glibly adopted the C-R slogan "The personal is political." Which got us not very far when we were discussing how the world works. Some women sneered at the ("male") Left; others busied themselves campaigning for women, on the theory that any female "victory" was desirable . . . and not just desirable but (absolutely) good. (These are two words that never got defined: *power, success.*) In that value-free space, we celebrated individualism. Secretly, we judged.

We never had a good, open, honest fight. We treated one another like cripples. We were afraid of all the enormous words: *good* and *evil* were two we didn't use. Not out loud, anyway. Feminists who were trying to work out a political-feminist-economic analysis were accused of behaving like men —speaking, that is, from their heads rather than their guts. Loath to allow our differences to surface, we were all passionate sensibility and no tensile sense.

Work. Most of us were trying to figure out what we were going to be when we grew up. Who was doing better work— the woman who worked in a child-care center for a minimal wage, or the woman who earned $50,000 a year writing advertising copy? (The child-care person said, "I'm tired of doing a service job for a slave wage"; she envied the advertising person. The advertising person said, "You're helping people. I'm writing garbage." But she didn't give up her job.) We never defined what was *better,* because we never defined what was *good.*

Some of us were on the threshold, hustling for jobs, beginning to make our presence felt in the larger world. Women who were trapped (in bad marriage, in indecision) and those who felt they were at the mercy of a brutal economic system didn't want to hear about the accomplishments of women who were beginning, in their own terms, to "make it."

And, paradoxically, women who were busy raising young children—and consequently unwilling or unable to work outside the home—were asked, "What are you doing with your life?" It was a no-win situation: we were expected to achieve, but not to talk about our accomplishments for fear that would disturb the equilibrium of the group and assault the egos of women who could not point to concrete achievements.

I'm talking about competition, of course. We never talked about competition. We pretended, airy-fairy, that it didn't exist. We lied.

Children were not, for the most part, regarded as accomplishments or achievements. One night, several of us read a story—in *Life,* I think it was—about women who had left their children in order to "fulfill themselves"—mostly, as I remember it, by throwing pots or driving trucks. Several women were appalled: *Who's minding the kids?* "I can understand desperation," Bobbie said, "but why do they have to justify it? Why do they come off sounding like Joan of Arc? It wasn't so hot when Gauguin did it." Bobbie was accused of not having compassion for her sisters who had made that difficult choice. She was told what a drag kids were; she was asked why she was "neurotically dependent" on her own kids.

Later Bobbie said (but only to Leah and me): "Compassion? What about compassion for me, for Christ's sake? I'm raising three kids *and* earning a living, how come I'm not allowed to say what I think? Why do we always honor the crazies—the suicides, the women who run away? If you're conventionally responsible, is that bad? And what does Anne mean, I'm 'neurotically dependent' on my kids? And I don't want to hear that kids are a drag from a whining woman who has a full-time housekeeper and has never changed a diaper in her whole privileged life. . . . And have you noticed that the women who are touting the most unconventional, radical life-styles are also the ones who are the most apolitical? They privatize everything."

I think Bobbie hit on practically everything that was wrong with the group. Compassion was reserved for wild, unconventional, or aberrant behavior—it was as if women were rewarded for acting out our own worst melodramatic fantasies. But: "Somebody from my kids' school asked me to give her kids a lift for a week, she's going into the hospital for an operation and her husband split. . . . And I said no. It meant going two blocks out of my way, and I'm tired of being used. . . . I'm so proud of myself for learning how to say no." It's impossible for me to think of that without cringing. "Compassion," a woman in our group once said, "is what got us into the mess we're in." And gleeful selfishness, the implication was, would get us out. (Out? Where to?)

When we went into the group, it didn't seem to matter that some of us were in therapy, and some of us—because we didn't believe that particular magic would work for us, or because we didn't have enough money, or because we had been that route with no return—were not. Later, it mattered very much. Women who were in therapy insinuated that women who were not were resisting self-understanding, or "externalizing internal problems," and, worse, that their not being in therapy somehow implied that women who *were* seeing shrinks were crazy. Now, the minute somebody says, "You think I'm crazy," you do begin to wonder. So the women who weren't seeing therapists began to feel both defensive and superior. We couldn't begin to make connections between therapy and feminist politics; we couldn't get the answers because the questions made everybody so defensive. Awful.

When Bobbie railed against privileged women, she hit on

two other issues we never discussed: class and money. ("No money to pay the rent this month," one woman said. "Don't tell me that, you'll make me feel guilty because I'm not going to lend you any," said privileged Laura. "I don't want to feel guilty.") Money made everybody feel nervous; and we pretended that class differences didn't exist or didn't matter.

Bobbie hated to hear people "whine." Women's lives are hard, and one of the reasons we formed a group was to give our indignation free rein and to allow our hurt to show in a protected environment. But without a sense of proportion? When a woman whose husband gives her $25,000 a year in alimony poor-mouths about how she can't afford to shop at Neiman-Marcus in the presence of women who can't ever afford to buy a steak, it's hard to take. I could give lots of other examples, not all of them having to do with money, all of them having to do with insensitivity. Each of us talked a lot more than we listened.

And that, strangely, was what was good about the group. Out of all that was bad came so much that was good. The group had the qualities of its defects. All that talking was more than cathartic; it was a way for us to take ourselves seriously. . . . When I look at that sentence, I can hardly believe it. I was thirty-six then. Is it possible that I'd never taken myself seriously? I don't think I had—not, in any case, since the painful, wrenching self-exploration of late adolescence. I had acted instinctively, or out of blind necessity, out of a visceral sense of what I needed to do to survive. Too little had been willed or chosen. I felt as if I were a person to whom things happened, not a person who made her life happen. I like, still, to feel that life's surprises can overtake me. But I don't like—don't choose —to be a victim of my own life.

I was talking about this to Leah, finding it hard to put what I meant into words, and she said, "Well, I have the feeling that before, though you functioned, every now and then you'd fall into a deep dark well and not know how you'd gotten there."

"And now?"

"Now you look before you leap."

"Or before I fall?"

"Or before you fall."

I'm making it sound as if everything good that came from the group was, if not accidental, a result of tension and abrasion. It's strange: I remember happy laughter, people huddled together for warmth, shared insights that produced a clear and lucid high. But those memories are blurred—and recede the harder I try to re-create them. The negative images have the sharp edge of definition; I understand and can analyze them better. I'm willing to admit that this shows something petty in me; and I allow for the possibility that time will give clarity and form to the positive things that went on.

As for now, this is what I'm sure of: I tested everything I felt and thought against what every woman in that group said. I defined my politics. I learned—looking at the choices other people made—the choices I wanted to make. (Or the choices I couldn't make because they were antithetical to my nature.) I was not—am not—nonjudgmental. I make no apologies for that. The judgments I make are the person I am.

That process of choice and self-definition did not end with the group. It didn't start with the group, either. But I grew up in the group. . . . Which, in many ways, was like a family: the weak tended to dominate and manipulate the strong. People who coped didn't command as much attention as people who screamed about their inability to cope. It wasn't fair. (Well, life isn't fair.) There are ways and ways of attracting attention to pain. One is to be (or pretend to be) weak; another is to act as if your strength is the only kind worth having. And one of the most unpleasant traits of human nature is to fasten on the weaknesses of a strong person and make those weaknesses the most important thing about that person. Why is it so difficult to understand that people are a complicated mixture of weakness and strength? I don't know. I do know that one comes to depend on a group as one depends on one's family, for a sense of one's worth—even when one does not accept the values of the group.

The group, like a family, forced each of us to declare—to ourselves—our own values. The group was the whole process of growing up, and growing out into the world, speeded up so much that it hurt. We all used the group to grow up—and to grow into ourselves. When that happened, we outgrew one another; we parted.

MORAL AMBIGUITY:
The Ambivalence
of Abortion
by Linda Bird Francke*

(1978)

The main thrust of the feminist movement, in all its historical manifestations, has been to recognize the value and to enhance the dignity of human life. At its best—its most noble and most useful—it has always said *no* to that which degrades and diminishes the quality of life: *no* to the sexual and economic exploitation of women and children in factories, mills, homes, offices; *no* to the slaughter of women, children, sons, lovers, husbands, and fathers in senseless wars; and *yes* to that which enlarges the possibilities of goodness. The main thrust of feminism has always been pro-life.

What an irony that feminists now find themselves locked in battle with people who describe themselves as "pro-life"; that we who have so passionately proclaimed, with all the authenticity of suffering, that our minds and bodies are inviolate find ourselves in bitter opposition to those whose rallying cry is the "sanctity of human life."

Feminists may protest that the highly organized, well-financed "pro-life" forces have been known to use violence to achieve their "pious" ends. We may say that—inasmuch as "pro-lifers" were remarkably silent when lives were being lost in Indochina and were silent on the issue of capital punishment —they are not pro-life, but merely antiabortion. But to say that

*Random House, 1978

is not to address ourselves to a real, heartbreaking question: have we become so brutalized by our struggles that we see abortion only in terms of expediency?

Now that our right to legal abortion stands in jeopardy, one is frequently given to understand that it is not expedient to explore moral and emotional ambiguities. Of course that is wrong. Now that we are at the barricades, precisely *because* we are at the barricades, when moral sensitivity tends to crumble in the face of action, I think we need to ask ourselves many questions. The consequence of not discussing the moral ambiguities of abortion is that we allow "pro-lifers" to catch the moral ball and run with it. We are afraid to say that abortion is terrible—for the woman whose body undergoes the trauma, and (I think) for the other life involved. Afraid to give our "enemies" ammunition, we whisper these things to one another; we are afraid to say them out loud.

Is it really so awful to admit to confusion and unhappiness over the issue of abortion?

That is what Linda Bird Francke did. In 1973 Francke, the mother of three children, had an abortion. Three years later, under a pseudonym, she published an account of her experience in the *The New York Times*, and she was roundly denounced, both by Right-to-Lifers and by women she describes as "pro-abortion zealots." Neither group liked her "line."

The truth is that Francke didn't have a "line." Her brief piece was a masterpiece of ambivalence: it spoke implicitly of her relief—and explicitly of her remorse. Like most pieces written for catharsis (Francke had originally no intention to publish), it had more of sensibility than of sense. In spite of its shortcomings, however—perhaps because of them—Francke's piece struck a nerve. The *Times* received hundreds of letters in response. *The Ambivalence of Abortion* grew out of those responses.

Like Francke, women spoke of relief; they also spoke of anger (sometimes turned inward, sometimes directed toward doctors, clergymen, husbands, lovers, men in general, mothers, fathers, and the women's movement, and the fetus); they spoke of anguish, grieving, remorse, physical and emotional estrangement from loved ones. Not a few of the women interviewed felt betrayed by feminists who'd led them to believe that abortion was "as easy as pulling a tooth."

Francke allows the hundreds of women interviewed—young, old, single, and married women—to speak for themselves. The interviews are revelatory, painful, vivid. But I would wish for more editorial comment. Francke addresses herself only to the emotional ambivalence surrounding abortion. She doesn't deal with moral ambiguity (or she chooses to regard morality and emotion as synonymous). I think I understand her difficulty. It is this: when one considers abortion as a moral issue, one is confronted with two absolute positions. *One*, the fetus is a human life, and abortion is, therefore, immoral. *Two*, women have the absolute right to control their bodies, and the placing of any limits on that control is, therefore, immoral. Unhappily, it is perfectly possible to have one's emotions *and* one's morality colored by both those positions—and the collision of absolutes throws one into the realm of relative morality, a realm from which it is next to impossible to write with any degree of clarity.

Francke chose not to wade into this messy territory, though she would undoubtedly describe herself as "pro-choice":

> Regardless of whether [a woman] chooses to continue her pregnancy or to terminate it . . . it is her decision alone. So it falls to all of us to support that decision with grace, safety, and understanding—and to live with it, and each other, as best we can.

Francke takes an "I'm okay/You're okay" approach: she hopes that, as a result of her book, "women who are suffering from guilt will feel comforted that others have suffered like them, and that women who feel guilty because they *don't* feel guilty will also find comfort in the stories of others who have no regrets."

Francke says that many abortions were a "life-style choice." What she means, by that deplorable jargon, is that some women chose to abort because—as they unhesitatingly tell us —they didn't want to be cursed with morning sickness while on a Caribbean vacation; they didn't want their graduate degrees deferred; or, chillingly, because the fetus was the "wrong" sex. I think such "life-style" choices are wasteful, frivolous—immoral.

I was also appalled by the number of women who became pregnant because neither they nor their insensitive lovers took the trouble to use contraceptive devices; I was even more appalled by the women who routinely use abortion as a contraceptive device—and astounded that these same women could righteously mouth clichés about "control of their bodies," when the idea of exercising "control" never seemed to occur to them before having intercourse. (I want to say that the notion that we have, or ought to have, *absolute* control of our bodies is a sloppy one. I have no "right," for example, to place my body in front of a moving car; I have no "right" to perform private bodily functions in public. Civilization—as well as good sense—implies a measure of restraint.)

If all of this sounds like fodder for "pro-lifers," one has only to read the testimony of women who were too young, too old, or simply too worn out by life to bear children without devastating physical and emotional consequences. Most of all, one has to read the testimonies of women who had abortions before abortion was legal. Their experiences were so savage, so degrading, that—at the bottom line—one can only say that this kind of brutality, this carnage, can never be allowed to occur again.

The trouble is that to say this is also to say that one life—the life of the unborn child—must be sacrificed to preserve the life of another. This is a very great trouble: unless one does a moral/intellectual tap dance (such as likening the right to abortion to the concept of the "just" war), there seems to be no morally tenable position one can take, no "pure" position.

As feminists, we tend now to focus our moral indignation on the fact that poor women will not be able to receive Medicaid funds for legal abortions. Here we seem to be standing on morally unambiguous ground: why should poor women be so unjustly penalized? We care about the quality of life; and giving birth to a baby that may be ill-fed, ill-educated, or physically abused does nothing to enhance the quality of anybody's life. But the other side of the moral coin, as amply demonstrated by Francke's interviewees, is that many poor women abort *because* they are poor; many women wanted babies but believed they couldn't afford them. Where should one direct one's anger? Toward the life-isn't-fair people who would *deny* women the right to abort, or toward the economic system (perpetuated, of course, by the same life-isn't-fair people) that allows poverty and affluence to coexist and *forces* women to abort? (One thing I didn't need to be convinced of before I read this book was that abortion does not cure poverty.)

I can imagine no circumstances under which I would have an abortion; I consider the fetus a human life. But I would also consider it immoral to bend my efforts to stop any other human being from having an abortion she deemed necessary. I hate the idea of abortion, but I hate even more the death of a woman by coat hangers or lye. I hate, that is to say, the idea of murder twice done.

We live in a secular, pluralistic society. I believe that Heaven is an actual place—as real as the physical headquarters of

Planned Parenthood. But the promise of a Heavenly Reward is cold comfort to those who do not so believe—and, even if I wished to, I could not impose my belief on others.

Young Bolshevist revolutionaries once said that murder was sometimes necessary, but never justifiable. That thinking informs my thinking about abortion—and makes it no easier to come to a comfortably unambiguous conclusion about it.

I have a teenage daughter. If she were to become pregnant, I would consider it a violation of her integrity to tell her that she could not have an abortion if she chose to have one; I would take her to a doctor—and I would thank God that we had legal access to a doctor who would not maim or butcher her. But if she were, of her own free will and without coercion, to choose to give birth to a child, I would consider it sinful not to support her in that decision.

To read *The Ambivalence of Abortion* is to be convinced that the problems raised by abortion cannot be satisfied by right-on slogans. What, for example, are the consequences, for the mother, of bearing a child to term and offering it up for adoption? Is this truly a humane solution, or does that mother also grieve and mourn the loss of her child forever? I think the real message of Francke's book is something philosophers and moral logicians have always known: the most painful moral struggles are not those between good and evil, but between the good and the lesser good.

IMAGINATION AND IDEOLOGY:
On Lies, Secrets and Silence: Selected Prose, 1966–1978

by Adrienne Rich*
(1979)

It's an unhappy fact of life and of prose that ideology tends to coarsen, and sometimes to fossilize, the moral imagination; it leaves little room for nuance or for play. In the writing of some (though by no means all) feminist theorists, insight becomes a bludgeoning rod instead of a lightning flash; and the greatest danger for the ideologue who is also political activist is not that she will become corrupt but that she will bore her readers into disaffection.

Example: In the foreword to this collection, Ms. Rich exhorts us "to question everything . . . to remember . . . to come together telling our stories . . . to look afresh." Of course; yes! But then, after having informed us, somewhat opaquely, that "women's culture . . . is active"—as opposed to the "deadly 'radical passivity' " of "twentieth-century white male capitalist culture . . . whose artifacts are the kind that lend to a deepening passivity and submission: 'Pop' art, television, pornography"— Ms. Rich proceeds from arguably reasonable premise to quite unreasonable argument: "Abortion," she says,

> has become the most visible and emotionally charged of all our efforts to speak for ourselves and to defend our own life. . . . A pornography of antiabortion literature and

*W.W. Norton, 1978

imagery exists: the fetus who will never disturb a mother's sleep; the fetishism of tiny fingers and toes. Feminists have responded . . . by demonstrations with coat hangers. . . . The debate [is] framed in terms of a morality, an ethic, a social conscience that is man-made and male-defined. The questions raised thereby (At what point is a fertilized egg a person? When does the soul start to exist? Shall abortion, if legal, be federally funded?) are inevitably male questions. . . . It is time that we frame our own questions on this as on every other issue. . . .

The tender conscience and the tough mind alike are confounded by this diatribe: are we not to consider the fetus at all when we approach the heartbreaking question of abortion? Are "tiny fingers and toes" less real—and less to be considered with fear and trembling—than coat hangers? Why are the ethical, moral, and juridical questions Ms. Rich mockingly mentions "male-defined?" (Either both men *and* women have souls or nobody has a soul; if we do—or do believe—we have souls, then it is not irrelevant to ask at what point the soul starts to exist.)

This passage of Ms. Rich's anthology reminds me uncomfortably of a remark made by visual artist Judy Chicago (in whose sculptural work *The Dinner Party* Virginia Woolf is represented by a three-dimensional ceramic dinner plate that looks like half a head of lettuce or a vagina, depending on which eye one closes). Bemoaning the lack of $2 million with which to build a ceramic room for her banquet table and plates, Ms. Chicago said that women would now be deprived of "the kind of monument to women's culture and achievement that there are all over Europe for men's, such as the chapel by Henri Matisse at Vence in France." Now, for one thing, I'd always thought that the chapel at Vence was constructed for the honor of God, and not to praise famous men; for another, I do not wish to be told that Matisse, Michelangelo, Donne, Yeats, et al, do not belong to me because I am a woman. If what feminism says is that women are fully human, then Vence belongs to me as much as Jane Austen belongs to me and as much as Georgia O'Keeffe belongs to me.

It is vexing to be told (as we are, again and again, in this book) that we must "frame our own questions on this as on every other issue." (What are "our own questions?") It's particularly vexing in the context of abortion, when battle-trench mentality seems to suggest to Ms. Rich that all philosophical inquiry is inappropriate (or "male-defined") because all questions are "man-made."

It's interesting, this about questions. In an introductory note to an essay about Anne Bradstreet, Rich says certain questions were "unavailable" to her when she wrote about the early American poet in 1966 "partly because of the silence surrounding the lives of women." Rich wishes she had asked, "What has been the woman poet's relationship to nature, in a land where both women and nature have, from the first, been raped and exploited?" I think we can agree that there was, in 1966, a silence surrounding the lives of women; and I suppose I could be persuaded that the question Ms. Rich raises in 1979 is a good one. But I don't know why she denigrates the questions she asked in 1966; the problems she then thought Bradstreet's life posed seem to me no less—and possibly more—compelling. Rich wrote then of Bradstreet's preoccupation with good and evil, of her struggle to remain in a state of grace, avoiding the peril of despair, while "rearing eight children, lying frequently sick, keeping house at the edge of wilderness." I like this essay. It is nice, precise. I'm rather glad, in fact, that Rich wrote it in 1966 and not in 1979, when her questions, I think, tend to become parochial.

I say parochial at the risk of damning myself as a creature of the "patriarchy." Having charged men with attributing universal importance to *their* concerns, and only tangential importance to the concerns of women, feminists of Ms. Rich's ilk now contend that only *women's* concerns are of universal importance . . . assigning to themselves the right, of course, to define "women's concerns." This implied reactionary separatism leads inevitably to the conclusion that there are no truly universal concerns, in which case, pity us all! Ms. Rich has moved toward a view of the world that obliges her to believe in "an inevitable process by which women will claim our primacy." "It is the lesbian in us who is creative, for the dutiful daughter of the father in us is only a hack"; "it is the lesbian in every woman who is compelled by female energy"; "women working in the common world of men are denied that integrity of work and life which can only be found in an emotional and intellectual [and, one assumes, exclusive] connectedness with ourselves and other women."

Is that not a parochial view? "I believe that a militaristic and pluralistic lesbian feminist movement is potentially the greatest force in the world today for a complete transformation of society." This is a statement, surely, that can resound only within the confines of a lesbian-feminist salon. The women's movement, Ms. Rich says, "is being fueled and empowered by the work of lesbians." I understand that that is different from saying that every feminist is—or must be—a lesbian; nevertheless, doesn't it have the effect of casting doubt on the credentials of all feminists who are not lesbians? Must I, in order to understand the "tangle of race and sex," go to bed with a black lesbian? Ms. Rich implies that I must. But that option isn't open to me; so—am I lost?

No; I am bored to read again that "both middle-class marriage and factory work enslaved women"—bored because to say that is to tell only part of a complex truth and part, also, of a terrible lie. (A bad marriage taught me, for example, how good a good marriage might be; but there is no room for my truth in Ms. Rich's rhetoric.) Boring to hear witches praised without being given reason to praise them. (Witches are very popular in certain quarters these days; but nobody seems eager to tell us exactly what it was they were supposed to have done.) It is boring to read casual references to matriarchal societies, "gynocentric" or "gynocratic" societies, when there is little real evidence that such societies ever existed—claims for them appearing to rest more on desire than on scholarship. Boring to hear more whining about ironing. (Ms. Rich's excesses provoke me to my own: why the hell doesn't she just buy drip dry?) Boring and possibly corrupting to read that "to be maternally with small children all day . . . requires a holdingback, a putting aside of . . . imaginative activity." (What of those of us who have been made more honest by our children, more courageous, and—dare one say it?—happier? Ms. Rich, by the way, insists upon the right of lesbians to have and to raise children. All very well. But how, exactly, does one go about this? Look for a suitable sower of the seed in a telephone book? If women don't want to be regarded as breeders, why should men wish to be viewed in that peculiarly agricultural light?) Finally it is boring to read what has become an unexamined platitude: "The nuclear family is a principal form of social fragmentation." (I haven't noticed that the extended or joint family in India has done much good for women—unless one counts Mrs. Gandhi as a good; and Ms. Rich hasn't noticed that the nuclear family can be, as it was in Vietnam, a unit of resistance against the "white male capitalist culture" she so much deplores.)

Which brings me to that paper word *patriarchy* (which, in its wildest forms, results in such abuses as *patriarchitecture*, meaning, as you might have guessed, buildings designed by men). The word eradicates real differences and distinctions; it is the enemy of nuance. Here is an example: Rich contends that "it is characteristic of patriarchal society" that "the mystical and aesthetic . . . are regarded as separate and mutually exclusive" from the "practical and political realms." Was this true of the Medicis? Is it true of Islam? of the Ayatollah Khomeini? What does one do with the fact that *the same* "patriarchists" who inveigh against abortion fight—as hard as Ms. Rich does—against pornography? My reading of Ms. Rich's book does not even tell me whether I may assume there are any qualitative differences between my son—poised on the brink of adulthood, scared, brave, kind, uncertain—and Idi Amin.

There are good things to be said about this book (though I have been too impatient to go on about them): an acute, unmuddled, aphoristic essay called *Women and Honor: Some Notes on Lying;* a long lovely passage about Emily Dickinson that evokes, as has nothing else I have ever read, the poet of the "intense inner event" working in her "white-curtained, high-ceilinged room." This essay reminded me that Ms. Rich was/is a poet—but, alas, Rich's eccentric reading of Dickinson's love poems ("they are about the poet's relationship to her own power, which is exteriorized in masculine form") reminded me that Rich is, unhappily, also a polemicist, her respect and love for the written word betrayed by her ideology.

I leave to the end my own biases, my own philosophical and visceral disagreements with Rich. "Powerless," she says, "women have been seduced into confusing love with false power—the 'power' of mother-love, the 'power' of gentle influence, the 'power' of non-violence, the 'power' of the meek who are to inherit the earth." The concepts she enumerates here only to dismiss are provocative and profound; they are the ideas upon which (whether one accepts or rejects or wrestles with them) our understanding of goodness and purpose rests. I believe (I try, that is, to believe, and sometimes I succeed) that the meek will inherit the earth. I believe it because a man said it—a man who, let it be acknowledged, never rebuked women for being female or urged them to be feminine. Ms. Rich has offered me nothing more bountifully mysterious.

Rich says, "The woman whose psyche is still heavily involved with the father, brother, teacher, or other male figures out of her past" is "enthralled to maleness." I am "heavily involved" with my father—a cranky, sick, stubborn, loving, contentious old man (he loves me); I love my brother, the most decent man I know (and he flies to me when I am in trouble, and better yet, when I am not); I am forever in the debt of the teacher who loved me undemandingly when I was a frightened, awkward girl, and whose death, 20 years after the fact, I still mourn; and I love, with all my damaged heart (damaged, many times, by men; yes) my good son (who loves his sweet fiery sister). If I were to abort or silence my love, I would lose, not only the men I love, but my past, my present, and my future.

A TROUBLED PEACE:

What The Woman Lived: Selected Letters of Louise Bogan, 1920–1970,

Edited by Ruth Limmer*

(1974)

There is much nourishment in this book, and there is much moral splendor. In the letters Louise Bogan wrote to her contemporaries and friends—which form a stunning commentary on the arts and letters of her time—there is generosity, wit, humorous detachment, gossip, suffering, gaiety, mature irony, brilliant and meticulous criticism and insight, perverse prejudice, growth, despair, contradiction: *life.* These are the letters of a woman too reticent and austere ever to become a cult figure, a poet too private and self-effacing ever to inspire heroine worship. Louise Bogan inspires something very much better, I think: love.

Bogan's place as a lyric poet is secure—Auden said of her that she wrested "beauty and truth out of dark places"; but her poetry is not confessional, she does not glue people to her with her suffering. With characteristic generosity, Bogan wrote to one of her correspondents that she admired Marianne Moore because Moore had "gone on, fought through, and endured." Bogan herself was not a wallower in the muck of suffering; she was never one to display her wounds as if they were stigmata. She fought and endured with the aid, she said, of "the jolly grinner in the soul" who keeps "even misery and malevolence sane." Her sanity and her dignity inform and ennoble every

*Harcourt Brace Jovanovich, 1974

page of this remarkable book. (Remarkable, among other things, for its narrative cohesion: the letters span fifty pulsing years, and are more vivid, fresh, and unpatterned than formal autobiography.)

Louise Bogan died (in February, 1970) at the age of seventy-two, of a coronary occlusion. She had the death everyone fears: she died alone. She died uncelebrated. Less than a year before her death in her New York apartment, she had written to her good friend and literary executor, Ruth Limmer, that her collected poems, *The Blue Estuaries,* seemed "to have fallen down that deep, dark well. Not a review!" (Chin in the air, she added, "This doesn't bother me much.") She had been passed over for the Pulitzer prize—"Well, I'll never receive that accolade; not enough time left. But I do not weep." And, poor all her life, even in her final years she continued to long, modestly, for "a slight margin of economic safety."

Poetry reviewer for *The New Yorker* for thirty-eight years, she retired less than a year before her death. From letters to Ruth Limmer we learn how painful and difficult her bread-and-butter work had been for this incorruptible critic. "Remember: this takes *courage.* But I'll come through! . . . I've exorcised the demon! I'm free! No more A.M. weeping. No more *fear.* The books go back to the magazine tomorrow."

In her final decade she suffered the last in a series of "seizures of pure depression" that had necessitated confinement in sanatoriums. Two years before her death, she wrote: "I simply don't know one other person . . . in the company of whom I can listen to music. That is bad—and strange." When she was seventy, after most of her intimates had died and her "circle of friends in New York City [had] rapidly dwindled," she described her days in a letter to poet Rolfe Humphries: "Maidie [her daughter from her first, early marriage] I see once a week; and I visit a literate youngish psychiatrist twice a month. But I get pretty lonely. This is a new feeling, for I have always been pretty vigorous and self-sufficient. A slight failure of nerve, no doubt. . . . But I hate it, and wish it would go away."

A slight failure of nerve! Most people would whine more mightily if they'd scratched a finger. Her approach to life was to get on with it. There is much here that is painful . . . terrible, as life and death are terrible. But the letters, and Bogan's life, are wonderful and thrilling—exhilarating. And not only because she left behind a fine body of work ("Get it all into the work," she was fond of saying, ". . . the work is *everything*"), but because of her joy and exuberance, her sheer vital force. Despite bouts of intellectual and visceral pessimism, she exemplified what she herself longed to believe in: "the tenderness and strength of the human heart." *

"Mankind is nuts," she once remarked. But, "How good life is! How complicated! . . . I love and revere life; and intend to keep on being vulgarly alive just as long as possible." She hated people who were "fixed and finished" and she never saw an excuse for boredom. Approaching sixty, she wrote to May Sarton of her "delight in objects, both natural and artifacts . . . the delight of the collector . . . the delight of the naturalist (which I never had, when young, except in flashes, but which makes me scrutinize everything, from flowers to rocks on the shore, in these later years); the delight of the amateur in the arts (the piano and embroidery); the delight of the cook and the housewife. . . . All these are substitutes, I know; but they keep me alive and not only happy but occasionally full of joy." To John Hall Wheelock she wrote, "I cannot believe that the inscrutable universe turns on an axis of suffering; surely the strange beauty of the world must somewhere rest on pure joy!"

None of it came easy. "You know, as few others do," she wrote her friend Edmund Wilson, "that I am a housewife, as well as a writer; I have no one to sweep floors or get meals, or get out the laundry, or, in the case of sickness, make eggnogs and squeeze orange juice. All these tasks are very good for me, but they are tasks I never can allow to slip; and in the crisis of illness, I have no free time. Please bear all this in mind." (Could Wilson have understood the struggle that underlay these words?)

Lightheartedly she wrote, "How fortunate the rich and/or married, who have servants and *wives* to expedite matters." And casually she wrote, a year after her second marriage had ended acrimoniously in divorce, "Wifehood is too damned full of hero-husband-worship, for one of my age [thirty-eight] and disabusedness." Of course, her intelligence grasped the paradox that lies in those parallel remarks; but one senses that she —who bore onerous responsibilities singlehandedly—grasped incompletely the irony of woman's situation; and that is abrasive to a feminist consciousness. Her daughter remained her friend all her life, and that is no small thing.

To poet Theodore Roethke she wrote: "I had a child, from the age of 20, remember that, to hold me back, but I got up and went just the same, and I was, God help us, a woman. . . . Forgive me if I sound melodramatic, my pickled pear." (I love that "pickled pear.") Whenever Bogan began to sound even slightly maudlin or pompous, her wry self-mockery asserted itself with delicious aplomb. She despised what she called "ego-airing."

Roethke was then twenty-six; Bogan was thirty-eight. They were lovers: "One would think that I was too old for all this. A second blooming, and the bough can scarcely bear it. He is very, very large . . . and he writes very very small lyrics. . . . We . . . have indulged in such bearish and St. Bernardish antics as I have never before experienced. . . . Well! such goings on! A woman of my age!" She did not expect it to last; she was able, all her life, to look back upon her eight-year affair with joy. She always reckoned—even when she was sixty-three—that "swatting down love" was an offense against life: "In my declining years, I feel this should be done *only* when love becomes a menace to life and limb! A direct hazard, like a hole in the ceiling or the floor!" She knew that love offers itself in a variety of forms, and she treasured all its manifestations: "[William] Maxwell is really an exquisite human being; and I wish there was something between love and friendship that I could tender him; and some gesture, not quite a caress, I could give him. A sort of smoothing. . . . I simply love him like a brother."

Not least of the virtues of these letters is that Bogan's enthusiasms and antipathies, her passions and perceptions, are so pungent and singular that one is constantly forced to test one's own assumptions and values against hers—which has the salutary effect of obliging one to look hard and clear at things imperfectly observed and thought out. I love Bogan even when I'm quarreling with her, as I do when she discusses the relationship between art and politics. A "violent pacifist," she feared any kind of orthodoxy: "I don't like quintessential certitude," she wrote to her friend—and lifelong political antagonist—Rolfe Humphries. "The reason I get so mad at the comrades is that they always sound as though they had discovered everything yesterday. . . . When I was a child . . . even I knew that the system was iniquitous. The only point I can make is that there seemed to be nothing I could do about it, and, since the days of the barricades have gone out, there still seems to be nothing. So, although you tell Edmund [Wilson] that my ideas of social justice are depraved, I tell you that I want a little peace, a little troubled peace, in which to finish out the time allotted to me in life as a human being." Although she recognized the need for radical reform, she was never able to bring herself to join any movement for social change. She hated, with equal passion, the "horrid little utilitarian Roosevelt administration ideas" and the Presbyterian, stuffed-shirt crowd at *New Masses* magazine. Most of all she despised self-aggrandizing political actions: "Hemingway was having such a hell of a good

time looking at a *war,* and being disgustingly noble about it.
. . . All full of the milk of human kindness, and the virtues of
the dear *peasants* and the brave civilians. I don't see him doing
any labor and union helping at home, however. I suppose an
automobile strike isn't colorful enough for him."

She held out for "pure art"; in the end, she said, politics were
"sand and gravel": "What we suffer, what we endure, what we
muff, what we kill, what we miss, what we are guilty of, is done
by us, as individuals, in private. . . . I know that it is a lousy
system. . . . But . . . to hell with the crowd. To hell with the
meetings, and the public speeches. Life and death occur, as
they must, but they are all bound up with love and hatred, in
the individual bosom, and it is a sin and a shame to try to
organize or dictate them." Still, external realities revealed to
her the ambiguity of her own position: "I understand now,"
she wrote, after Maidie and she had been evicted from their
apartment and she was without money or resources, "that all
the spirited uppishness in the world wouldn't have stopped
. . . my landlord . . . from throwing me into the gutter, and I
could have sat and quoted middle-class gush about the necessity for gracious living . . . and that would have been a laugh."
Two years before her death, she was persuaded to read a poem
("To My Brother Killed") at a Vietnam peace rally. It was her
first, and only, overtly political act.

Have I said that these letters are fun? The spirit of playfulness that enlivens them derives, I think, from Bogan's conviction that "saints should be . . . able to run a convent and dance
every day before the Lord, and have visions and ecstasies, but
also a fine, firm, human and tough point of standing." Bogan's
letters reveal her to be, essentially, a religious ecstatic with a
great deal of good common earthy sense.

DOROTHY SAYERS:
FEMINISM
AND INDIVIDUALITY

(1974)

"It's not the tragedies that kill us," Dorothy Parker once said, "it's the messes." And she added, not irrelevantly, "I love Sherlock Holmes. My life is so untidy, and his is so neat."

Women's lives are messy; mystery novels are "neat." Indeed the charm of good detective fiction lies in its mathematical exactness: everything comes out all right in the end. It's no wonder so many of the best mystery and detective novels are written by women; for what is so seldom true in the ragged cloth of a woman's real life is true in these engaging parables: blame is righteously assigned, justice and truth triumph—there are no loose ends. Not only does this form of romantic fiction satisfy the hunger to return to the sanguine naïveté of happy-ending nursery fables, but also—in the right hands—it serves the requirements of morality as well: a superb mystery writer must have a passion for balance and order, a determination to right the wrong, and a severely logical mind.

The most austerely intelligent, the wittiest, liveliest practitioner of the tidy art of detective fiction, was—although her irritably individualistic nature led her to reject the label—a feminist. Generally acknowledged to be one of the greatest mystery writers of the century, Dorothy L. Sayers—who wrote more than a score of short stories, more than a dozen full-length mysteries—is perhaps best known for her stunning

Wimsey-Vane trilogy: *Strong Poison* (1930), *Gaudy Night* (1935), and *Busman's Honeymoon* (1937).

Ingeniously plotted, meticulously crafted, these novels are deliciously happy-ending romances starring a feminist hero—Wimsey—as well as a feminist heroine—Harriet Vane. For anyone with a taste for comedies of manners, the eminently rereadable Wimsey trio is a perfect wallow in bliss. But there is substance as well as glitter: these novels reflect their author's serious concerns.

Born in 1893, four years before Queen Victoria's Diamond Jubilee, at Cathedral Choir School, Oxford, where her father was headmaster, Sayers became a first-rate medievalist (she translated Dante) and a theologian (her miracle play, *The Man Born To Be King,* outsold her mystery novels in her lifetime); she died in 1957. Sayers the theologian and Sayers the feminist are present in her detective fiction; all her work was of a piece.

When we first meet Sayers's heroine, Harriet Vane, she is standing trial at the Old Bailey for the poison-murder of her lover, Philip Boyes, a thirty-six-year-old "boy genius" who wrote literary works of "an advanced type." Twenty-nine-year-old Harriet has for seven years earned a substantial independent living by writing mystery novels (for which "unwomanly" behavior the presiding judge damns her with faint praise). The judge is at some pains to point out that the fact of her "immorality"—Harriet had lived with Boyes for a year—is not *necessarily* proof of homicidal tendencies.

Harriet admits to having quarreled with her lover shortly before his death: after having represented himself as conscientiously opposed to marriage, and after having badgered Harriet to live with him, Boyes at length offered to "make an honest woman" of her. Instead of being "decently grateful," Harriet was, perversely, inspired to wrath: "I quite thought he was honest when he said he didn't believe in marriage—and then it turned out that it was a test, to see whether my devotion was abject enough. . . . [He] made both himself and me ridiculous. . . . I couldn't stand being put on probation." These sentiments are incomprehensible to the court; what damns Harriet more than the watertight circumstantial evidence against her is her refusal to behave like a "natural woman."

Enter rich Lord Peter, amateur detective, who is not only fanatically certain of Harriet's innocence but inordinately attracted to this stubbornly honest woman. Peter, one of whose endearing traits is that, unlike most men, he's always able to see "what the fuss is about," immediately pegs Boyes as a conceited prig who couldn't forgive Harriet for making more money than he did, nor forgive her for writing books that sold while his own went unappreciated. Harriet, Boyes felt, ought to have been ministering to *his* muse with unselfish devotion, not making money for both of them with her "independent trash."

As Sayers was to write in a later essay, few angry compassionate voices are heard saying that *poor* women must not toil in backbreaking work alongside their husbands: "The objection is only to work that is pleasant, exciting, or profitable. . . . The keeping of an idle woman is a badge of superior social status. Man must work, and woman must exploit his labor. . . . And if the woman submits, she can be cursed for exploitation; and if she rebels, she can be cursed for competing with the male: whatever she does will be wrong."

In real life, Harriet would no doubt have been made to suffer for the crime of "unwomanliness"—surely as threatening to her judges as the murder of an inconsequential writer—and her stiff neck would have graced the end of a hangman's rope. But this is never-never land, where right is done: Peter, the agent of justice, delivers Harriet from the scaffold, and promptly asks her to marry him.

But Harriet is frightened of marriage, because she conceives of it in terms of surrender; and she is resentful of having to be grateful to Peter, who enjoys the advantage of being her protector. Beholden to him, Harriet is not Peter's equal. Believing that his proposal is a rich man's whim to possess something notorious and therefore extraordinary, that she is the mirror of his magnanimity, Harriet wants nothing more than to "get out of all this and be left alone."

Sayers's casting is inspired. Her lovers are antagonists. Harriet, the daughter of an impecunious country doctor, is common, rebellious, unsure, and dislocated. Peter is impossibly rich and wears the arrogance of caste lightly. Harriet is no Cinderella; the last thing in the world she wants is a Prince Charming. Peter's generosity sticks in Harriet's throat like crumbs from a rich man's table. And yet—and yet—this is the story of love between equals.

In the first Wimsey-Vane novel, *Strong Poison,* Lord Peter, Sayers's incomparable Hound-of-God supersleuth, is—with his silly-ass-about-town pose—distinctly off-putting. And, in fact, Peter's detractors (among whom are Edmund Wilson and W.H. Auden) have called him "a priggish superman," "a chattering icicle in an eyeglass." (This last and wittiest description was written, characteristically, by Sayers herself and put in the mouth of another of her characters.) Peter cultivates fatuity. He is imperturbably urbane and possessed of the kind of courtesy that sometimes suggests "God Almighty condescending to a black beetle."

Sayers, it is clear, regards her silk-lined aristocrat with amused affection; in a speech given in 1940, she described the prototypical Englishman as having a "sense of superiority and security, strong insularity, plus a passion for the exotic, for adventure and romance, practical executive ability plus a curious dreamy imagination."

She might have been holding the mirror to her creation, Peter Death Bredon Wimsey (born 1890), younger brother of the richest peer of the realm; graduate of Eton and Balliol; unofficial diplomat-at-large for the Foreign Office; musicologist, bibliophile, cricket player, and (to the gratitude of all succeeding generations) criminologist. With his beautiful manners (Peter's mother writes in her diary, "I believe if he were in Inquisition he would exert social talents to entertain executioners"), with that extraordinary self-assurance that being born into the English upper class confers, with his odd combination of garrulousness and inaccessibility, his stylized drawl and ready wit, he is bound to drive earnest people to despair.

Peter's appeal, nevertheless, to a certain kind of romantic imagination is total. He is very much in the British fire-and-ice tradition—like a charming forties Leslie Howard giving a perfect imitation of a frivoling fool while all the time, in his secret identity, searching after the good and the beautiful and the true.

Sayers herself took little pleasure in earnestness, remarking that just because a thing is dangerous doesn't make it any less funny. Erudite Peter, who can talk esoteric nonsense, issue forth sonnets, and deliver himself of encyclopedic information with equal felicity and impeccability of style, must be seen as the creation of a woman whose passion for words inclined her to indulge any twaddle as long as it was nicely put; and as the product of her abiding love for England (Sayers's chauvinism was as casual as it was defiant, though mercifully tempered by a realistic sense of humor); and, above all, as a reflection of her attraction to men and women who bore the stamp of eccentricity, to unique individuals with a clear calling and vocation.

Connoisseurs of eccentricity will delight in Lord Peter; and romantics will understand that his smooth, defensive, highly polished surface is camouflage. For Sayers, eccentricity was indeed a recommendation—but the men she loved had, like Peter, also to be brilliant and accomplished. We are told by writer Vera Brittain (a contemporary of Sayers's at Somerville College, Oxford) that young Sayers had an unconcealed passion for Sir Hugh Allen, director of the Oxford Bach Society and Orchestra, a man with a reputation for *enfant terrible* eccentricity. Sayers was to be seen at choir practice "gazing at him with wide adoring eyes . . . as though she were in church worshiping her only God."

If Sayers's massive intelligence seems inconsonant with hero worship, we must remember that Sayers the theologian was fond of saying that love of a person is capable of leading one into love of God, because romantic love convinces one so intensely of the reality and power of Divine Love. Wimsey and Vane are forever quoting divine-and-human-love John Donne at each other; and more than one critic has acidly remarked on Lord Peter's resemblance to an Anglican version of God. Sayers disarms criticism by her gift for self-mockery, which saved her from becoming ridiculous: she didn't stay moonstruck with Sir Hugh (who may have provided the inspiration for Lord Peter) for long; at term's end, and in his presence, says Brittain, "she caricatured her idol with triumphant accuracy and zest."

While paragon Peter is often mistaken for Sayers's alter ego, it is much more likely that if Sayers resembled anybody, it was Harriet Vane; but men, having paid Sayers the compliment of saying she wrote like a man, have been unwilling to acknowledge this tough-minded woman's regard for another tough-minded woman—albeit a fictional one. (When, at the height of her fame, Sayers was asked by a male admirer how, in spite of the fact that she had been raised in a household dominated by women, she was able to make the men in her novels talk like real men, she replied acerbically that she'd had the good sense to have them talk like humans . . . and that she would be pleased if male novelists would try to return the favor occasionally.)

Carolyn Heilbrun, in her perceptive essay "Sayers, Lord

Peter, and God,"* has noted that Lord Peter may be "every woman's idea of the perfect man." Harriet Vane, on the other hand, is hardly every man's idea of the perfect woman. "Prickly," "unsentimental," "unattractive," "incomprehensible," are some of the adjectives that have been applied to Peter's paramour. Critic James Sandoe calls her "the Vane," as if she were a disease, and would probably agree with the gouty curmudgeon in one of Sayers's short stories who says, "a woman who pretends to be serious is wasting her time and spoiling her appearance." It is indeed a measure of Sayers's genius that many men adore her novels even as she is telling them, with superb grace and aplomb, that every myth they cherish about women is false.

For *Gaudy Night,* her "Oxford" novel, Sayers—who was one of the first women to get an Oxford degree, graduating in 1913 with First Honors in Medieval Literature—drew upon her own happy experience at Somerville College. "The University is a Paradise," said her beloved John Donne; and Sayers agreed with him. Indeed, women had fought so hard to enter its precincts, it must surely have seemed as if they were entering heaven itself.

In 1935, which is when the action of Sayers's most famous novel takes place, the women's colleges were a celibate, and a sheltered and genteel, heaven. In Sayers's day, academic women were forced absolutely to make a choice between a profession and marriage. *Somerville College,* a history of Sayers's school written by her friend Muriel St. Clare Byrne, reveals that, of all the tutors, librarians, and bursars from 1894

*This essay, which first appeared in "The American Scholar" (1968) and has been reprinted in *Lord Peter,* an Avon collection of Wimsey short stories, is as insightful, I think, as anything ever written about Sayers: it is a shrewd and sympathetic account of many of the known facts of Sayers's life, and a pleasure to read.

to 1921, only two—incredible as it may seem—were married.
It is no wonder that Vera Brittain spoke of her dons as "lonely
Olympian women . . . who lived Spartan ideals of justice,
endurance, and self-sacrifice." (In a less rhapsodic mood, Brittain complained that the difference between the women's colleges and the men's at Oxford was—literally—the difference
between prunes and iced pudding. Academic women soared to
Olympian heights on a Spartan college diet of gristly mutton,
boiled potatoes, and tepid rice pudding—at a time when the
men's colleges were as well known for their meringues as for
their academic excellence.)

Gaudy Night is Sayers's tribute to these learned and clois-
tered women. This formidable mystery also embodies—although Sayers is far too stylistically elegant to dish up ideology
as rhetoric—her unnerving radical views about love and about
work. One wonders how many captivated men have had their
consciousness raised by this clever woman simply because she
bewitched them into having to know "whodunit." The person
"whodunit" in *Gaudy Night* is a woman. In her unlikely villain,
Sayers embodies all that which, as a feminist and a scholar, she
felt bound to fear and to loathe.

Harriet returns to her college reunion carrying the notoriety
of her murder trial around with her like an albatross. But "to
be true to one's calling," she feels, "whatever one's emotional
follies, is peace." What Harriet sees of marriage confirms her
belief that it's work that really counts: she sees brilliant scholars
of her year, their minds muddled and gone slack, their spirits
broken under the yoke of traditional marriage. The celibate,
amiable, and uncompromising dons, on the other hand, whose
sole allegiance is to fact, seem to her to have achieved peace
with honor. For Harriet—whose costly messes with "Love"
have taught her to value honesty and detachment above all
qualities—Oxford is a refuge from the abrasive personalities of
other people. She is tempted to devote herself to "the narrow

serenity" of that haven where "the fact that one had loved and sinned and suffered and escaped death was of far less moment than a single footnote in a dim academic journal."

Sympathetic readers may feel that a misguided Harriet is crucifying herself on a cross of her own construction: having established a dichotomy between the emotions and the intellect, she is determined not to give way to the demands of the flesh, lest integrity of mind suffer. But neither Harriet nor Sayers was being arbitrary, or inventing polarities where none existed; they were relating to the strictures and imperatives of a society in which one chose *either* to marry *or* to enjoy "the creative life of the intellect."

Harriet's peace is short-lived. A malevolent spirit is at large in the University Paradise. Anonymous letters advise the dons that they are not fit for decent society, that unless they leave men alone, horrible things will happen to them. "No man is safe from women like you . . . unnatural women, harpies," writes the "Poison Pen," who all the evidence suggests must be a college woman. This villain lurks around the darkened quadrangle at night to whisper messages into the ears of visiting males: "We murder beautiful boys like you and eat their hearts out."

To poor Harriet, who is convinced that the Poison Pen is one of the dons whose malignity is the outcome of soured virginity and starved appetites, all the dons begin to look abnormal. She begins to view the cloister as a coven; she finds herself believing that the villain is either a "man-hater" or a "man-trap." The reader, inclined to view the situation through Harriet's eyes, also regards the crimes as the outcome of repressions due to celibacy. This is not only because Sayers is a master of bafflement, but because our conditioning has inclined all of us—and Sayers counted on this—to share Harriet's subterranean fears and suspicion of "unnatural" women.

Into this volatile situation comes Lord Peter. Regarding him as a dangerous alien, Harriet is only infuriated by his reason-ableness and right-mindedness. When the Warden asks Peter if he is interested in the question of women's education, he nicely replies: "Is it still a question? It ought not to be. I hope you are not going to ask me whether I approve of women's doing this and that. . . . You should not imply that I have any right either to approve or disapprove."

Nor does it simplify matters that, all at once—"like falling down a well"—Harriet becomes intensely aware of Peter's dynamic physical attractions. To the despair of most critics, Peter never uses this as a weapon against her; although she confesses that if she once gave way to Peter she'd go up like straw, Wimsey never descends to caveman tactics. He is one man who does not believe that it is every woman's secret desire to be raped. Male critics, no doubt of the mind that a little wholesome brutality would have put prickly Harriet right and been far more manly than Peter's scrupulous regard for his lover's physical integrity, petulantly declare that, in this respect at least, Peter is so eccentric as to be downright crazy.

Flying in the face of his own self-interest, Peter advises Harriet that "if you want to set up your everlasting rest, you are far more likely to find it in the life of the mind than the life of the heart." (Sayers's critics have interpreted this delineation of Lord Peter as sheer perversity on the writer's part, refusing to recognize that Peter's un*macho* character is not merely a fortuitous artistic shot in the dark but a calculated feminist statement.)

Peter is about as "protective as a can opener." He recognizes the fundamental truth that the protector has it all over the protected: "A desire to have all the fun," he says, "is nine-tenths of the law of chivalry." When Harriet protests that he would, in spite of his demurrals, prefer "some nice little woman who adores being protected," Peter says he will have none of it: she "would always be deceiving me, in the kindest manner, for my own good; and that I could not stand. I object to being

tactfully managed by somebody who ought to be my equal."
Peter allows Harriet to run her own risks in her search for the
identity of the Poison Pen, refraining from offers of help and
advice: "I know that if you have put anything in hand, disagree-
ableness and danger will not turn you back, and God forbid
they should." That is an admission of equality; Peter may be
the one man on earth who would not snort with amusement
if he were to hear his beloved say, "I could not love thee, dear,
so much/Loved I not honor more."

The situation that gives rise to the disclosure of *Gaudy Night*'s
villain—and that allows Sayers to articulate her feminist beliefs
—is this: a male instructor, with a wife and children to support,
has written a fallacious paper, suppressing information that
proves his contention false. A female don, without regard for
the well-being of his family, has been instrumental in having
his degree, and therefore his livelihood, taken from him. His
wife stands by him, takes his side.

The academics assembled for *Gaudy Night*'s denouement
discuss these questions: What comes first—one's children or
one's job? Are one's children one's job? Is it moral to sacrifice
professional honor for the sake of women and children? Should
one marry unless one is prepared to make another human being
a full-time job? When principle leads in one direction, and
compassion in another, which must be sacrificed, principle or
compassion? Is charity toward the unprotected a virtue if it
results in the rewarding of unsound work?

Sayers's beleaguered dons feel that publishing self-serving
lies must not be overlooked, "not," as Harriet says, "for ten
wives and fifty children." "If anybody did a dishonorable thing
and then said he did it for one's own sake, it would be the last
insult. How could one ever feel the same to him again? . . .
Once you admit the principle, the consequences must follow."
A don is honor-bound to see that unsound work is unrewarded;
she must do her proper job regardless of consequences. If,

however, she were truly compassionate, she would thereafter concern herself with "what happened to that unhappy man and his family." "If the domestic responsibility is to take precedence over the public responsibility, then the work should be handed over to someone else to do. . . . Children have to be clothed and fed"; but "if one takes on personal responsibilities, one owes a duty in that direction. If one's job interferes with them, perhaps one should give up one's job." Only a few "rare people . . . don't look on themselves as jobs but as fellow-creatures. . . . *People who make some other person their job are dangerous.* "

The sternness of the views expressed by the dons may be seen as an integral part of their essential loneliness: these were voices crying out in a political wilderness; feminism as a social movement was, in Sayers's day, for all practical purposes as moribund as one of her celebrated corpses. Lonely people who have had to make difficult choices without support tend to see things in a harsh, uncompromising light. On the other hand, the very basis of all these *work-versus-love/charity-versus-principle* arguments may be seen as elitist—and elitism is a charge with which, sooner or later, anyone who loves Sayers (as I do) must contend . . . as one must also contend with Sayers's belief, upon which rest all her arguments, that scholarship is in fact "objective," and not colored by ideology or cultural norms.

It is clear that Sayers regarded these fierce women, not one of whom would place personal loyalties above professional honor, with unflinching admiration and love. Seen through her eyes, these are Spartan women who guard the gates of their University Paradise, achieved at such great cost, with flaming swords. She holds them in awe for the exercise of the "ruthless impartiality of . . . splendid isolation." They apply a single stern standard—"If there's any subject in which you're content with the second-rate, then it isn't really your subject"—to both men and women. Because, Sayers is saying, they serve the truth without pity and without rancor, one is safe with them.

The villain, therefore, as Peter has understood all along, is not one of the dons. She is acting, not out of sexual repression, but out of an animus against dons and scholars that proceeds from her having made another person—her husband—her job. She is this woman: "I wish I could burn down this place . . . where you teach women to take men's jobs. . . . It's women like you who take the work away from the men and break their hearts and lives. . . . You'd destroy your own husbands, if you had any, for an old book or bit of writing. . . . If [my husband] had been a thief or a murderer, I'd have loved him. . . . It would do you good to learn to scrub floors for a living. . . . [Love] means sticking to your man through thick and thin and putting up with everything. . . . You haven't the guts to do your proper job in the world. . . . Wives and mothers may rot and die for all you care, while you chatter about duty and honor."

The Poison Pen is the wife of the man dishonored and exposed by a principled don. She is a woman unprotected and alone, forced to scrub floors for a living, a "scout," or domestic, for the college staff.

Now, it goes against the class-conscious grain to accept as a villain a working-class woman, and to admire as heroines members of a privileged academic elite. Indeed, Sayers was an elitist; the elite she recognized was composed of "people really devoured with the passion for making and discovering things"—artists, scholars, scientists, craftspeople, engineers, mechanics, carpenters. She loved those best who did their job best: "Once lay down the rule that the job comes first and you throw that job open to every individual, man or woman, fat or thin, tall or short, ugly or beautiful, who is able to do that job better than the rest of the world."

Furthermore, Sayers knew that there is no image better calculated to promote tenderness in the male breast than the sweet "little woman" whose job is another person, whose mission is to stand by her man, no matter what. Sayers took that tender image and flung it back in the face of its creators, knowing that it served to brutalize women, to make them dangerous to themselves and to others.

There is an intensity of feeling in *Gaudy Night* that can be best understood in the light of Sayers's bitter reproach: "There is perhaps one human being in a thousand who is passionately interested in his job for the job's sake. The difference is that if that one person in a thousand is a man, we say, simply, that he is passionately keen on his job; if she is a woman, we say she is a freak." Sayers herself was one of the lucky ones; successful at work she loved, she also enjoyed a happy marriage.

Sayers was married for thirty years to a war correspondent, Captain Oswald Atherton Fleming, who is unfailingly described, by those who knew him, as "dashing." (That this dashing man wrote a cookbook—dedicated to his wife, "who can make an omelet"—is proof that life sometimes copies art: Sayers was apparently able to find a real-life man as unstereotypical as Wimsey.) It is to her credit that, in spite of an apparently felicitous marriage, Sayers never ceased to identify with those women the world called "freaks"; *Gaudy Night* is her brief for those "unnatural" women.

Gaudy Night also provides the epiphany for Sayers's lovers: it was Peter, foreseeing the consequences of his investigation, who told Harriet that "of all devils let loose in the world there [is] no devil like devoted love . . . love's a nervous, awkward, overmastering brute; if you can't rein him, it's best to have no truck with him." Peter might have used Harriet's fears about the celibate life to coerce her into the marriage he ardently desired; nevertheless, he did not cringe from the truth—the unpalatable truth potentially damaging to him—that the villain was a Devoted Wife and Mother.

Harriet, for her part, sees that her lover has a just and generous mind, that the qualities she admires in her beloved dons—honesty and detachment—are his as well. He has allowed her to risk her life, canceling her debt of gratitude; they are equals. But she will not consent to be Peter's wife if it means that she must become the caretaker of his happiness, if she must make him "her job": " 'Tell me one thing, Peter. Will it make you desperately unhappy if I say No?' 'Desperately? . . . My dear, I will not insult either you or myself with a word like that. I can only tell you that if you will marry me it will give me very great happiness.' "

Busman's Honeymoon—A Love Story with Detective Interruptions—is Sayers's delectable answer to the cynics who insisted that this marriage of two independent humans was doomed to be resolved in the divorce courts. In it Sayers takes on thorny problems with delicious wit: can two people marry with no sacrifices on either part, with neither person being impoverished or diminished? Does affection corrupt judgment? She tackles Peter's endemic male vanity; and she slays the serpent in conjugal paradise—possessiveness. She also describes physical passion in prose that manages to be delicately discreet and virile. ("The only sin passion can commit is to be joyless.") It is likely that even the sternest critic of marriage, entranced by Sayers's peculiar magic, might feel that Peter and Harriet have achieved love with honor.

Sayers's reputation as an artist is secure. But she has continued to infuriate critics whose resentment of class structure finds a focal point in rich Lord Peter. Sayers's feminism was as radical as it was individualistic; yet she confessed herself unmoved by the vision of social revolution. She wrote between two world wars; like all of her generation, she was a permanently misplaced person. The terrible upheavals of the First World War, which destroyed the rigid stratifications of an ordered society, may have inspired her with a misguided longing for the rooted comfort of tradition, for the security of a structured society in which everyone knew her or his place. But the pleasure she took in a mythical England in which people of all classes moved "like chessmen upon their allotted squares" was the pleasure of a hungry girl whose nose is pressed against the bakery window; she may have been an elitist, but she was not a snob—she had not a condescending, or a patronizing, bone in her body.

From a novelist's point of view, Peter's enormous wealth is a stroke of genius: accountable to no man, he may follow the path of righteousness with divine single-mindedness. From a feminist point of view, however, Lord Peter's wealth may be interpreted as a cop-out: Vera Brittain tells us that the central feminist problem of her time was "how a married woman without being inordinately rich can have children and yet maintain her intellectual and spiritual independence as well as having . . . time for the pursuit of her own career." It must be admitted that Sayers funked the question.

Harriet maintains her independence, all right, but Peter's inordinate wealth frees her from having any preoccupation with the perils of domesticity. It's true that Peter rejects the status symbol of an idle wife and that he would be aghast at the thought of gifted Harriet managing a household; it's also true that he has the means to provide her with eight servants and a housekeeper. Sayers managed to solve the problem in her own life; perhaps she is to be forgiven for obviating the struggle in the Wimsey-Vane never-never land.

Sayers's feminism derived from her attitude toward work: "Every woman is a human being—one cannot repeat that too often—and a human being must have occupation if he or she is not to become a nuisance to the world." Because of her frequently reiterated belief that "what we ask is to be human individuals, however peculiar and unexpected," she had a great distrust of mass movements, which she equated with forced unanimity. Devoted to the idea of individual excellence, she resisted the idea that she was a member of a class.

When the pioneers of university training demanded degrees, and men demanded to know why women should want to know about Aristotle, a vexed Sayers replied: "The answer is *not* that *all* women should be the better for knowing about Aristotle—still less . . . that they would be more companionable wives for their husbands if they did know about Aristotle—but simply: what women want as a *class* is irrelevant; *I* want to know about Aristotle." She rested her hopes not on concerted political activity but on the power of the enlightened individual to effect change; the brain, she said, was the "great and true, sole androgyne."

It is easy to charge her with arrogance. But it is difficult, while recognizing her limitations, not to love her. The world she created in her superlative fiction is a world of passion and order; she wrote beautiful fairy tales, fairy tales that were also morality fables. She was determined to find truth and beauty in the same place. Toward the end of her life she put away the Wimsey-Vane fable and devoted herself almost entirely to theology. For her, finally, the most profoundly exciting and terrifying mystery drama of all was God-made-human. Her God-Jesus was a feminist who "took women seriously, rebuked without querulousness, never patronized, condescended, nagged, flattered, coaxed, never urged them to be feminine or jeered at them for being female." (He sounds, as a matter of fact, not at all unlike Lord Peter.) She was God-obsessed; but not pious.

A literary acquaintance gives us this picture of Dorothy Sayers in her sixties: "Miss Sayers is a cheerful, gregarious lady, who owns as one of her chief recreations motorcycling." It is easy for me to imagine this "true androgyne" zipping up to heaven on a motorcycle and entertaining her aristocratic, feminist, Anglican God with her "peculiar and unexpected" combination of erudition and wit. Left behind in the messy world, we may comfort ourselves with the mathematical/logical truths of the Wimsey-Vane novels, with the beauty of Sayers's legacy of a paradise where they all lived happily ever after.

III.

Culture Heroes

JOAN DIDION:
ONLY DISCONNECT
(October, 1979)

When I am asked why I do not find Joan Didion appealing,
I am tempted to answer—not entirely facetiously—that my
charity does not naturally extend itself to someone whose lavender love seats match exactly the potted orchids on her man-
tel, someone who has porcelain elephant end tables, someone
who has chosen to burden her daughter with the name Quintana Roo; I am disinclined to find endearing a chronicler of the
1960s who is beset by migraines that can be triggered by her
decorator's having pleated instead of gathered her new dining-
room curtains. These, and other assorted facts—such as the
fact that Didion chose to buy the dress Linda Kasabian wore
at the Manson trial at I. Magnin in Beverly Hills—put me
more in mind of a neurasthenic Cher than of a writer who has
been called America's finest woman prose stylist. (Thinking of
Didion's drapes, it occurred to me that in the worst of all
possible worlds, Franny Glass might have grown up to be Maria
Wyeth of *Play It As It Lays.* Her faith in the Jesus Prayer
permanently misplaced, and possessed of no secular equivalent
to fill the vacuum, in her second incarnation Franny is Maria,
a fragile madonna of acedia and anomie. This feeling was
confirmed when I reread all of Didion, an activity that, trust
me, is roughly akin to spending several days in the company of
Job's comforters.)

I chose first, for no particular reason, to read an essay from

Slouching Towards Bethlehem, "Some Dreamers of the Golden Dream." In this essay, Didion reports, or purports to report, on the murder case of one Lucille Maxwell Miller, who was convicted by the State of California of having killed her husband by dousing him with gasoline and allowing him to burn to death while he slept in a Volkswagen she had been driving.

Until I sat down to write this essay, I could not, in fact, remember whether Lucille Maxwell Miller had been convicted or acquitted. Now, unlike the heroines of Didion's fiction, I do not regard memory as an affliction; I remember. I remember in part because I have no choice, but also in part because (unlike Didion's heroines, whose fate depends less upon memory and volition than upon selective amnesia), I believe that without memory there is no civilization. To complain ("I am so tired of remembering things") of remembering is to express a wish to be dead, to return to some pre-Edenic state in which good and evil, right and wrong, do not exist. It is a wish to erase not only one's personal painful past but our collective past—which, in turn, is an invitation to believe that we cannot, individually or collectively, affect the present or the future.

I remember; so why didn't I remember what was surely a salient fact to Lucille Maxwell Miller if not to Ms. Didion? The reason—and I ask you to understand that this is directly related to lavender pillows and matching lavender orchids—is that Didion was not in truth engaged in reporting about Lucille Maxwell Miller; Didion was reporting on Didion's sensibility, which in this essay, as in all her essays, assumes more importance than, say, the existence of the electric chair. What happens in this essay is that Lucille Maxwell Miller is convicted —by Didion—of wearing polyester and Capris, of living in a house with a snack bar and a travertine entry, of speaking in clichés, of having a picture window and a family room and a husband nicknamed Cork, of frequenting the Kapu-Kai Restaurant-Bar and Coffee Shop, and of never having eaten an artichoke. Lucille Maxwell Miller's real sin—a truly, as it turned out, mortal one—was to live in a subdivision house in the San Bernardino Valley and to hope to find "the good life" there, instead of in Brentwood Park or Malibu. Unlike those heroines of Didion's novels, Lucille Maxwell Miller never floated camellias in silver bowls to stave off encroaching madness or corruption—no such exquisite desperation for her; she found a "reasonable little dressmaker" instead. The crime for which Didion indicts Lucille Maxwell Miller is of being tacky —of not, that is, being Didion. This, you see, is where the lavender pillows come in: the body of Lucille Maxwell Miller's husband—burned black—offends Didion less than the fact that Lucille Maxwell Miller wore hair curlers. It isn't Didion's sense of morality that has suffered a blow, it's her sense of style. . . . Which is why, although I have nothing in principle against pretty houses or lavender love seats, Ms. Didion's lyrical angst strikes me as transparently ersatz. What I mean to say is Didion writes about Lucille Maxwell Miller—and her loyal baby sitter, and her friends, and her admittedly silly lover—as if they were mutants. No; she writes as if her subject were the Pillsbury Bake-Off Contest.

No; in fact, her subject is always herself.

Now that I've gotten that off my chest, I'd like to talk a little about Ms. Didion's highly acclaimed style before I move on to her politics.

Didion's "style" is a bag of tricks. Some of the effects she produces are quite pretty, even momentarily beautiful. But make no mistake: these are tricks—techniques—that can be learned (I don't know why they have evoked so much wonder). If, for example, I put Al Capone and sweet williams in the same sentence, I can be fairly sure that a certain number of readers will be jolted by the juxtaposition—their eyes will cross, and they will assume that they are in the presence of genius. They will be wrong, of course, because unless I use this technique to draw them into meaning, I will have cheated them: a magician can pull a rabbit out of a hat and get away with it; a writer's job is to tell us what the rabbit was doing in the hat in the first place. And, as Didion will gladly acknowledge, she is interested only in the *what* (the "empirical evidence"), not in the *why*.

Didion uses the Capone-sweet williams trick often, sometimes with dazzling effect:

"In the years after Luis was shot water hyacinths clogged the culverts at Progreso."

"Hear the doomed children celebrate all things bright and beautiful, all creatures great and small." (*Doomed* is the trick word here.)

"Look at the slut on Easter morning. Marin had a straw hat one Easter, and a flowered lawn dress." (Slut/flowered lawn: it works.)

"What makes Iago evil? some people ask. I never ask." (What makes those sentences work? I ask. Cadence, I answer. What do those sentences mean? you may ask. Don't.)

From *Play It As It Lays:* "I used to ask questions, and I got the answer: nothing. The answer is 'nothing.'" As soon as Maria Wyeth ascertains that the answer is "nothing," she segues to "Damson plums, apricot preserves, Sweet India relish and pickled peaches. Apple chutney. Summer squash succotash." That juxtaposition of nihilism with all the ripeness and plenitude of the physical world—the emptiness/cornucopia syndrome—is what passes for style. (Any recital, litany, of fruits, vegetables, and old-fashioned flowers is evocative—although, with Didion, we are never sure of what; anyone can learn to do it: read a Burpee catalogue.)

"The acrid string of weeds breaking under them . . . was stronger than all the roses and jasmine gardenias in the whole of Mercy Hospital."

"Alcatraz Island is covered with flowers now: orange and

yellow nasturtiums, geraniums, sweet grass, blue iris, black-eyed susans . . . candy tuft. . . ."

You see how it works.

Sometimes it doesn't work.

As in: "Carter could not remember the soft down on her spine or he would not have let them put needles there." Carter is Maria's husband, and, in the real world, he would—anyone would—have let "them" put needles in the spine of Maria's retarded child Kate, soft down or no, if he thought the needles would help. I am not being perversely literal-minded. I am concerned here with truth, as well as with fact, and the fact is that Didion is being perversely sentimental, dismissing the truth in order to achieve effect.

(I am also not unaware of the danger of confusing Didion with the narrators of her novels. I am aware of the danger, but I discount it, because the sensibility of her female narrators is indistinguishable from that which informs her essays.)

Her style has been acclaimed as spare, lean. Not so. The emperor is actually wearing more clothes, more finery, than his structure will support. As in (from *A Book of Common Prayer*):

> That was August.
> Boca Grande is.
> Boca Grande was.
> Boca Grande shall be.

That is padding—elegant padding, if your taste runs to that sort of thing, but padding nonetheless. It sounds good; it doesn't signify. "World without end, Amen" (from *the Book of Common Prayer*) sounds good—gorgeous—too; but it signifies: we know from the context what we are meant to feel and to understand. When Didion pulls one of her Boca Grande tricks, we are not meant to understand anything (except, perhaps, that even white girls have rhythm).

Here is another kind of trick, a trick used to round off a paragraph or an essay that threatens to be going nowhere. From *The White Album:* "James Jones had known a great simple truth: the Army was nothing more than life itself." Nonsense. Tell it to the Marines. Look hard at that capricious sentence and it wilts—for the very good reason that there is no truth in it, only contrivance. . . . Actually, as I think about it, it's worse than that: there is just enough truth in that sentence for it to slip by unnoticed. Sentences that contain half-truths should not be allowed to slip by unnoticed. As Didion herself says, "The consciousness of the human organism is carried in its grammar."

"I never expected you to fall back on style as argument," BZ says to (boring) Maria Wyeth just before he dies his curiously antiseptic sleeping-pill death, a death as cool and clean as Ali McGraw's in *Love Story.* Vomit, excrement, the mess attendant upon even this least harsh of suicide methods, would have been technically inappropriate for Didion's ending to *Play It As It Lays:*

> I know what "nothing" means, and
> keep on playing.
> Why, BZ would say.
> Why not I say.

One would be hard-pressed to imagine even self-absorbed Maria uttering these words while lying in BZ's mess—blood on the sheets—in the bed they share while he ends his purposeless (boring) life.

Didion uses style as argument.

Sometimes her tricks appear to be merely cheap, when in fact they are pernicious: "I live in a house in Hollywood in which, during the late thirties and early fifties, a screenwriters' cell of the Communist party often met." In that house is "a vast Stalinist couch." How does Stalinist deco differ from

Trotskyite deco or Leninist deco? one might ask. This is an example of Didion's using style as argument: one cannot imagine her calling attention to a "vast capitalist couch." Style as argument: the house, she says, "suggests the particular vanity of perceiving social life as a problem to be solved by the good will of individuals." Didion uses the "vast Stalinist couch" to illustrate her dearly held belief in the futility of all human endeavor—particularly if it originates from the Left.

Her style . . . her eye: about Boca Grande (the inspiration for which is said to be Panama), Grace, the rich narrator, says: "There is poverty here, but it is obdurately indistinguishable from comfort. We all live in cinderblock houses." Oh, no. The eye that sees no difference between the cinderblock houses of the poor and the cinderblock houses of the rich is a cold, voracious one; it is, furthermore, astigmatic. One does not have to have lived in a Central American country (I have), one has only to read *Newsweek* to understand that there are certain very real differences between the cinderblock houses of the rich and the cinderblock houses of the poor. Earthquakes, for example: the esthetically unpleasing cinderblock houses of the poor collapse during earthquakes; the esthetically unpleasing cinderblock houses of the rich do not. One assumes that that is a matter of some concern to those who live therein. (One might also mention plumbing. Didion does not.) I don't want you to think I am belaboring this; you may argue that Grace/Didion is being ironic when she compares the cinderblock houses of the poor to the cinderblock houses of the rich. That defense won't play: for irony to be effective, it has to start from a definable and recognizable moral base (think for a moment of Evelyn Waugh, and, whether you accept his moral premises or not, you will understand immediately the point I am trying to make); irony lacks pungency as well as passion if it lacks context and does not draw us into meaning.

Didion makes it a point of honor not to struggle for meaning. (I have yet to meet anyone who has offered a satisfactory explanation of the first and last sentences of *A Book of Common Prayer:* "I will be her witness." "I have not been the witness I wanted to be." Witness to what? one asks. Some ask. I no longer ask.) I do not require that a novelist eradicate all mystery, which is in any case impossible: think of Graham Greene, who tells us everything we need to know about his characters; we are still left with a sense of the ineffable, and no one can quarrel with that or with Greene until and unless God tells us why He permits suffering and evil. Think also of the existentialists, and in particular of Camus, who spent a lifetime exploring the absurdity of the human condition—and left us with so keen a sense of exhilaration as to amount to hope. Compare the sensibility of the existentialists to that of Didion —which also stems from the 1950s—because while Didion chooses to call attention to that which is ludicrous (Huey Newton spouting rhetoric), the existentialists, and Camus in particular, chose to call attention to that which was and is tragically absurd. The difference between the ludicrous and the absurd is the difference between the mirror (Didion) and the void (Camus). Reports from the mirror are likely to be jaundiced, puling, and debilitating; reports from the void can, not so strangely if you think about it long enough, inspire courage and the will to act. You will remember that transcendent moment when Camus's Sisyphus, bound to his absurd fate, poised on top of the mountain, sees his rock, his burden, plummet to the earth; at that moment, lucid and aware, Sisyphus knows that he will once again and forever push the rock, the burden, up the mountain; but in that moment, wrestling with meaning, he becomes truly human. The essence of human dignity resides in that struggle for meaning. (Another point in Sisyphus's favor was that he didn't whine, even though the gods neglected to place a swimming pool on top of the mountain for his refreshment.)

Now listen to Didion:

"I prefer not to know."

"The meaning continues to elude me."

"Nothing applies."

"Trying to find some order, a pattern, I found none."

"Almost everybody I meet in San Francisco has to go to court at some point in the middle future. I never ask why." Why?

"None of it mattered."

Nothing matters, Didion writes. What one hears is, "Only what I have to tell you matters." And, for Didion, only surfaces matter.

Didion is like a latter-day Scarlett O'Hara: she will think about whatever it is she thinks about tomorrow when she dabbles her toes in her pool, all the while calling attention beguilingly to the hairshirt she has fashioned for herself . . . which may explain why so many male critics find her adorable.

"What is, is," Werner Erhard tells his fans. "All connections," Didion tells her fans, are "equally meaningful and equally senseless." It does not say much for us that those are the messages we like to hear. Part of Didion's appeal, I am convinced, lies in her refusal to forge connections (notably between the personal and the political or between the personal and the transcendental). In spite of the sense of dread that suffuses her work, it contains this implied message of (false) comfort: if Didion—who is so awfully smart—doesn't trouble to make connections, why should we? "What is, is." In *Play It As It Lays* we are told: "Everything was happening exactly the way it was supposed to happen." "I am not much engaged by the problems of what you might call our day, but I am burdened by the particular, the mad person who writes me a letter." Few among us would raise three cheers for the mad person who writes us letters (Didion is not alone in preferring frangipane to obscene phone calls), but, leaving that aside, the point to be made is that—I don't know how else to explain Didion's appeal—readers find Didion's fatalism and her fashionably apocalyptic outlook comforting. If the plague is indeed coming (I ask you again to think of Camus), what is there to do but wait, curtains drawn and migrainous, contemplating—if we are lucky enough to have them—our roses?

While I am sure that Didion would deny that she romanticizes insanity (indeed, she reproaches Doris Lessing for celebrating the logic of the madhouse), her revulsion against the struggle for meaning is so overwhelming that, in the world of her fiction, only the cruel, the blindly sentimental, or the mad are functional and/or attempt to interpret data or analyze facts. "They [the unfeeling keepers of Maria's daughter, Kate] will misread the facts, invent connections, will extrapolate reasons where none exist, but I told you, that is their business here [in the loony bin]." In *A Book of Common Prayer* Grace says, "Our notoriously frequent revolutions are made not by the *guerrilleros* but entirely by people we know. This is a hard point for the outsider of romantic sensibility to grasp." Grace—who owns 59.8 percent of the arable land of Boca Grande "and about the same percentage of the decision-making process in La República"—is drawn to the lonely, witless, wandering American Charlotte because, among other things, Charlotte has no interest in "the reform of the Boca Grande tax structure." In Didion's moral universe, to be interested in tax reform is to be truly crazy. (I would find this point of view funny if I didn't find it dangerous.) Any attempt at political analysis is rendered perversely romantic. Grace stays in Boca Grande (which for all practical purposes she owns) because her days "are too numbered to spend them in New York or Paris or Denver imagining the light in Boca Grande, how flat it is, how harsh and still. How dead white at noon." It ought to be clear from this that it is Didion who is perversely romantic, and it ought to be clear that what she romanticizes is privilege and terminal lassitude. What contempt Didion has for those who "look for the sermon in the suicide, for the social or moral lesson," for those who "interpret what we see"! For Didion, the *only* appropriate response to suicide, revolution, to all the ills the flesh is heir to, is "vertigo," "nausea." (Of course it *hurts* to be crazy, but the pain is somewhat assuaged if you own a country; orchids provide some surcease from pain, too.)

Now, Didion tells us, many times, and in many ways, that her mind "veers inflexibly toward the particular."

To *what* in particular? Here is where we must look hard at Didion's politics. (I see now that I have been writing about politics all along—style and politics being, at least in Didion's case, apparently inseparable.)

Didion is interested in "personalities." And she reduces politics to personalities. She has been called a minimalist; better to think of her as a trivializer. In her devastating essay (from *The White Album*) "James Pike, American" (an essay that might even be said to have some "ideas," though Didion professes not to have, and not to wish to have, "ideas"), Didion scores some good acerbic points about a man foolish enough to drive "into the Jordanian desert in a white Ford Cortina rented from Avis with an Avis map and two bottles of Coca-Cola." Well, of course that's folly. But Didion—let us at once call her a reactionary—cannot then refrain from telling us that earlier Pike was in Baltimore for the trial of the Catonsville Nine. I guess nobody's ever told her that an idea—or a cause —is not responsible for those who believe in it. By way of demolishing Pike, she manages to reduce the trial of the Catonsville Nine—an event of some political (and perhaps even spiritual) significance—to a grotesquerie. Similarly, when she reports—selectively and superficially—on the Black Panthers, on campus disorders, she zeroes in on the most foolish of spokespersons, making a mockery of the causes that inspired good men to good action by ridiculing the worst of the best. Children playing odd games, she calls campus protesters, committing a sin of omission: these "children" were playing for their lives (Kent State?); the fact that there were con artists and idiots and tricksters among them does not alter that fact. (Because Jerry Rubin is now in love with hot tubs are we to believe that all protest against our criminal engagement in Vietnam was inspired by lunatics?) It is because Didion does not believe that human beings can modify or transform the world that she is obliged to call attention—in a series of verbal snapshots, like a Diane Arbus of prose—only to the freaks of the 1960s. In *Slouching* she writes trenchantly about one Comrade Laski, a self-styled freelance revolutionary with no discernible goals: "I am comfortable with the Michael Laskis of this world, with those who live outside rather than in, those in whom the sense of dread is so acute that they turn to extreme and doomed commitments; I know something about dread myself, and appreciate the elaborate systems with which some people manage to fill the void, appreciate all the opiates of the people, whether they are as accessible as alcohol and heroin and promiscuity or as hard to come by as faith in God or History. . . . You see what the world of Michael Laski is: a minor but perilous triumph of being over nothingness." For Didion, all "pain-killers"—heroin, God, the march on Selma, the gin and hot water and Dexedrine she guzzles to write her deflating essays—are alike. They are, she tells us, alike, but clearly she finds—and we are meant to find—her own pain, and her own methods of alleviating her own pain, far more consequential and lovable than those of others.

Didion turns this dirty trick—the trick of discrediting a cause by discrediting the advocates of a cause—against Joan Baez, too ("Where the Kissing Never Stops"): Baez "did not want . . . to entertain; she wanted to move people, to establish with them some communion of emotion. [Of course this might be said of any performer, but never mind.] By the end of 1964 [Baez] had found, in the protest movement, something upon which she could focus the emotion. She went into the South . . . [to] Negro colleges . . . always there where the barricade was. . . . She is the pawn of the protest movement." The *pawn*? Because Didion seems incapable of believing in, or exercising, volition and free will, she very neatly projects this quality onto Baez, who, admittedly, has been guilty of uttering some mushy-minded platitudes in her time (the writing on some of her album covers is quite as adolescent as Didion says it is). Didion is wicked—okay, brilliant—when she writes about the "children" who came to Baez's peace school; they "were not," Didion says, "very much in touch with the larger scene." But what does Didion believe to be "the larger scene," and how does she perceive it? We do not know. More importantly, the fact that Baez has both entertained people and attempted to alleviate human misery counts for nothing in Didion's scheme of things.

Didion turns her gift for mockery against the poor old Center for the Study of Democratic Institutions, too. She is wonderfully witty about the center's "ectoplasmic generality"; and one must concede that there is something inherently ludicrous in Dinah Shore's earnestly discussing civil rights with Bayard Rustin.

(There's something inherently ludicrous about the Jaycees, too: they wear funny hats. I'm the first one to laugh at a good joke; but I don't see that their funny hats give us the right to laugh at their avowed desire to "open our neighborhoods to those of all colors," and I don't find their concern with youth centers and public health clinics corny—and even if I did, I wouldn't find integrated neighborhoods and youth centers and public health clinics corny.)

Didion, who lives somewhere in Ayn Rand country, makes

fun (in *Run River*) of the character who "stood up for the little fellow and for his Human Right to a Place in the Sun"; she makes no apology for the character whom she quite truthfully describes as a "robber land baron."

How come, I'd like to know, her art of deflation is never put to use against those in power? When Didion deigns to mention the ruling class, she puts *ruling class* in quotes—which ought to tell us something about the woman who voted for Goldwater.

To assert that there was much about the 1960s that was bizarre, ludicrous, hedonistic, and muddle-headed is like coming out in favor of white wine in carafes and fresh daisies—most of us recognize the obvious when we see it. Many of Didion's observations about the self-serving "children" of the 1960s are dead accurate; but that doesn't give her the right to fiddle while Watts burns. In "Los Angeles Notebook" Didion writes, "At the time of the 1965 Watts riots, what struck the imagination most indelibly were the fires. . . . The wind [that damned Santa Ana that blows through her novels and her essays] shows us how close to the edge we are." To the edge of what? What *is* the apocalypse? And who, or what, has brought us to this place? Do not look to Didion for answers.

"Of course," Didion says, pandering to our worst instincts, our careless and selfish desires for political quietude, "we would all like to 'believe' in something, like to assuage our private guilts in public causes, like to lose our tiresome selves." The essay in which that sentence appears was written in 1965: Vietnam. In 1965 Didion told us that "all the ad hoc committees, all the picket lines, all the brave signatures in *The New York Times* . . . do not confer upon anyone any ipso facto virtue." Well, whoever said they did? Believing as I do in original sin, I am not so crazed or so simple-minded as to believe that human nature can be redeemed by an act of Congress; but I also believe that the consequences of not acting are as drastic as the consequences of acting: one marched because it was right and fitting to do so, and one allowed Providence to handle the rest. One acted upon the principle —the principle being in this case that the war in Vietnam was atrocious, as was the bombing of children in Alabama—and allowed the consequences to take care of themselves.

What Didion does in her essays she does also in her novels: in *A Book of Common Prayer* she parodies a Kunstler-like political being who defends the "Alameda Three" and the "Tacoma Eleven," who has an Andy Warhol silk print of Mao and who makes of having cocaine a civil libertarian issue. I think it's fine and dandy to poke fun at radical chic—I rather like it when someone like John Simon does it, because, say what you will about Simon, he operates from a moral base, however eccentric, and he includes the words *right* and *wrong* in his vocabulary. But Didion is incapable of divorcing *radical* from *chic;* she hangs out with a sorry crowd.

It's true that Didion occasionally ridicules the rich; it ought not to follow that this gives her the right to express contempt for the poor. In *A Book of Common Prayer* Charlotte (whose daughter Marin is another empty-headed "revolutionary," Patty Hearst-style) conceives an idea for a boutique in Boca Grande: "Needlepoint canvases of her own design and Porthault linens, the market for which would have seemed limited to Elena, Bianca, Isabel, and me [La República's oligarchy]." "Think," Charlotte says, "of a lath-house crossed with a Givenchy perfume box . . . gardenias." All very well; but then we are treated to this: Didion's narrator has "no patience with the fact that almost no one in Boca Grande would cross the street to be inoculated. They were all *fatalistas* about cholera. Cholera was an opportunity for God to prove His love." If you are a Didion fan, you may be inclined to see this as Scathing Honesty ("Didion writes so tightly it cuts the flesh": *Vogue*);

I see it as myopia. Didion does not see very clearly from the vantage point of whatever luxury hotel she happens to be staying in. I have seen people lining up for cholera shots, and I have seen people die of cholera, and I am here to tell you that Didion is lying.

While I'm on the subject of cholera, I'd like to make two more points, one of them obvious. Didion sees the death of one damaged child as infinitely moving: "They put shoes on her feet. Red shoes." She sees the decimation of an entire populace by cholera as a matter for scorn. I call that writing sentimental; I call that sensibility nasty. The second point: Charlotte is capable of performing noble, self-sacrificing deeds: she helps to inoculate the *fatalistas* against cholera, risking her own life to do so. Admirable in truth. However, what we get with this is Didion's insistent, insidious—and aristocratic—perception that the only good deeds are those so private as to escape the general notice. All virtue resides in acts so private that only the participants can understand their significance. Read *A Book of Common Prayer* again, and you will see that what is implied is that having politics paralyzes the potential for performing good deeds: to swallow Didion it is necessary to swallow the notion that all acts of virtue are—*must be*—divorced from politics. . . . I wonder if Didion is acquainted with the Manichaean heresy.

Didion—reporting from what she calls "the quintessential intersection of nothing . . . the hard white core of the world" (her vanity table)—is obsessed with the child trapped in the fridge, the "children burning in the locked car in the supermarket lot," the honeymooners killed in their thermal blanket by a coral snake. Yes; this is the stuff of nightmare. How mean-spirited would it be to point out that this is also the stuff that calls attention to Didion's Exquisite Sensibility? It's hard to fault people for their obsessions, but Didion's proclivity for "aimless revelation" does tell us something: to attach oneself only to the unanalyzable incident (especially when one's subject matter intersects with the political passions of our times) is to prefer to love one's pain; it is to caress and nourish one's pain, to find it of infinitely more value than the pain of "acquaintances [who] read *The New York Times* and try to tell me the news of the world."

"The notion of general devastation had for Maria a certain sedative effect. The rattlesnake in the playpen, that was different, that was particular, that was punitive." No. For the enthralled reader, I think, it works the other way around: the reader can enter into Maria's obsession with the rattlesnake in the playpen—which after all he never really expects to see except in his dreams—and, thus sedated, dismiss the "general devastation" as irrelevant to his life. The reader derives a certain masturbatory pleasure from contemplating events over which he has no control, and which he cannot be expected to analyze rationally.

Didion is the lyricist of the irrational. Some people find that charming. I do not.

So far I have spoken of the obvious. Now I want to move on to Didion's more subtle and covertly political messages, to a place where Ayn Rand's characters Howard Roark and John Galt—both rugged individualists whose religion is laissez-faire capitalism—would find themselves at home. In a nicely written and apparently harmless essay, "Many Mansions," Didion expounds (and she does it well) on the sterility of the Governor's mansion in California—an enlarged version of a tract house that Jerry Brown, with a rare show of good sense, has chosen not to inhabit. Didion expresses a preference for the old deserted Victorian mansion in Sacramento, with its secret rooms and hiding places, its gingerbread and grace. And its marble pastry table. Didion, if we are to believe her, alone among all the visitors to the Sacramento mansion, understands about

marble pastry tables: "There is no way to say this without
getting into touchy and evanescent and finally inadmissible
questions of taste, and ultimately of class." Oh, come on! Does
one have to be upper class to understand about marble pastry
tables? My grandmother, who came from Calabria, understood
about marble pastry tables; so do I, and I live in Brooklyn in
a cosmetically renovated tenement. Julia Child talks about
marble pastry tables in *McCall's,* for heaven's sake. Is Didion
the only classy lady around? Why does she ruin a perfectly good
essay with a gratuitous comment on class and the philistinism
of the bourgeoisie?

She is tricky. In her essay on the Getty museum she exalts
the Little Man—at the expense of egalitarianism. First she
says, and she is right, "The Getty tells us that the past was
perhaps different from the way we like to perceive it. Ancient
marbles were not always attractively faded and worn. Ancient
marbles once appeared just as they appear here: as strident,
opulent evidence of imperial power and acquisition. Ancient
marbles were not always bleached and mellow and 'tasteful.'
Ancient marbles once looked as they do here: as if dreamed by
a Mafia don. . . ." Then she spoils it: "The Getty advises us
that not much changes. The Getty tells us that we were never
any better than we are and will never be any better than we
were and in so doing makes a profoundly unpopular political
statement." What a quirky moral to draw. "The Getty," she
says, is "a museum built not for those elitist critics but for 'the
public.' Here was a museum that . . . need never depend on
any city or state or federal funding, a place forever 'open to the
public and free of all charges.' On the whole, 'the critics'
distrust great wealth, but 'the public' does not. On the whole,
'the critics' subscribe to the romantic view of man's possibilities, but 'the public' does not . . . the Getty [is] a palpable
contract between the very rich and the people who distrust
them least." My dear, tell it to the taxi driver who can't get

gasoline for his cab. (And now think of *The Fountainhead* and of Howard Roark's reasons for blowing up a public housing project—and of the poor who approve, in this cloud-cuckoo world, of his blowing up the housing project designed to benefit them, the rich and the poor acting in collusion against the "liberal critics"—and you will see that we are dealing with kindred, so to speak, "minds.")

And, not so incidentally, Didion indicts the dreamers of "the American Dream" for "F.H.A. housing" *and* "the acquisition of major appliances. . . ." How can one tell such a woman that she is confusing necessity with greed, treating them as if they were the same?

Here is another *Fountainhead/Atlas Shrugged* epiphany: Didion is at the Hoover Dam. She thinks about water a lot. Not about the *politics* of water, she is quick to point out (maybe she never saw *Chinatown*), just about . . . water: "I just stood there with my hands on the turbine. . . . It was a peculiar moment, but so explicit as to suggest nothing beyond itself. . . . That was the image I had always seen, seen it without quite realizing what I saw, a dynamo finally free of man, splendid at last in its absolute isolation, transmitting power and releasing water to a world where no one is." Well, if she chooses to regard a turbine with awe commensurate with that usually reserved for the contemplation of the ark of the covenant, that's her business. But why are critics so eager to celebrate a writer who celebrates a world "free of man"? I am defeated by my own question.

She tells us ("On the Morning After the Sixties"), "If I could believe that going to a barricade would affect a man's fate in the slightest, I would go to that barricade, and quite often I wish that I could, but it would be less than honest to say that I expect to happen upon such a happy ending." If you can believe that, you'll believe anything. The only happy ending for Didion is an unhappy ending. There's a lot I could say about barricades (as opposed to swimming pools), but I am now sick of Didion's paeans to the futility of human endeavor, her elevation of pain to a sacrament, and, in any case, I doubt that Didion's myopia would permit her to *see* a barricade if it were put up smack in the middle of her lavender sitting room. (What I would like to see is an essay by her that begins, *On the morning after the uprising in the Warsaw ghetto* . . .)

I suppose something should be said about Didion's essay on the women's movement, but not by me. What interests me more than her trivial and trivializing essay on women's liberation is that she sometimes expresses notions that would not be at all alien to the staunchest of feminists: "Women don't ever win. . . . Because winners have to believe they can affect the dice." If that is not a tacit admission that women are relatively powerless, what is? Of course, her female characters are all "strikingly frail" (emeralds complement their fragility beautifully), their eyes are too large for their faces, and, honey, they cry a bucket. Delicate pieces of machinery, humor is alien to them. And look closely and you'll see that none of her female characters has any female friends ("There existed between [Lily] and other women a vacuum in which overtures faded out, voices became inaudible, connections broke"). And Didion weeps for them, weeps for them. Which is probably why I love one sentence in *Run River* in which Didion allows herself to see some humor in their general incompetence: "Somebody holds the door open for Lily in a hardware store, and she thinks she has a very complex situation on her hands"; in a novel that closely resembles a gothic, that is a truly funny line.

"She had always smiled that way at men she did not know . . . wanting them to want her, recognize her as the princess in the tower." Alix Shulman might have written that sentence.

There is an essay about Georgia O'Keeffe that I find wonderful, an essay that is as "feminist" as anything in *Ms.:* "Some

women fight and others do not. Like so many successful guerril-
las in the war between the sexes, Georgia O'Keeffe seems to
have been equipped early with an immutable sense of who she
was and a fairly clear understanding that she would be required
to prove it. . . . At the Art Students League in New York one
of her fellow students advised her that, since he would be a
great painter and she would end up teaching painting in a girls'
school, any work of hers was less important than modeling for
him." Could one ask for a better denunciation of cultural
oppression than that?

(I can't resist quoting something Gloria Steinem once called
out to a journalist on her way to interview Didion: "Ask her
how come, if she spends all her time crying and swimming and
struggling to open a car door, she finds the energy to write so
much?")

"Things said out loud for her had an aura of danger so
volatile that it could be controlled only in the dark province by
those who share beds." I know few women for whom this
sentence would not resonate; it speaks to a particular truth of
women's condition, it is all too true. As is Didion's description
of Maria's abortion and her subsequent horror at the waste, the
fetus in the pail. (If I have seemed, up to now, to be unfair to
Didion, if I have neglected to say that her conservatism can
sometimes be a refreshing antidote to doctrinaire radicalism-
by-rote, to the shiny new baubles of current public opinion
. . . if I have not acknowledged that some of her sentences leap
off the page and find their way to the heart, in which her
sentiments have already, inarticulated, been lodged, it is because that is a path well worn: when a writer has been so much
overpraised, it is difficult, if not pointless, to join the chorus.)

Didion writes about Newport: "The very houses are men's
houses, factories, undermined by tunnels and service railways,
shot through with plumbing to collect salt water, tanks to store
it, devices to collect rainwater, vaults for table silver, equip-

ment, inventories of china and crystal and 'Tray cloths-fine' and 'Tray cloths-ordinary.' " That is, again, a "feminist" construct; and it reminds us that feminism, at its most useful and least cranky, is synonymous with good sense and clear vision, with sanity.

Still, for Didion to have any sympathy with anyone who aligns herself with any cause, any movement, is too much to hope for. She informs us balefully that she feels "radically separated from most of the ideas that seem to interest other people." Like Grace in *A Book of Common Prayer,* she is *de afuera*—the outsider: "I have been *de afuera* all my life." I think she wears that singularity like a badge. "I am different" translates into "I am superior." (When I came of age in the 1950s, everyone one knew was an Outsider, and proud of it; and every Outsider belonged to a privileged Inner Circle of Outsiders, and then we grew up.)

That coddled singularity/superiority is, I am afraid, one of the reasons readers love Didion. To delight in her sensibility is to say, "I'm different, too—better than other people. I see that she sees what I see."

Didion, who can manage, maddeningly, to sound smug and remorseful at the same time, tells us that she has no opinions: "In New York [on a book tour] the air was charged and crackling and shorting out with opinion, and we [she and Quintana Roo] pretended we had some. Everyone in New York had opinions." To pretend to carry no mental baggage at all makes one a voyeur at the party, a detached onlooker at the execution. There is a precariously thin line between voyeurism and decadence; and I am bound also to conclude that Didion, the participant-observer—at Hollywood parties, at the Manson trial, etc., etc.—titillates her readers with faint whiffs of decadence that emanate not only from the observed but from the observer—a poseur who does indeed have consistent opinions, although they are disguised as instinctual, idiosyncratic reactions to ephemeral phenomena, and thereby rendered less threatening and more winsome.

The reason I don't love Didion, after all is said and done, is that I need to be told forthrightly what a writer loves, or more precisely, what she values. I don't like to be seduced by indirection.

We know she loves—or is obsessed by—water. (There is not a day, she says, that she does not think of lifesavers "and what they are doing, what situations they face, what green-glass water."(She also—wouldn't you know it?—gets seasick.) There is in addition not a day that she doesn't think of the Hoover Dam and of the Quail Reservoir in Los Angeles County: "I knew I had missed the only vocation for which I had any instinctive affinity: I wanted to drain Quail myself." (Delirious overstatement; but then again, one of the things Didion can be said to love is delirium.) She loves swimming pools—which, she would have us believe, are "a symbol not of affluence, but of order, of control over the uncontrollable." And she loves orchids and greenhouses (all her life she has "craved the light and silence of greenhouses . . . all my life I had been trying to spend time in one greenhouse or another"). That's nice. She has been enamored of "yellow theatrical silk" curtains, too. That's nice. And she loves John Wayne and she loves Rhett Butler.

Like all writers with an apocalyptic turn of mind, she, like Lily in *Run River,* values a golden past never precisely defined; she has nostalgia for "a place of infinite possibilities for faith and honor and the grace of commonplace pleasures"; and she has dreamed of an unattainable "just-around-the-corner country where the green grass grew."

In an essay called "Self-Respect," she lets us know that she abhors "sins of commission and omission, the trusts betrayed, the promises subtly broken, the gifts irrevocably wasted through sloth or cowardice or carelessness." These are pretty sentiments, prettily expressed; but her sense of tragic regret rings hollow to me; it is as nonspecific as her proposed remedy: "The willingness to accept responsibility for one's own life is the source from which self-respect springs."

"Except on that most primitive level—our loyalties to those we love—what could be more arrogant than to claim the primacy of personal conscience?" Then to what *does* she give primacy? If not to personal conscience, to authority? To a "social code," she answers: "I want to be quite obstinate about insisting that we have no way of knowing—beyond that fundamental loyalty to the social code—what is 'right' and what is 'wrong,' what is 'Good' and what 'Evil.' " But to what social code? Framed when, and by whom? *for* whom? How can I trust her when I do not know the answers to those questions? When she and her family talk about "sale-lease-backs and right-of-way condemnations, we are talking in code about the things we like best," she says—"the yellow fields and the cottonwoods and the rivers rising and falling and the mountain roads closing when the heavy snow comes in." I can't trust that. I can't trust her because when she talks about "the long golden afternoons that [are] no more" in her native Sacramento, her language is suffused with that peculiar sentimentality one associates with an Englishman who once enjoyed the glories and the privilege of the Raj—an imperialist mentality is at work here, a gentlemanly, aristocratic sensibility that obdurately ignores the realities of class and economics and remembers only the long shadows on the green grass on a summer afternoon. Both are real—the golden afternoons and the sale-lease-backs (the money); Didion dismisses half the equation.

Her idea of peace, or of salvation, is to retreat to a place like Guyamas or Alcatraz, where there is no "vanity"—which is to say, a place where there is "no trace of human endeavor."

(Then what is she doing at those Hollywood parties with "gangsters" and "fags"?)

Tell me how I can love a woman for whom New York in the 1950s—the city of "the shining and perishable dream"—was F.A.O. Schwarz and Best's and dancing to the music of Lester Lanin and crying at Toots Shor's and Sardi's East.

She has trouble, she says, "maintaining the basic notion that keeping promises matters in a world where everything I was taught seems beside the point." What was she taught? For what, exactly, does she repine? What are those "extreme and doomed commitments" for which she professes love? From what magic kingdom is she in exile?

In the 1960s, she says, "no one at all seemed to have any memory or mooring." But to what is she moored?

What she is moored to, of course, is her angst. And her angst is not the still point of the turning world.

Anyone whose love is reserved almost entirely for the past can have only disdain for the present. And can consequently not be trusted to tell us the truth.

Make no mistake: I too am interested in visits to the interior. I know that what happens in the recesses of the human heart is at least as interesting as what happens at the Center for the Study of Democratic Institutions. Yes, everything begins in the human heart. But the human heart is not vacuum-packed. The pulsebeat from any breast, however armored, is felt, not just in private contracts—"doomed commitments"—between private persons, but in Selma, in Haight-Ashbury, in Vietnam, in South Africa, in East New York. Reports from those locations are also reports from the heart. And Didion's heart is cold.

Well, I have spent a long time now in Didion's world. "The baby frets, the maid sulks [or would, if I had one]. I . . . lie down."

GODFATHER II:
OF Families AND families
(1974)

When my radical friends cottoned to the fact that I was a
Godfather I junkie, I was quick to anticipate and disarm criticism by arguing that while it was possible for a *lazy* audience
to understand from *The Godfather* that Mafiosi went around
knocking off only one another in internecine wars, making
offers that couldn't be refused only to other pestilential pigs,
leaving the rest of the citizenry to go about their God-fearing
ways in peace, an *intelligent* audience could easily extrapolate
the truth from Coppola's film—which is that the Mafia ruins
small lives, destroys innocent grocers as well as rival dope-
dealers. *The Godfather,* I said, bore witness to the bitter truth:
evil, hydra-headed, renews itself and triumphs in the end; in
America, the Corleones win.

To which my radical friends said, *Bullshit:* "Don Corleone
and Sonny and Michael were all so damned attractive. They
were killers, but one liked them just the same. Their evil was
mitigated by their charm." And my brother said, "You liked
it because you're Italian." And of course my friends, and my
brother, were right. I had not, after all, seen *Godfather I* six
times for the pleasure of witnessing the triumph of Evil over
Good. I saw it because, in spite of its celebrated violence, it was
perversely comforting and warm; it had a uniquely tender,
cradling quality. Each time I saw Don Corleone die his rose-
garden death, I was set squarely in that fabled place where

families honor, respect, support, and protect one another, *touch* one another, forgive one another their sins. Viscerally I understood the Corleones better than, say, the Louds (and I liked them better, too). *The Godfather* nourished the notion that there was someone, some force, who could absolve guilt and make all the hurt go away, someone whose accepted authority could gentle and sustain us.

"Heresy," my feminist friends snorted. "You are talking about patriarchal families who have no remedy for pain, families that smother you, that protect you because you're their property. Step out of line and see what they do for you." My critical intelligence—and my own experience as a third-generation Italian—told me they were right. And yet I returned, as if on a pilgrimage to an atavistic part of my nature, to the courtliness of Don Corleone, to the sanguinity and vivacity of Sonny, to the magnificent reserve of Michael—that eloquent stillness that promised everything, that promised absolution. *Godfather I* created a world analysis could not sour. I felt embraced by the film, and not just because I so rarely see the pungent gestures and rich rituals or hear the rude songs, the lyrical-vulgar dialect of my childhood, reflected in literature or art: I have a vestigial yearning to believe, damn it, that there is a safe, redemptive place, a landscape where everyone knows his or her place, where one follows, with benediction and grace, the yellow brick road to the shrine of approving family gods.

And then Coppola, in his extraordinary sequel to *The Godfather*, did more to challenge my cherished conviction that the family can be a Salvation Army than did all the harangues of my radical friends.

Consequently, *Godfather II* gave me an attack of spiritual indigestion similar to the heartburn I invariably suffer after Italian weddings. I return, always, from a family wedding blood-warm, warmed by "the blood." I think of the extravagant assurances we have all ritualistically exchanged: "You are our blood," we tell one another, "We will love you whatever you do, we are here for you." And then I think of the work some of those men with whom I've danced the tarantella and exchanged blood-love do in the world (it's not pretty); and I marvel at my capacity to be seduced by the passion and authority and vigor and charm of men whose work I cannot love. And I think—looking at their wives, who have reaped the traditional rewards of traditional lives—What would have happened to those warm, smiling women if they had chosen separate identities, if their paths had violated the ethic of *la famiglia*? Would, in fact, their men have been there for them? And then I think of my brother, who is a just and generous man, whose authority I *do* accept, who can outcharm Sonny any day of the week, who *is* always there for me, who stills my restlessness and makes me feel safe, as no one else in the world can make me feel safe. And I think of my gentle father, who has learned painfully to love his maverick daughter, who defends me even when he finds my life incomprehensible. And then I think of a few bitter women, sitting outcast and alone, who are tolerated merely because they are "the blood," but who are not protected, not loved, because in some way they have violated the sacred rules of this large, lusty family composed of good men and bad men, of strong women and selfless women. I think of the strength of Italian women, of strength perverted and strength preserved. And I am painfully confused. I want all of these people to love me, to comprehend me; I want none of them to constrain or confine me. And I know that what I want is impossible.

I would be surprised if Coppola were not also a victim of the hopelessly ambivalent feelings about family—about the bonds that both heal and mortify—that all second- and third-generation Italians suffer. I think *Godfather II* must have been a painful film for Coppola to have made.

Politically, *Godfather II* is as explicit and forthright as *God-*

father I was elliptical. It bludgeons us with what its predecessor hinted at. It says, with a specificity that leaves little room for a gentler interpretation, that we are one nation under capitalism, and that under capitalism, the Enemy is One—and the enemy includes corporate business, members of the United States Senate, organized labor, and the Mafia. It is, as Pauline Kael has aptly said, "an epic vision of the corruption of America."

Psychologically, *Godfather II* is kaleidoscopic—some have said muddled. But its confusions are *our* confusions, its malaise *our* malaise. *Godfather I* was an almost elegiac film. *Godfather II* is an ice bath. After three and a half hours spent inside the second-generation Corleones' conspiracies and psyches, I felt as if I'd been savaged, betrayed, cheated. I've spoken to Italian friends and they agree: Coppola, who gave us in *Godfather I* the romantic family idyll we all craved, forced us in *Godfather II* to test all our own troubled, troubling feelings about family. What he gave us was not entertainment, not a mythical romance that released us, briefly, from the oppression of our singularity and aloneness, but necessary pain.

There was a kind of golden aura about Brando's Don Corleone, even as he was plotting to destroy half the population of Harlem. He was a luminous goon. There, but for a few wrong turns of fate, one felt, goes a real sweetie pie of an Italian poppa. One could imagine being caressed by his caring; he was the prototypical daddy of our nursery dreams—the powerful man of the world who wipes the tears from the eyes of his babies and acts always, and only, to protect his cherished family. He was, literally, the God/Father. Don Corleone was a rock against whom one might lean. The Michael of *Godfather II* is a defoliator, a glacier. There is, about Michael, everything dark, dank, and pernicious. Charity is inimical to his nature; he feeds on the blood, not only of his enemies, but of his family. He kills his dopey older brother Fredo, destroys the womanhood of his sister Connie, and shuts his wife, Kay, out of his heart and his life and robs her of her children. As *Godfather II* ends, he is absolutely powerful and absolutely evil, locked in the solitary confinement of his own corruption, without warmth and without pity.

How well Coppola knows that in Italian families the blood calls to the blood; how devastatingly he deals with the fact that a sister needs, above all things, the approval of her brother to remain whole. When thrice-married Connie approaches Michael (on her knees) and says, with palpable self-loathing, Everything bad I have done to myself I have done to hurt you because you killed my true husband and turned me into a whore, she begs to be allowed to return to the family, *to take care of Michael,* in order *to redeem herself.* Now, for one brief (shameful) moment, I felt my heart leap: the family is back together again! Reunion! Fortunately, I was sitting next to my sister-in-law, who has lived through enough Italian melodramas and vendettas not to be so easily gulled. She introduced a note of raucous sanity into my mindless sentimentality: as Connie groveled and Michael bestowed his icy benediction, my sister-in-law yelled, *"Right? There's always some woman around to pick up the pieces!"*

I would like to have seen a woman like my sister-in-law portrayed in *Godfather II*—a strong Italian woman, that is, with a built-in bullshit detector. I'm sorry that the woman who *named* Michael (who pronounced him evil) was the quintessential WASP Kay. When Kay can no longer pretend to herself or to Michael that she is innocent so long as she is ignorant, when she aborts Michael's dynastic successor, her bitter reproach is couched in words I find unacceptable: "I won't," she says, "be part of your two-hundred-year-old Sicilian thing any longer."

My Calabrian chauvinism notwithstanding, I wish Coppola hadn't allowed Kay to imply that Sicilian families have a particularly bad odor. Clearly *Godfather II* tells us that crime Families stink to heaven. But what about our need for *family*? Coppola's film says brilliantly and unambiguously that the end preexists in the means—that a single small maggot of corruption, given enough filth to feed on, becomes a devouring multi-headed dragon: I gave you Don Corleone, Coppola says, and I permitted you to love him; but you should have been smart enough to know that evil breeds greater evil, and that the end result would be Michael, would be devastation.

But does Coppola not believe that families can heal? My brother and my father—who are good men—inspire me to believe. Does Coppola? I don't know. I don't know because *Godfather II* doesn't tell us. It tells us about a killer Family; its ambiguities spring, I think, from the fact that the bleakness of its vision cannot wholly disguise Coppola's need to believe. But the need to believe is not the same as belief itself. There is a tension between the need and the conviction. *The Godfathers, I* and *II,* reflect that tension, that anguish.

One thing is certain: Coppola understands the terrible hunger of second- and third-generation Italians. Caught in the limbo between the old ways and the new ways, we all want what we are quite sure we cannot have: we want to suckle forever at the family breast. I think he also understands the hunger of all Americans to believe in the goodness of human nature. What Coppola says to that is, Forget it. Bad people are bad people.

What men do in the world resonates in their bedrooms. If one's work in the world is evil, one's "love" for one's family turns into something obscene. The Michael Corleone who has a prostitute butchered to compromise a defiled and defiling senator is incapable of loving *any* woman. The protection the Corleone men offered their women was predicated on the ignorance of those women; and those women, who cultivated blindness, reaped their own destruction. The price they paid for being sheltered was the loss of their souls. I have known women like that. As long as they remain mute and unprotesting —as long as they care more for pasta than for politics—they are happy. As one is happy in a dream. The Corleone men created a dreamworld for their women; they locked them into pink and pretty closets. The closets were roomy—there was space enough for laughter and lust and love and fun. I know those closets; I know that it is possible to stay in them forever. But, for most of us, eventually the world impinges. Mama Corleone, who never questioned, never stepped outside her defined and defended world, died relatively happy in her Skinner-box closet; but even she, at the end, had a glimmer of recognition that her acquiescence had helped to produce that which Kay called "unholy, . . . an affront to God."

If *Godfather II* has a moral, it is that you cannot feed evil men and expect to be nourished by them. Evil men are never "good family men." The myth that Italian-Americans have helped to perpetuate ("Joey Gallo brings his mama roses every Sunday") an Italian-American has helped to destroy. Americans have found that myth irresistible; in these lean and hungry times, when people huddle together for warmth, when robust folk heroes are the vivid symbols of our weary desires, audiences may find Coppola's iconoclasm unforgivable.

THE SUBJECT
IS ROSELAND

(September, 1977)

In the mid-'50s, when I was hanging out at Birdland a lot, two young secretaries I worked with hung out at Roseland a lot. Birdland was then on the east side of Broadway at Fifty-second Street, and Roseland was on the west. But, while we were within geographical hailing distance of each other, we felt ourselves to be light-years apart. Over there, Helen and Julie, my office pals, were doing the fox-trot and the tango, dreaming of winning fhe Harvest Moon Ball contest; they were planning their trousseaus and filling the hope chests they would bring to the men they had not yet met. I was listening to Sonny Rollins and Miles and Basie and Joe Williams, wondering when my here-a-while-gone-a-lot-longer jazz-musician lover would come back to me again, and dreaming of living with him in pictur-esque poverty in what real-estate agents had just begun to call the East Village. Helen and Julie were appalled at the risks they thought I was taking (I was exhilarated by the risks I knew I was taking); and I wouldn't have exchanged one smoky, hot, jazz-filled night for a year of what I believed to be the watery-white, middle-class music and singles angst of Roseland.

Everything changed. Birdland shut down forever. Helen stopped going to Roseland when she met a gynecologist at Democratic campaign headquarters in Flushing and acquired a diamond that matched in taste—and very nearly in size—the circular bed in the window of Gimbels she had her eye on. Julie stopped going to Roseland when Helen started to have satin sheets custom-made for her circular bed. I stopped seeing my jazz musician when I fully understood that he was not going to leave the comfort of his home (and his middle-class wife) to live in romantic poverty with me in the East Village. Roseland moved around the corner to Fifty-second Street between Broadway and Eighth; who, I would have said, cared?

Dumb question. If I'd had my wits about me when Helen and Julie and I were pursuing our separate after-work lives, I would have understood that the world of Roseland was as unique—and arguably as captivating—a subculture as the one I was in love with. Much to my own surprise, I myself am beginning to care a lot about the place Lou Brecker, Roseland's owner, conceived and created fifty-six years ago.

I came to Roseland when Ismail Merchant, who was preparing to produce a film titled *Roseland,* invited me to hang out. I thought it would be fun. (Also, I love the idea that everything is connected, the notion that the past circles back to embrace us . . . and I was intrigued by the prospect of visiting the place I had once calumniated as a dumping ground for people who were not really living the '50s.)

Merchant and director James Ivory came to Roseland because Don DeNatale, a dancer-actor who is kept in gold-studded denim by his various ballroom and extra-ballroom activities, had a bit part in Merchant-Ivory's *The Wild Party.* DeNatale invited them one night when his hustle group (a two A.M. staple at Muscular Dystrophy telethons) was there. Merchant and Ivory brought with them novelist Ruth Jhabvala—who knows a rare microcosm when she sees one. Jhabvala, a Polish Jew who'd lived in India for twenty-five years, was, from the moment she entered the front door (admission $3.50), overwhelmed by the physicality of Roseland. Here she found the raw material for her first "American" screenplay.

It was the dancing shoes and the testimonials that initially titillated Jhabvala's imagination: the first thing you see when you enter the place is the Roseland Wall of Fame. Enshrined in glass, tenderly preserved, are the dancing shoes of celebrities and Harvest Moon Ball winners who have danced here: Betty Grable, Katherine Murray, Don DeNatale, Chita Rivera, Eleanor Powell, Sandy Duncan, Ray Bolger, George Raft, Benay Venuta, Joel Grey, Joan Crawford. (Say all of that is "camp," and the Roseland regulars won't know what you're talking about.) Next, a glass case containing written testimonials invoking God's blessings on the Breckers ("We love you. You are our second home. We'd be lost without you.") Then, the Honor Roll of couples who've met and married here. (Mr. and Mrs. Frank Cesare, married 1926, head the list.) There are two places to go from here—*out*, if you're put off by tarnished nostalgia, or, if like me you catch a whiff of glittery geriatric excitement in the ballroom beyond (there are very few youthful Helens and Julies at Roseland nowadays), down to the lounge and into the ladies' room. There transformations occur: bag ladies shed layers of clothes and emerge in extravagant whipped-cream chiffon confections, circa 1940. Late-middle-aged Bendel's matrons apply makeup in loving Felliniesque slow motion. Narcissism makes egalitarians of all—the lonely ladies of means who buy comfort for the night, the poor in spirit and in purse who find the illusion of glamour and fullness in the tacky-opulent ballroom that beggars description: bulbous brass chandeliers, which actor Conrad Janis describes as "not quite Miami Renaissance." Bunting—purple, red, faded. A Godfather bar, plastic roses. A neon American flag over the bandstand. Sitting-out chairs, tables where regulars who come to feast on food and spectacle gather. Some Roselanders never dance at all. Helen Hayes, DeNatale says, frequently comes just to sit and look. Ballroom dancing is a spectator sport, DeNatale says—don't *mention* the word gigolo to him.

Merchant-Ivory films with screenplays by Jhabvala *(Shakespeare Wallah, The Householder, The Guru, Autobiography of a Princess)* are both lyrical and acute, informed by a merciless vision, but drawn gently. Their "Indian" films, resonant with nuance, explore the complexities and ambiguities of the subcontinent, where reality and illusion tangle; India, for them, is not so much a country as a state of mind. It will be interesting to see this sensibility brought to bear on Roseland—where reality seems altogether suspended.

Teresa Wright and Lou Jacobi are going over their lines. In one of three interrelated stories, Wright plays a genteel widow and Jacobi an uncouth widower who, with some reluctance on either side, connect at Roseland where the illusion of perpetual youth blurs the reality of what they can bring to each other. The ballroom has been cleared for this scene. On the sidelines, Screen Actors Guild extras and Roseland regulars mingle. Is that woman with a widow's hump and orange hair and a dead-white *Vogue* face and rhinestone-studded glasses a regular or an extra? They all look desperate and importuning—the extras, one supposes, because they are hoping the improbable/possible will happen . . . the camera will single them out, they'll be given a line; and the regulars . . . well, how else can you look when you have a sixty-five-year-old head on a graceful twenty-year-old body, and you're about to do the Peabody with slender hips that are brittle with age? You know all those almost-well-dressed old men one sees on the street(dapper, oily) who don't seem to be anybody you'd ever know, and you can't imagine what they do or did for a living but you're not sure you really want to find out? They're all here at Roseland. Whether they're extras or regulars, one cannot be sure. The man with the impeccable blue suit and the white ventilated shoes who asks a twenty-four-year-old production assistant to go to Florida with him ("Like a daughter I'll treat you") turns out to be both a regular *and* a SAG extra. Everything overlaps—a surreal collage.

The production crew is bemused. Everybody is talking about happiness. A sociologist who teaches at John Jay theorizes, for anyone who will listen, about the motivations of women who come to Roseland. (She herself came to watch a night of filming and, addicted, stayed to work as a gofer.) What her theory amounts to is that if an eighty-year-old woman can hire an almost-young dancing instructor (plus other, less orthodox, services), why not? Roseland is more fun, she says, than a senior-citizens' club, less desperate than a singles' bar, "because these people know they might die tomorrow, so it's only one night that's on the line—at a singles' bar it's the rest of your life." One of Merchant's assistants wants to bring her recently widowed mother here: "It's better than watching TV all alone. . . . It's nice to know I'll have someplace to come when I'm sixty." All the people seem intent on believing that Roselanders are happy—it's like insurance for *their* old age. Meanwhile, you get the feeling that everyone expressing these sanguine sentiments would rather drop dead than be found dancing here.

Don DeNatale tries to disabuse me of this notion: "Good dancers come here. Some young ones, too. It's a sport. Older women hire dancers, and everybody's happy. See that woman in gold lamé? She's a psychiatrist. She comes here to relax. I'm her dance instructor. The woman in red chiffon is a physical therapist; she takes care of stroke patients. It's cheaper than spending your money complaining to a doctor or a lawyer or a shrink, isn't it? I won the Harvest Moon Ball here when I was seventeen. I took seventh place in the London Dance Olympics. *I'm* happy."

I don't know what the London Dance Olympics are, but I know it would be a mistake to reveal my ignorance to DeNatale, and a worse mistake to ask him in what year he won the

Harvest Moon Ball contest. Like everyone else who comes here regularly, DeNatale is not what you'd call forthcoming about his age. (He has the face of a Spanish aristocrat, a hint of the Orient around his eyes, and a mod haircut, which refutes his elegance but achieves—in this dim light—its purpose: it makes him look younger.)

Nothing is what it seems to be here. Everybody is playing a part patterned on somebody else's real life, and the real-life models for the parts are in the room, too; it's confusing. DeNatale is playing Roseland's emcee in the film. Actor Christopher Walken plays a dancer, special friend, and companion to a wealthy woman of a certain age. Walken is breathing his role. During a break in the shooting, he echoes, almost word for word, DeNatale's sentiments: "No, of course the people who come here aren't neurotic. . . . It's a sport. . . . They're happy. Well, at least no more neurotic than you or I." DeNatale nods his approval. Watching these two is like watching an amoeba split, multiply.

Walken goes back to the set, where he rehearses a scene with Helen Gallagher. Helen Gallagher's dancing shoes are enshrined in Roseland's Wall of Fame. Now she is playing a dance instructor and Roseland regular—which she once was. (It is not going to be difficult for Jim Ivory to coax "natural" performances out of these actors.) Character actress Lilia Skala is on the ballroom floor, swooning in the arms of an aging actor who is, according to the script, about to have a massive coronary. He is totally believable in his role; but, then, a quarter of the male population here seems to be a tango away from a coronary.

There is a choreographer here—a good one—Pat Birch. But she seems redundant. By now I am beginning to be able to tell the extras from the regulars: the regulars are better dancers. Regulars ask crew members to dance: orthopedic shoes dance with sneakers; sneakers dance with golden slippers. One man dances alone all night, in a corner of the underpopulated ballroom, smiling, and looking—it's true to say—absolutely happy.

By eleven thirty, I've had enough of this twilight zone. I look for my daughter, whom I find pinioned against a wall, being clutched at by a fiftyish woman with a rose appliqué on the lapel of her sequined pants suit; she is earnestly explaining that the greatest thrill of her life would be to win the $5000 lottery at Roseland. My daughter looks frightened: her captor is beginning to complain querulously that she was "caught" by the camera dancing with a "twerp" the other night; ordinarily, she doesn't dance with "twerps." She's a secretary in a law office; she has her dignity to maintain: "Some of the people here have no dignity." She is echoing the words Teresa Wright said to Lou Jacobi during the filming earlier—when, of course, she was not present to hear them. She rummages in her pocket for a rose she has had, pressed in plastic, since Roseland moved here twenty years ago. "I suppose," she says, "everybody comes here for a different reason. What does it matter, as long as they're happy?" Those words are not unfamiliar: I've seen them on the first page of Jhabvala's script. The last words the law-office secretary says are, "I'll never be old, as long as I come here, never."

Geraldine Chaplin is sitting in the lounge, knitting. Her movements, on camera and off, are precise, fastidious, and minimal. She plays a bewildered, lonely woman, younger than most who come to Roseland, who has allowed herself to be brought here by friends after her husband has deserted her. It is a quiet, subtle performance, unlike her gaudy one in *Nashville*, which I tell her I liked a lot because it reminded me of my worst excesses as a journalist; it made me laugh. After a very long pause, she says, "That's nice." After a longer pause, she says, "I like that." She knits a row and says, "I wasn't copying anybody." Chaplin has been variously described as shy, aloof, serene. Serene people make me nervous.

Everybody at Roseland looks nervous, edgy, this afternoon; this is not an afternoon place. When the Roseland regulars aren't here to provide a focus for everybody's ruminations, a kind of gloom settles over the production crew. Whose happiness can they dissect?

In the midst of chaos, Ivory directs quietly ("tenderly," one actress says). "It's like India," he says, "you love the place, but you despair of getting anything done." The afternoon is stretching into the evening. People are beginning to perk up: soon the regulars will arrive.

Conrad Janis, whiling away time between takes, muses, "Anything can happen here, don't you feel that? I feel as if everything that's happening here happened to me in the past. I have to keep reminding myself I'm on Fifty-second Street and Broadway. Why do I feel like I'm on a boardwalk in eighteenth-century France?" The first regulars drift in, and Conrad smiles in anticipation: "Look, even the lighting is tender, nothing harsh. It's a four-in-the-afternoon weakening sunlight. The saddest part of the day. It's always the saddest part of the day here." He springs to his feet, humming a waltz, and takes a sequined lady in his arms.

JANE FONDA:
EVERYWOMAN
WITH A DIFFERENCE

(1978)

Dressed, without regard to fashion, in severely plain utilitarian blue denim, she loped gracefully along, her long sexy stride and that abundance of frizzy tangled honey-colored hair making her clearly recognizable, even from the back—which was all I saw of her, as I panted far behind, my lungs, congested with bronchitis, slowing me to a snail's pace. She stopped, saw that I was laboring painfully to keep up with her, and doubled back to relieve me of my suitcases. "That's okay," she said, "I'll carry these and take care of getting us on the plane. You just take it easy." I liked her so much for that—a vital female animal, she displayed none of the contempt of the healthy for the infirm. But the next day, when I had occasion to comment on her unflagging energy, she drawled, "Well, I don't ever have any horrible diseases, like *bronchitis*, or anything."

On the flight from New York to Los Angeles, recognizing my abject fear of flying, she offered to hold my hand on takeoff. *How nice!* I thought. She *is* good. But later, when I ordered a double Scotch on the rocks to take the edge off my fear, she said to the stewardess, in a voice unmistakably tinged with mockery, "I'll have a double *orange juice* on the rocks." Then she turned to me and said softly, "There's very little I'm afraid of." And the next morning, when she introduced me to her four-year-old son, Troy, she said: "Hi, hotlips. This is my friend Barbara. She's afraid of airplanes, isn't that silly?" "I told you

153

not to call me hotlips, dummy," Troy said—and rammed his head into her flat stomach.

The first words she had said to me, grasping my right hand in both of hers, were: "I'm *very* happy to know you." A simple declarative sentence, and no more than courtesy dictated—but she said the words with such ringing conviction, I actually believed her. The last words she said to me, a day and a half later, were: "Thank God, you're the last interview I have to do for three months."

Jane Fonda confounds me.

With her straightforward gaze, her bold, uncompromising certainties delivered in a voice that brooks no nonsense, Fonda ought to be drawn in clean, unfinicky lines. But all my thoughts about her are convoluted. She reacts, as one interviewer has said, to many gravitational pulls. There is both more and less to her than meets the eye.

I wanted to like her (and, to tell the truth, I wanted her to like me); it didn't happen.

Her answers to interviewers' questions have been variously interpreted as niggardly or antagonistic or glib or very much to the point (*her* point). She talks—in that rich, fruity, authoritative voice—with a kind of practiced passion. (She has said it all before; all the questions, she says, have been asked before.) When her answers are ample (they are seldom effusive, and always carefully measured), they sound more like those of a political campaigner or an evangelical proselytizer than those of a woman engaged in self-exploration or the pleasures of dialogue. She sometimes answers the questions before you have had a chance to ask them—and, frequently, without the appearance of caring whether they were the questions you might have chosen to ask had you been given a chance. Her curiosity about the people who are curious about *her* is, for all intents and purposes, nonexistent. She makes no secret of her dislike of journalists, although she woos the press when it is politic for her to do so. "The reporters who seem the nicest are always the ones who stick it to me," she tells her public relations woman. (She is talking about me: she thought I was "nice"—and used that as a reason to guard herself against me.) Determined not to be burned again by journalists, she hardens herself against intimacy, although—even when she seems most armored—she protests that she is "always relaxed." She regards herself as "an example to other people," as living proof that it is possible to be wife, mother, superstar, and political activist. Being an example obliges her to present herself as absolutely happy, whole, full of what she calls joyous certainty. She does not welcome questions that intrude upon that certainty, and fends them off with accomplished ease. Nothing arouses her ire so much as a writer who presumes to take an imaginative leap into her consciousness. "I will never allow a novelist to interview me again, *ever*," she says. (She is talking about British writer Margaret Drabble, who wrote what most people considered a very sympathetic portrait of Fonda.) "All novelists are interested in is uncertainty; they don't believe anyone has a sense of purpose. I am *not* uncertain. I am *not* neurotic. I am in complete control of my life."

So formidable is her personality it seems almost a failure of taste to wonder if her life can possibly be as "stable, harmonious, and wonderful" as she claims it is. Transfixed by her intense, intimidating blue gaze, it requires rather more than the usual amount of courage to ask her if all is what it seems. What she calls her "automatic self-censoring device" acts to preclude her from revealing vulnerability, from exposing self-doubt.

I have never met anybody who exerted so little energy to be charming.

"Here," she says, flinging open the door of her compact station wagon, "are my groceries." She exhibits seven supermarket bags as if they were trophies, certainly as if they were more representative of the life she has chosen than seven Academy Awards. "There's a turkey in that one—which I'll cook myself—and there's stuffing and there's . . ." She recites her grocery list. Then, as we climb into the battered seven-year-old vehicle for a drive from her house in Santa Monica to her son's play group in the neighboring beach community of Venice, she recites another well-worn litany: "I have been up since seven thirty A.M. to make breakfast for Troy and Vanessa. [Troy is her son by husband Tom Hayden; ten-year-old Vanessa is the child of her first marriage to French film director Roger Vadim.] I had to shake Troy to wake him up. I had to tell Vanessa to brush her teeth six times. She is stubborn and obstinate, just like me when I was a kid. . . . We had a health-food breakfast. We always have a health-food breakfast: tortilla toast, bacon, buckwheat, granola. Troy understands that junk food is a political issue." (He does? That's more than any four-year-old of my acquaintance understands . . . and, later in the day, Troy's behavior will suggest that Fonda is perhaps too sanguine about her son's political sophistication. Later in the day, Troy will whine and kick her in the shins and punch her in the stomach and demand, "Where's my candy, dummy? Where's my candy, dummy, dummy? I want my candy." This unseemly display will occasion some embarrassment on Fonda's part—and, unless I am very much mistaken, will account for an increasing chill factor between us; I am not meant to witness such an incident.) So Jane goes, on and on, discussing her child-centered, husband-centered plans for the day. I feel as if I am with a middle-class suburban mother. But every time my eyes are drawn to her profile—that strong jaw (so like her father's) that Hollywood moguls wanted, years ago, to break and re-form into the prevailing fashion of insipid prettiness—I am jolted by the recognition that this isn't just any housewife: this is the woman whose acting lights up a screen. This is Jane Fonda, who can't escape being Jane Fonda, no matter how plebeian her activities.

John Steinbeck once wrote that Henry Fonda imposed "an iron slavery" of discipline upon himself. Jane has inherited more than her father's looks. She has imposed an iron slavery on herself, too.

Just now, it consists of Fonda's presenting herself as Everywoman. But she is Everywoman with a difference.

She lugs her dirty clothes to the cleaners—somewhat ostentatiously, perhaps; she refuses all offers of help ("I'm never tired")—and she does not allow herself to see that this public demonstration of domesticity is, for all who witness it, an Event. One of the ironies of Fonda's position is that everything this superstar does to convince people she's ordinary serves merely to convince them that she is an interesting anomaly, and to call to herself the very kind of attention she claims not to want. She washes her own dishes. (One young journalist who watched her do so told me, "Somehow I kept getting these vibes: 'I am Jane Fonda. I am Jane Fonda washing the dishes. See Jane Fonda wash the dishes.' And yet she *does* wash the dishes. It was like watching her play a role in the movies. Very convincing, and you knew she was living the part—but it was still a role.")

She stands on supermarket lines—in a transparent tie-dye shirt through which her firm breasts, made famous in the erotic science-fiction film *Barbarella*, are clearly visible. (And yet Fonda speaks with repugnance of the days when she allowed herself to be a "sex object.") She takes Troy to the Y for swimming lessons and takes her turn as "mother's helper" at his preschool play group—where his best friends are named Ozone, Huckleberry, and Pooh. (She forgets the teacher's name.)

She lives in what her father laughingly refers to as a "shack."

The shack, given Southern California's insanely escalating real-estate prices, probably has a market value of $100,000. Originally purchased for $40,000, its value has been considerably enhanced by an elegantly designed redwood platform in the back garden, which she and Hayden use for gatherings of members of their political organization, the Campaign for Economic Democracy (CED)—a multipurpose grassroots organization that grew out of Hayden's unsuccessful campaign for the United States Senate and whose aims are either liberal or "revolutionary," depending on who is speaking or who is being spoken to. When she is not at residence in Santa Monica, she has the option of retreating to a one-hundred-and-twenty-acre ranch in Santa Barbara, where her kids can ride horses and where her tenant, singer Cat Stevens, pays an astronomical rent to live in a house she describes as a "redwood-and-glass magic fantasy," but which Hayden refuses to live in because it is "elitist and disfunctional." The ranch doubles as a hideaway and as a center for chapters of the CED.

She defers to her husband and plays the coquette with him in a way that suggests she has just read, and subscribed to the ideas of, Marabelle Morgan's *Total Woman*—and she shares ideas with him and plans the future with him in a spirit of determined reciprocity that suggests she is a recent convert to feminism.

While she regales all comers with stories of how she has chosen to forfeit affluence and privilege for the joys of working within a loving community of political activists and organizers ("the most wonderful, brave, committed people I have ever known"), she is also an acknowledged member of the Hollywood aristocracy. Even John Wayne, with whom she told me it was inconceivable that she would ever work, because he so much detested her antiwar activities ("He wouldn't want to work with *me*"), consented to present her, with fond asides and expressions of admiration, an award from the Hollywood

Women's Press Club in Los Angeles. She esteems grape-pickers who make $80 a week ("They lead heroic lives"); and she invites Julie Christie to Thanksgiving dinner.

It seemed to me, when I was with her, that Fonda was comfortable with people she regarded as oppressed, with the organizers of the oppressed, and with the Hollywood aristocrats with whom she grew up—and didn't quite know what to do with anybody who fell in between those extremes.

She and Hayden were preparing for a visit from a "fundamentalist Baptist ranch owner" she had met on a movie set in Wet Valley, Colorado. She professed to have loved her life among "the People" in Wet Valley—evenings at Frank's Bar, laughing and singing Rotary songs with the ranch owner, whose working-class origins she was quick to call attention to. Meanwhile, as she prepares for a visit from her friend and his wife and their six kids, with whom she intends to share the simple pleasures of Universal City and Disney World, she chats familiarly on the telephone with Marlon Brando—whose every excess she dismisses peremptorily. "I've had a crush on Brando since I was seventeen," I say. "He knows all about Indians," she says. Suspending disbelief, I ask, "Why does he make rotten pictures like *Missouri Breaks*?" "For *fun*," she says curtly. The question displeases her. "My daughter has a crush on Al Pacino," I say. "Tell your daughter," Fonda says, "that Al Pacino is *only* an actor."

Being "only an actor"—even a great one—is not, by her lights, a consummation devoutly to be desired. She is, however, willing to make exceptions: her father, for one, even though they have in the past publicly disagreed over politics. She calls him an "absolutely decent" man. Her brother, Peter Fonda, is another exception. He comes in for a fair share of her love in spite of his yacht and his easy living (manifestations of the materialism she deplores in others less dear to her) She chooses to regard Peter as "a visionary and a mystic Long before I became involved in politics, Peter understood the cultural movement of the sixties and was a part of it." She speaks with pride of Peter's film *Easy Rider. Easy Rider* was, of course, a celebration of the drug culture (and Fonda deplores "opiates"). It was also a savage put-down of the very people Jane now courts and seeks to unify in a "progressive political coalition." But these inconsistencies do not seem to trouble her. Peter, she says, is a "cosmic thinker." He "feels inequities so viscerally he doesn't know what to do about them. . . . He feels helpless and impotent." (But Fonda, except when she is talking about Peter, has no patience with political apathy. Blood, evidently, is stronger than politics.) I find her loyalty endearing, refreshing. Jane Fonda—who refers to herself as A Political Woman, "utterly convinced" of the justice and the ultimate triumph of her cause—believes in "economic democracy" (yachts for all or yachts for none), but allows herself to love Peter, yacht and all. If this is an inconsistency in her nature, it is a natural and an appealing one.

But Fonda has been spending years trying to eradicate all the inconsistencies, and all the contradictions, in her life: "Until 1968, I was very unhappy. I was thirty years old, and I had nothing to show for it. I knew in my heart that nothing I'd ever done could earn me the respect of the people that *I* was beginning to respect—civil-rights activists and antiwar people. I didn't want them to dismiss me as irrelevant. I didn't want to go out as the kind of person I was. When I was married to Vadim in France, I was part of the international jet set—but I never enjoyed it. I don't like small talk, I don't like cocktail parties, I never knew what to say to any of those people. I spent a lot of time by myself. I went to bed early when parties were going on downstairs."

Her discontent took her to India—for three weeks: "India was where a lot of interesting people—Mia Farrow, the Beatles

—were going to find new things. All I could see was poverty, disease, starvation, and the terrible indignity of people having to beg. I ran into American kids doing their mantras, heads shaved, wearing beads and saffron loincloths—and I couldn't share their lives. I flew directly from Bombay to Beverly Hills . . . and I remember seeing a news headline at the L.A. airport about American Indians taking over Alcatraz . . . and I felt again what an outsider I was, what a peripheral person I was. . . . All the time I was living in France, I hated being an expatriate. I wanted to be an American; I *am* an American. No one will believe this, but when I was in France I defended our country. I couldn't stand foreigners saying we were bad people. I felt that I didn't have the right to criticize till I came back here, to put myself on the line. . . . I came back to find a life."

Performing superbly in highly acclaimed and valuable films like *They Shoot Horses, Don't They?* and *Klute* didn't satisfy Fonda's hungers. She found "a core to her life" in political activism.

And she met radical Tom Hayden. Thirty-seven-year-old Hayden is cool, serious, aloof. Fonda says he has an "impish" humor; I didn't see it, and most of his associates have failed to notice it, too. Vadim, who counts Brigitte Bardot among his ex-wives, has been described as "intelligently decadent." It is difficult to imagine two men more unlike each other.

Fonda's association with Hayden—to whom she says she will be married "forever" ("This is it; this is really it. I am very very lucky")—exacerbated her sense of the contradictions inherent in her life. "I felt like a goody-good who lived up on the hill, out of the fracas and above the smog, coming out of my ivory tower to dole out money for causes and to use my fame to attract people to rallies. I felt that living in Beverly Hills was creating a contradiction in my life that would become more and more severe. By temperament I am not a person who can do things by half. I knew that I would have to alter my life, to live in a way that was as close as possible to the lives of average people."

In 1973 Fonda married Hayden, and they bought their "shack" in Santa Monica, where she is surrounded by assembly-line workers, writers, hippies, plumbers, and, such are the vagaries of life and real estate in Southern California, millionaires—among whom is temporary resident Vadim, with whom bilingual Vanessa spends much of her time. Fonda acknowledges that her neighbors were "leery" of her when she first moved in, but she thinks they began to like her when she became pregnant with Troy, and she thinks they accept her now: "I schlep around just the way they do; I don't have servants." She does, however, have hangers-on, one of whom was watering her plants when I visited her. She said he was "a member of our organization" and immediately launched into a diatribe against being served—and looked profoundly embarrassed. "I throw out my own garbage. . . ."

Mellow Jane, happy in her shack a block away from the unpolluted ocean, with its wraparound porch, rooms painted in bright kindergarten primary colors, and the kind of eclectic-organic decorating I always, for some reason, associate with the houses of untenured Harvard professors: some really fine antique furniture; some comfortable thrift-shop furniture (which Troy and his playmates shove around the living room at will); the Fonda-Haydens' double bed (a mattress covered with Madras cloth plopped unceremoniously down in the middle of the bedroom floor) surrounded by dozens of plants; wall-to-wall books in the dining room, whose refectory table I admired (and which Fonda said was "just a place to eat on"); moderate-sized cluttered children's bedrooms (a dollhouse in Troy's bedroom, which he does not use; a lot of Superhero dolls, which he does play with); everything altogether pleasant, designed for nuclear-family living, and a far cry from Beverly Hills elegance. Although Jane compulsively details the inadequacies of her house—no insulation, some rattling pipes—for all practical purposes, it might just as well be a fortified mansion. A friend of mine whose sister had lived and worked with Hayden called on Jane and Tom once—and Jane effectively barred the door. "As if," my friend says, "I was a beach bum. I knew Tom very well; but it took me an hour to establish my credentials, and if a friend of Tom's hadn't wandered by—a friend who knew me from the old days—I'd never have gotten in to see him." One can't blame Fonda for trying to protect her privacy; but it's hard to see how she can, on the other hand, pretend that she's just Plain Jane, easy and accessible to her neighbors.

The forty-year-old woman who claims, now that she's found "a reason to live," not to fear aging or loss of good looks, the woman who throws out her own garbage (and who greeted Hayden, after a four-day absence from him, with an Edith Bunker narrative of how their German shepherd, Geronimo, tore up the garbage sacks), has traveled a long way.

But perhaps not so far as she would like people to think. In the bad old days, before Hollywood took her back to its bosom, the pre-Watergate days, when Fonda was "graylisted" for having spoken on Radio Hanoi and for entertaining soldiers with vaudevillian antiwar skits, her critics called her the Red Guard and Miss Grim. Even people whose politics were roughly in alignment with hers accused her of being a spectacular nag and of having an ideology, but little humanity. Now that she has become less strident—which is surely as much a function of the times as of her own personal evolution—she brims over with the milk of human kindness. She has, she says, "an almost perfect life—in these days of permissive sex, swinging and open marriage, I have a happy, monogamous marriage. But I suffer every day of my life for other people—not just poor people, but people whose lives have dead-ended, who have nowhere to go,

who have no sense of purpose, who are deprived emotionally
. . . it breaks my heart to see that pain, those wasted lives."

Declarations like that can be heard as humane, even as
saintly, or as sanctimonious (and/or rehearsed). What I find
more revealing are her (few) spontaneous utterances. "Sharon
is having a baby," one of her CED friends called out to her as
we were entering her house. *"Terrific,"* Fonda yelled back.
"Another child for the Revolution." Dear me. I marched, too,
and no one has ever accused me of leaning to the Right; but
I have seldom heard a less humane, more knee-jerk ideological
response to the birth of a child. And what, precisely, did she
mean by the "Revolution"? No matter how much she talks
(and talks and talks), I still find Fonda's politics liberal-left-
fuzzy. She let drop (and appeared to regret it immediately) that
Hayden might be running for the California State Senate. I
came prepared to like and to admire Fonda; but in my more
cynical moments it seemed to me that all of her politics had
become a means to that end. The end itself is not despicable,
and can't be said to cast doubt on Fonda's sincerity. What is
disconcerting is that few of Hayden's old friends can figure out
exactly what the Fonda-Haydens are up to—or whether
Fonda's housewifery is a means of endearing herself to Hayden's constituency. It's perfectly possible, of course, that all
things are true—that she delights in her approximation of a
middle-class life *and* that she's playing it for all its political
worth. What I find disconcerting is her reluctance to admit she
can't escape being Jane Fonda. She always has the prerogatives
of privilege and wealth to fall back on; she can never be Ms.
Average; she is as trapped in her circumstances as the rest of
us are. She is in an extraordinarily difficult position: she is
idolized, petted, cosseted—and she has chosen to throw in her
lot with those less privileged than she, whose approval she
earnestly seeks. (She went bananas when the studio sent a big
car to pick her up at the airport; she spent five minutes protest-

ing that she didn't require anything but a taxi.) She says it all works together harmoniously. I admit that I'd have liked her better if she had once said, "It's hard. I can't be all things to all people." What in fact she said was: "I don't have the luxury of retiring to lick my wounds . . . I don't need to. I'm a role model. I have no wounds . . . to speak of."

Her mother was a suicide. She slit her throat when Jane was twelve. Jane says that her childhood was "idyllic." She and Peter scrambled around in the country, playing cowboys and Indians ("I wanted to be the Lone Ranger"). Later, when her father moved to New York to star in the long-running stage hit *Mr. Roberts,* she roamed through the canyons of Manhattan with tomboy abandon. When I asked her about her mother's death, she spoke of it flatly, and without emotion. Her personality, she says, was "fixed" by that time, stamped with the happiness of her earlier childhood, so that she was not hideously scarred. But a schoolmate at Emma Willard, a posh prep school in upper New York State, remembers wildness and despair. Jane was first told that her mother died a natural death. When a classmate told her the actual circumstances of the death, Jane went beserk: she screamed and broke things and carried on and was, in general, as well she might have been, inconsolable. Supposing Fonda's schoolmate's story to have been accurate (and I have no reason to doubt her), why did Fonda see fit to conceal from me, as she has concealed from others, the fact that she was, not unreasonably and certainly not unbecomingly, acutely miserable, distraught, and bitterly unhappy at the time? Why did she have to protest so vehemently that she was *not* like Brooke Hayward (the daughter of actress Margaret Sullavan, another apparent suicide), who considers her mother's death the most important fact of her own life? It often seemed to me that, in her determination not to reveal any weakness, Fonda succeeded in rendering herself far less likable and far more one-dimensional than if she had acknowledged pain. (And if she does despise her own pain, how can she really love the pain of others?)

What Fonda did say about her mother may go a long way to explain her concern with the bread-and-butter issues of feminism: "My mother was outgoing, friendly, gregarious, a woman with lots of potential and no way of expressing it. She could have been a great businesswoman. She lived in a time and in a society that placed primary emphasis on youth and beauty. When her youth and beauty deserted her, her friends deserted her. She had nothing." The emotion Fonda did not allow herself to bring to her mother's death she brought to an economic analysis of women's condition (she is happier with the abstract—and safer, perhaps—than with the specific): "Women are treated with no dignity; they get no wages for housework, no workwomen's compensation; they have nothing to protect them. If their husbands leave them, they have nothing. According to the Bureau of Labor Statistics, only seven percent of American families fit the Ozzie and Harriet mold —you know, where the husband works and supports the wife and kids, and the wife stays at home. . . . And the lack of adequate child care is tragic. . . ." Fonda has managed, in a way, to sanitize her mother's death. She blames neither her mother nor her father for what happened: "If you live in a society that represses generosity and courage and social responsibility and fosters competition, competition is what you'll get. I don't believe these failures are part of human nature, just as I don't believe that greed is part of human nature. If you alter social institutions and social priorities, you begin to change people's basic nature. . . . We live in a society that sets men against women. . . ."

Her P.R. woman arranged for me to meet Fonda at Queens College in New York City, where she gave a lecture—her thirteenth in as many days—to students who were prepared to love her before she opened her mouth. She endeared herself to the kids immediately (and I think surprised them as much as she energized them) by telling them that they were "a sleeping giant. . . . There are social reasons for your apathy; the fault is not in you. In the sixties, we lived in a yellow submarine. Now—because we're afraid of getting hurt—we live in singles' bars. If you're frightened, you have reason to be: you have unemployment staring you in the face. We have to devise means by which the majority of the people have more control over the economy—and that can be done without socialism. . . . You can do it."

After that peppy beginning, Fonda started talking about agribusiness and multinational corporations—and about the sun (the immediate relevancy of which was obviously lost on most of her audience): "We have to move quickly to keep the sun from being monopolized and metered by large corporations. We have to create a public solar corporation, which will be good for the environment and provide jobs. We have to protect small businesses and make them competitive. . . . Don't turn your rage inward—get mad instead. Work for economic democracy. The future belongs to us. Use your bodies, your pennies, and your voices to work for it."

Since nobody present seemed to understand exactly what Fonda meant by "economic democracy" and since it was unclear to what constructive end the anger she had urged upon them could be put and since she hadn't enough time to tell them how to use their bodies, their pennies, and their voices to secure the future, there were a lot of bewildered faces gazing up at Jane Fonda . . . who disarmed criticism by saying she had to "quick catch a plane to be with my kids" . . . and left to something less than a standing ovation.

On the ride to the airport, I kept wondering who it was Fonda had reminded me of. Then I got it: Robert Redford in

The Candidate—the same charisma, the same appeal to youth, the same soft-at-the-core, open-to-interpretation populist politics.

I had just heard Jane Fonda give a campaign speech.

On the flight to L.A. (economy class—millionaire Fonda disdains first-class frills), Jane told me more than I wanted to hear about the multinational corporations, and less than I already knew. (I think she would have delivered the same monologue to a Democrat, a Republican, a Communist, a Nobel prize winner, or a little white mouse. When Fonda is politically wound up, she is sublimely unaware of the individuality of her listener.) Somewhere over the Grand Canyon, she consented to talk about acting:

"I might some day do a trivial movie just for the heck of it, just for fun—but only if it doesn't take up a whole lot of my time. I'd do it to make money for our organization. It's more important for me to make films that have a message—like *Julia*. I thought I did pretty good playing the part of Lillian Hellman in *Julia*, even though I had to act the part of a fearful woman —and I don't know that kind of physical fear. Playing the part of a writer wasn't so hard—what I did to prepare myself for it was I read *The Children's Hour* up to about the middle of the second act, and then I wrote the rest of it myself, as if Hellman hadn't completed it. So in *Julia*, when I was acting Lillian sitting at the typewriter, I actually *was* a writer. . . . All those cigarettes I smoked in *Julia* were made of lettuce, by the way. I don't smoke. . . . People always think I'm going to be a drag on the set because I'll preach politics all the time. But you talk to Jimmy Caan. I just did a movie with him and we had a ball. I can dig his humor. I don't alienate people who aren't like me. I don't talk politics with them—I bear witness by the way I behave: I am never late. I will never agree to work overtime unless I ask the crew if they want to first. I deal with the people around me democratically. I don't pull an egocentric movie-star trip. I try never to be nasty or grouchy. I try to remember to be an example—just like when I'm at the supermarket and someone asks me if I want to go to the head of the line, I say no—usually I say no. Of course there are exceptions. . . . I want to be like everyone else. . . ."

At the time of our meeting, I had just seen a nonedited version of *Coming Home.* To my surprise, Fonda, who coproduced the film, told me she was considering cutting the lyrical love scene from the final edited version or substituting another scene: "Clumsier lovemaking would be truer, it ought to be fumbling and awkward; that stuff was too pretty." It *was* beautiful, which seemed to me a good reason for keeping it in. One of Fonda's associates despairingly agreed: "Jane," she said, "wants to cut that part because Hayden is jealous. He doesn't want her naked body on the screen—and we're having a hard time convincing her that cutting it will ruin the film as a love story."

"Tom reads all my scripts," Jane says. "He has a better eye than I have. He zeroes in on what's wrong."

After dinner, which she ate with a hearty appetite, Fonda turned her back and curled up to read a script. Left to my own devices, I began to chat with a middle-aged woman across the aisle, who, for no special reason other than that of propinquity, told me about her four kids, her needlepoint, her trip to Europe. It was a pleasant way to pass the time. Our plane hit an air pocket. A little kid who'd been wandering up and down lurched into me and spilled a Coke in my lap. Then he climbed onto my lap and played with my necklace until he got bored. A young Englishman from another section of the plane came to sit in the empty seat next to me (the man he'd been sitting next to snored) and talked to me about his job.

Fonda raised her eyes from her script and swiveled around: "How do you do that?" she demanded.

"Do what?"

"Get people to be friendly with you."

"It's what people do on airplanes."

"They don't do it with me," she said.

"The stewardess just told you she loved you in *Julia.*"

"She was talking to Jane Fonda the Movie Star."

"But you are Jane Fonda the Movie Star."

Fonda returned to her script.

This is what I remember most vividly about the next day we spent together, the day before Thanksgiving:

Her eyes turned three shades darker when she was with Hayden. She blushed like a girl when she greeted him. The smile she had for him erased the lines in her face. Sitting, beaming up at him, she flung one leg across the other in a gesture that was clearly invitational and provocative. They never touched—and still I felt like a voyeur. For the first time since I'd met her, she seemed genuinely happy, at rest.

Her eyes filled with tears when Troy called her a four-letter word: "He's cross. His demands aren't unreasonable—they're all reasonable demands, I'm just not with him enough. Those damn movies that keep me away from my kids! I was in Europe making *Julia* when Troy changed from diapers to a potty and from a crib to a bed. . . . Vanessa's been cutting classes at school. She thinks it's weird that people are around here all the time interviewing me. She doesn't want her mom to be different from other moms. Yeah, I'm sad. I'm deprived and they're deprived. But we'll make up for it. Tomorrow we'll go to the ranch and be all alone for four days—no telephone, no people, just us. . . . Really our relationship is terrific. They won't rebel against me, I'm sure of that. . . .

Tom's with them when I'm not, and Vadim's often with Vanessa, and a wonderful Vietnamese Political Woman is with them when none of us is here. . . ." She suddenly remembers that sadness is weakness, pulls herself up short, and begins to talk about the need for day-care centers. . . . From the next room, Hayden says, "Jane, I'm trying to convince some political organizers to join us for Thanksgiving dinner." For a moment her face falls, then she says, "Hey! Ask them if they wanna meet Julie Christie."

DICK CAVETT:
"'YOU CAN TELL
I'M NOT A WISECRACKER,
CAN'T YOU, HONEY?'"

(1978)

In her book *Venice Observed*, Mary McCarthy said of Paolo Sarpi, an obscure seventeenth-century monk, that he was "witty, sarcastic, ceremonious, spare in utterance, dry." "I *never* tell a lie," Sarpi is supposed to have said, "but the truth not to everybody." When assassins hired by the pope very nearly made a martyr of him (a dagger was skewered through his head), Sarpi quipped, "I recognize the style of the Roman curia." He was punning on the word *stilus*, which in Latin means both "style" and "dagger."

I find Sarpi's humor comforting and reassuring. This kind of wit, which manages to be both playful and bleak, is a way of touching unpleasant reality without resigning oneself to it. It is also a way for a man who has the kind of mind that Yeats describes as "gentle and sensitive" to remain sane.

I am thinking of Dick Cavett. The talk-show host from Nebraska has been accused of being condescending, self-congratulatory, "cultish," and superior, of talking too much and of talking too little, of being a "prissy Yalie, a bland WASP pancake who plays Little Lord Fauntleroy" (that elaborately muddled description would, I'm sure, delight Cavett, who has a perfect ear for language, and who, furthermore, is generously inclined to laugh, even when the joke is on him). He has been called arch, cute, coy, an artful dodger, remote, detached; more than one critic has charged him with using language as a barrier, and with using wit as a defense to insulate himself from the emotional demands of people around him. When journalists are at their wits' end—as they not infrequently are after a session with Cavett—they are reduced to grumbling that he is all seductive shuck and jive; whether they regard him as an entertainer or as an intellectual—or as one masquerading as the other—they invariably end their interviews with a dying fall: Cavett, they say, has "enigmatic appeal."

I find him charming and provocative, both on the TV screen and in what may or may not be Real Life. I don't say he's *not* enigmatic—he's as mysterious as the next person; but after one has reached the age of four and a half, it seems to me, perfect transparency becomes a bore. Honesty, however, is never boring, and, like cagey Sarpi, Cavett—while he may not tell the truth to everybody—doesn't, so far as I can determine, tell lies either. One detractor has said that a parodic air attaches even to Cavett's serious moments—when, for example, he asked Abba Eban if he'd let his daughter marry an Arab. It is also true that he parodies himself—and can quite clearly be seen to observe himself doing it; he is also gracefully willing to let his opponent play the game with him, as an equal partner. He doesn't take himself entirely seriously. Whether or not that gives him the right not to take anybody else entirely seriously is a good question. I think he does, when he interviews serious people, provided that they are not given to rhetoric or cant and provided that they have a sense of humor. "Humorlessness is something I don't understand," he says. "I find it hard to admit that someone exists who doesn't have a sense of humor, even though I've met a few." When *he* is being subjected to scrutiny, he tries out dodges—mostly, I think, for the pleasure of seeing whether he can get away with them, and also to test the mettle of his interrogator. He's mischievous. He is so constituted as not to be able to disregard the element of silliness that lurks even in the most dangerous and serious of issues, and in serious and sincere people, too. "I wish I could think who it was," he says, "who said, 'Because I am frivolous, do not assume I am shallow, any more than because you are *grave*, that you are profound.' Isn't that wonderful? No, I didn't make it up. It sounds eighteenth century. Dr. Johnson, I presume." He does sometimes deflect questions that are personal. When I asked him a question that I deemed impertinent, he said, quite sympathetically, "There are no impertinent questions; there are only impertinent attitudes." But he didn't answer the question.

Cavett is an inveterate, almost compulsive, punster (a talent he pretends to despise) with what he calls "an. unconquerable streak of pessimism." (When writer LeRoi Jones said he didn't particularly like being called a "spade cat," Cavett said, almost as if the words were forced out of him by something beyond his control, "I can understand that. The old maid living in the apartment above me lives with a spayed cat.") He is mocking, playful, and serious. "Do I have to be consistent? Can't you be things by turns? Hmmm, let's see; what do they say? That I'm all surface, bland, disengaged . . . that I skitter away from feeling by using irony? The right combination of those things in the right person could be attractive, couldn't it? It's a *lit*tle irritating if you see it as a *crit*icism, because you want to be told (a) what's wrong with it? and (b) how do you *know* that's what you're seeing? If someone says there's only surface, it implies he knows what's underneath. Maybe he's seeing all there is to see. Maybe when people think I'm skittering because they've struck a nerve, it's because I didn't understand the question, or because the question made me think of something more interesting than the question. What *is* the deep that I keep hiding from people? I'm willing to keep hiding it if I feel justified, but I'm not sure what it is. Do they want me to say I once burned a dog and hit an old lady and knocked a cripple's wheelchair out from under him? . . . Yes; I *knew* you'd ask me

when I did that: that was last summer, all in the same day.
. . . Do you suppose people want to say, 'I really like him in
spite of his being a pedophile?' . . . Shall we leave that one
alone?"

Cavett tends to take any question (or any answer) in seven
directions, which may account for the abstracted look one
sometimes sees on his face when he interviews guests on his
show. (Sometimes, however, the glazed look comes from his
gazing at his producer's cue cards; it means his inspiration has
dried up, or that he'd rather be in New Orleans.) I find talking
with him like being with a wonderfully entertaining dinner
guest who is not only practiced in the art of conversation but
who also exhilarates you by making you feel not only that you
are understood but that you understand. (When I left Cavett
after several hours of interviewing, *I* felt clever.)

I met him in the offices of Daphne Productions, his production company (named after his dog), which coproduces *The
Dick Cavett Show* with New York's Public Broadcasting station, Channel 13, WNET. Chris Porterfield, who was Cavett's
roommate at Yale, produces the show. Cavett is suspicious of
instant intimacy; most of his friends—among whom are Robert and Lola Redford, Woody Allen, and Jean Stafford—are
friends of long standing. The associate producer of *The Dick
Cavett Show* and Cavett's assistant are both highly intelligent,
individualistic women—as, not so incidentally, is his wife, actress Carrie Nye. Cavett has been denigrated for many things;
no one has yet seen fit to charge him with being afraid of strong
women.

His jaw was tense; his eyes were wary, emotionally committed to nothing at all. He was eating *sushi* with chopsticks. I had
been warned that he would "give nothing away," and that I
could expect to have only forty-five minutes of his time. Neither proved true. I was also asked not to smoke in his presence.

Cavett doesn't smoke, doesn't drink, nor—as I found out when I asked him if, in lieu of chain-smoking, I could pop a ten-milligram Valium—does he rely on tranqs. Because, generally speaking, I find ascetic or austere behavior both admirable and off-putting, I told him I felt as if I were walking into Thomas Merton's cell. He beamed. I asked him if he had any other health fetishes like his ridiculous and unfounded prejudice against tobacco. He relaxed.

"No, not really. . . . What would it do to me, by the way, if I took a tranquilizer? Can you describe the effect? The *nice* thing about tobacco is that you *know* it causes cancer. You can't be sure about anything else. One doctor's meat is another doctor's poison. . . . That reminds me of one of my favorite puns. H. J. Kaufman made it in the course of a poker game at the Algonquin. They were discussing the Peloponnesian Wars or Herodotus or somebody like that and Kaufman said, 'One man's Mede is another man's Persian.' It's a *vis*ual pun, of course; isn't it *won*derful? . . . It's strange, isn't it; here we are in a time when faith has been lost, supposedly, and the world is an uglier place, and all the so-called blessings of technology turn out not to be blessings at all, and the food and the water are all poisoned, and there-*is*-no-health-in-us . . . and yet we see people in the park, running, as they say, for their lives. . . . I run a *lit*tle bit, but I don't get my running shoes on every day. My guess is that jogging will probably delay your coronary for two years, but on the other hand you'll have spent those two years jogging. What dreadful black ironies we're faced with! . . . Are you *sure* this is an interview?"

"You may be enigmatic," I say, "you're certainly not intimidating."

"I get intimidating as time goes by; I tend to grow before your eyes and become ty*ran*nical. I'll let you know kindly when I'm about to become tyrannical. . . . I *love* being interviewed on TV. I liked being on Susskind's show with Phil Donahue and Stanley Siegel. Some side of me that hadn't been used for a while came out—maybe Siegel brought it out, and the presence of the audience, and everybody ganging up on everybody else. I was accused by Susskind of being enigmatic, of not revealing myself. Siegel said the key to TV was to re*veal* yourself, to bring the show alive. I asked him if he would urinate on television. That was a serious question. Where *do* you draw the line? Somewhere between urination and the failure to disclose yourself, I guess. The trick is to get to where the line *is.* Siegel gets analyzed once a week on the air by a shrink who's not his *real* shrink. . . . What am I doing now? Am I once again proving that I'll reveal anyone's secrets but my own? . . . The point is, if he's really going to reveal himself, why not let us see his real analyst—why have a show analyst that's good enough for the public and then go to your real analyst for the real stuff? . . . Yes; we can agree that that's duplicity and narcissism. D and N. He's into D and N. Some like S and M. . . . I feel a pun coming on. . . . You're right; there *is* no way to cope with puns; they're like the question that answers itself. I'm not wild about puns unless they're really brilliant. A compulsive punner is somewhat irritating and somewhat ill, according to at least one psychiatrist. I've been told punning is a prelude to schizophrenia. I was flattered the other day, though, because I said to S. J. Perelman, 'This must be a title of yours that I remember—either that or I made it up: *Down by the Old Maelstrom.*' He said, 'That *is* good.' Isn't it nice? The idea, I mean, that out of politeness, even, he'd say it was good?"

"I can't," I say, "conceive of the kind of mind—yours—that can hear *Oscar Wilde* and come up with the anagram *O lad, I screw.*"

"People who don't have the knack are overly impressed with people who do. Porterfield finds it astounding that I can look at *Alec Guinness* and immediately see *genuine class.* It's like magic to him.

"The only way I can understand that you can't conceive of my doing that is to compare your reaction to mine when I'm confronted with people who can look at a square root and give the seven versions of it or whatever. An anagram forms in my mind in about the time it takes to verbalize it, almost *in*-stantaneously. I promise myself I'm not going to do it anymore. . . . Weird. Well, that's about all I'm willing to talk about."

"Shall we quit?"

"Oh, no. I want to get to all the really heavy stuff. The touchy, delicate stuff I've never revealed to a living soul. . . .Your turn."

I had just interviewed Jane Fonda, and this dispiriting experience was very much on my mind. I asked Cavett, "Does it ever happen to you that someone you're prepared to like and admire turns out to be a rotten guest—or that he or she doesn't like *you*? And do you interpret that as a personal rejection?"

"Hmmm. I'm always reluctant to admit that someone doesn't like me till it's beyond the point of no return. You seem to be able to recognize it right away. I would have tried three or four more times. I tend to assume that I like them or they like me even when it's quite clear that the opposite is the case. The opposite of paranoia is what I've got. I imagine friends that aren't there. Why are all those friends following me? . . . Say, I just had a thought. I must ask a psychiatrist about this. What would it do to a *real* paranoid-schizophrenic if you put a real Nazi behind the couch? Know what I mean? Would the real Nazi be any more or less real than his imagined enemy?"

"Should we ask R. D. Laing?"

"I had a good answer for R. D. Laing once. He set me up with a straight line that was the most *won*derful of my life. Laing got a little irked at something, and he said, 'Well, you're going to say I'm paranoid because everybody is going around saying I'm paranoid.' And I said, 'No they're not, you're imagining it.' What an opening line—too good to be true."

On the "old show" (Cavett seems to find it hard to say the initials ABC—which is understandable, inasmuch as the network fired him when his ratings didn't stand up to Carson's), he often asked guests if they'd ever been in analysis.

"When I first came to New York and got into show business, I felt left out because *everybody* was in analysis. The other three people in a group of four were always saying, 'Well, my doctor says I shouldn't do this'—or, *rarely*, talking in*tell*igently about analysis. If they used jargon I'd just walk away and help myself to more avocado dip. . . . Oh, you read that line in my book, did you? Please let me repeat myself, it's so much fun. May I repeat myself? I can't stand jargon in any form. If we could just get the word *modality* out of the mouths of everyone who uses it! . . ."

"I never met anyone who used that word."

"Oh, boy, have you got the right friends. Well, I don't have any *friends* who use it, nobody *could*. Let's see, what were we talking about? Do I take it as a personal rejection when people are nasty to me on the show? I kinda liked it when Joanne Woodward told me that Werner Erhard gave me enough 'space' to hang myself. I like to be confronted; I like to be jarred. It gets away from the preparation aspects of the show. Let's see, what did I *really* feel at that moment? She'd told me before that she wasn't pleased with the Erhard show, so it didn't come as a total surprise. . . . I wasn't pleased with it either. I honestly don't know whether I think he's a charlatan or whether whoever headed est would do a certain amount of good, because whatever you do to people helps a certain number of them. . . . *No; not* including lobotomies. But I mean if you dumped a bucket of ice water on people's heads, a certain number of them would say, 'Gee, it worked.' Didn't I say that to Erhard on the show? I certainly *meant* to. Probably est is okay for you if you're healthy, but it's dangerous if you're not, and what would you be doing there if you were healthy? That show didn't please anybody—people wanted me to 'rip the mask of hypocrisy off his face'—if it *is* a mask, and if it *is* hypocrisy. I really couldn't be sure. I really didn't hold back anything I *felt*, unless it was not to admit to a native prejudice against *any*body who goes to *any* of those things. It's too cheap; it's too fast. It's the McDonald's of self-help. Can you imagine saying, 'I've got three days to cure myself, overnight and easy?' Or over light and easy, as the man said to the fried egg. Sorry about that. . . . Why are all these cure-alls hitting all at once? Are we living in such graceless times that we need an overnight pill? I asked Paul Weiss, my old philosophy teacher, about that; he didn't know the answer either, but he says that everybody *dim*ly grasps the idea that there is some fundamental answer or meaning below the surface that needs to be gotten at—which is the pursuit of the philosopher. None of them ever seems to reach it, though, which is why I'm suspicious. Eastern mystics spend a lifetime of discipline, and even then they don't claim success. Est claims success in two weekends. Nothing that good comes that easy."

But in his book *Cavett*, which he coauthored with Chris Porterfield, Dick wrote that if there were a God, the idea of Him would be so simple—so easy—that one would immediately grasp it.

"I may have changed my mind since then. I *think* I've decided that if there is a God, He's not for the many, but for the few that are capable of that kind of ratiocination. Rat-io-cin-*a*tion. That's one of those words you see written but only Bill Buckley speaks, isn't it?"

"Is God something you think about?"

"Not much. I remember once at a party at Yale some earnest girl at a mixer . . . why do you wince when I say *mixer*? Does that date me? Anyway, this girl said, 'What do you think about God?' and I said, 'God bores me.' That fixed *her.*"

"And I was just about to ask you the Meaning of Life."

"Damn it, I *knew* you were going to ask. I had the answer written down somewhere. It was on the tip of my tongue . . . wait a minute, it's probably on my desk somewhere. Now I've spoiled it. Sorry. . . . Patrick Buchanan once blurted out, when he was inveighing against PBS for being 'unfair' to Nixon, that educational television had all these 'radlib' programs. 'And then for a fig leaf,' he said, 'you have William F. Buckley.' What can he have meant? . . . Why do you suppose they use fig leaves, anyway? There's no mention of fig leaves in the Bible, is there? Any more than there is of an apple. Why the hell was it an apple that Eve ate? Why wasn't it a pear, or a plum, or a kumquat? We need to get hold of a Biblical horticulturist here, but of course we might not be able to get him to think. . . . You know that wonderful line of Dorothy Parker's? When someone asked her to use *horticulture* in a sentence, she said, 'You can lead a whore to culture, but you can't make her think.' Did you ever get to meet Dorothy Parker? I had a chance to, once, and I missed it. I've always regretted it. Don't you love that interview with her in *The Paris Review* where she says, 'You know I'm not a wisecracker, honey, don't you?' The fruits of religion is what we're talking about here. Or are we? What *are* we talking about?"

"Why would a man who doesn't think about God read *The Varieties of Religious Experience*?"

"I don't remember a thing about it; and, besides, it was a long time ago, and I was depressed. I was sitting alone in an apartment on East Sixty-eighth Street."

"What color shirt were you wearing?"

"I was afraid you were going to ask that. I doubt that I was wearing a shirt. I think I was wearing a T-shirt and socks. . . . Doesn't everybody think of God, or something? You're always left with the question of why it is that it has occurred to everybody in all cultures that there *is* something moving out there. . . . I guess the answer is obvious—it's because the earth is so full of mysterious forces, the dark, thunder. . . ."

"I thought the answer was much more obvious."

"What?"

"That He *is* there."

"Oh. But nobody *knows* that—except the ones you find it hard to trust. Who originated the joke—Lily Tomlin uses it in her show—that if you talk to God you're sane, but if He answers you're crazy? What politician would dare say, 'Last night as I sat in my room, suddenly I heard a voice'? Very unwise to say that. Yet the Bible is full of stuff like that and full of sudden conversions; look at Saint Paul and Saint Teresa. Wasn't Saint Teresa 'pierced to the quick with the arrows of God's love'?"

"Can you imagine that happening to you?"

"I can im*a*gine it happening. Actually, it happened to my grandfather, and *he* was no fool. . . . Anyway, it would depend on where the 'quick' is, and who does the piercing. And do you get an anesthetic?"

"In your book, you say you saw Christ's eyes move in a statue in Amalfi; then you sort of nervously move away from the subject and say, 'That's the end of *that* story.' Isn't that called skittering?"

"Oh; that's where I'm *con*sciously being that thing people accuse me of being—*sur*face. I knew you'd come up with an example sooner or later. I think maybe I did it on purpose to bug them. But maybe that's all I had to say on the subject. I just read the other day—and here I go deflecting the question from myself again—that that happened to Lord Kenneth Clark. He *skimp*ily describes an incident in a cathedral; he was not just moved by sublime architecture, but suddenly his entire *be*ing was radiated with this whole sensation unlike anything he'd ever experienced. He turned his back on it, he wasn't able to pursue it, his life was somehow not able to accommodate it. The man who reviewed Clark's autobiography said it was unfortunate that Lord Kenneth threw away a pearl of great price worth all his intellect and culture. Who's to say? . . . For God's sake, are you going to publish this? My mailbox will be flooded with tracts, I promise you. . . . Speaking of culture, what's that coffee container doing on my desk growing fungus; I don't need that, I have enough culture already."

"I didn't put it there."

"Of course you didn't put it there. You have the opposite of the opposite of paranoia. If you're going to be sensitive, you're going to have to leave. And come back again, of course. . . . What was the question?"

Somewhere along the line, I'd asked Cavett if he chose his friends on the basis of their being amusing. "I don't know *how* I choose my friends. I suppose if I were to look at a list of them I wouldn't find *any*one who didn't amuse me at least *part* of the time. . . . Can *you* imagine anyone who wasn't funny at least part of the time?"

"Hitler?"

"*Hit*ler. Now, let's see. Is there any evidence of the Hitler wit? Grotesque idea. There isn't a book of Hitler jokes. . . . People think I'm hallucinating, but I did see a book called *The Nixon Wit*. I saw it in a paperback in an upstate New York town, and why I didn't buy it I don't know. . . . Hitler. Can you imagine Hitler saying, 'Suppose Eva Braun had had one leg shorter than the other . . . ?' "

"How would that joke have ended?"

"I don't know; I'm no longer a gag writer. I have other unfinished gags like that: 'She took an overdose of birth-control pills, and . . .' There's *got*ta be a line for that. I once threw it at Neil Simon on the show; he couldn't finish it either. . . . Hitler and wit. . . . Fanatics wouldn't have a sense of humor, would they? People who say there's no time for humor either just don't *have* it or there's really something *de*finitely wrong with them. . . . Humor can be used to *de*vastating effect in political life. After Dorothy Parker characterized Dewey as the little man on the wedding cake, it was impossible *ever* to take him seriously again. . . . Humor and goodness and Hitler and wit. Hmmm. This is really a research problem. Shall we put it on the back burner? I knew you'd wince at that phrase. It comes from Mad. Ave., which gave us the dreadful phrase Mad. Ave. I really tend to take a question in all directions, don't I?"

After the easy give-and-take of a talk with Cavett, I was interested in seeing whether the good feelings our conversation generated would color my opinion of his on-the-air performance. When friends knew I was talking to Cavett, they inevitably called my attention to what they regarded as his most tasteless four seconds, which occurred when he was interviewing actress Liv Ullmann. (They were also good enough to remind me that I had then called Cavett a twit; and why was I singing his praises now?) Cavett asked Ullmann—whom he was loving with his eyes—whether she could prove her prowess as an actress by saying convincingly, "Dick Cavett, I love you." Ullmann said, "But I *could* love you—you give off a certain radiance. Two people can easily fall in love with each other while they're together. Couldn't you, over a glass of wine, feel that you were in love with me?" Cavett said dryly, with Ullmann all dewy vulnerability, "You'd have to wait in line"—hardly an adorable sentence. "You'd have to wait in line" is what everybody remembers and offers as evidence of Cavett's being unable to rise to extraordinary situations—in spite of the fact that he did say, almost immediately, "That was flippant. Of course I could." (Later he was to say, "I got so much more from her than I'd bargained for.") It is because Cavett is sometimes caught off guard that many people feel safer watching Johnny Carson—

who is always glib, always in control, and never, as Cavett sometimes appears to be, breathless and awed, as most of the rest of us would be under similar circumstances. Cavett—unlike Carson, always the performer—is both actor and spectator. With Carson, you know you're getting all there is to get. With Cavett, there is the promise of something withheld. Carson plays to the camera. Cavett plays to—sometimes with—his guests. He did so with Muhammad Ali. When the two were verbally jousting, Ali asked the camera to pan to his handsome, unmarked face, which he then lovingly caressed. He used his unmarked beauty as proof that he would never wind up in what Cavett perhaps not unintentionally called Queer Street. Cavett said, "Shaving for you must be practically like having an orgasm." There was an element of flirtation in the Cavett-Ali exchange; Cavett appeals to both sexes, and knows it.

One never knows what he might do or say next. That makes some viewers—who prefer late-night soporifics—nervous. On the other hand, he is not an emotion spiller—and that leaves other viewers hungry. He is neither "hot" enough nor "cool" enough to win over mass audiences.

I am watching Cavett at a taping of a show with Geraldine Fitzgerald. He is wearing cowboy boots, a turtleneck, and flannels. While Fitzgerald rehearses the song she will sing on camera, I try to read Cavett's face. It is in repose. But his expressive hands are outstretched, his blunt-edged fingers splayed, as if to help her or enter into her feeling. Occasionally, Cavett steals a look at colleagues in the studio audience to read *their* faces. He meets my eyes with a smile that, for all its being barely perceptible, is warm and welcoming. He briefly exercises his temper. The lights are too bright, he complains; and he dismisses peremptorily the crew's protestations: "That's too damn bad, fellas, I can't work like this, and I'm the one who's gonna be on camera."

Afterward, in his office, I ask him how he thought the taping went, and how he decompresses after a show.

"Sometimes after a show you're in a very good state but can't turn it to any good use; other times after a show, good *or* bad, you don't hear what anybody's saying to you, you just keep thinking, why did I—or didn't I—do this or that. You're not back out of whatever half of your mind you use on the air and back into the half you use off the air, if they are in fact separate. . . . I wish you'd never brought this up. Maybe I'm not decompressed and that's the answer. . . . I was *hop*ing you'd ask me whether Hitler had a sense of *hu*mor. . . . I can never tell how a show went. You can be fooled. Very strange. You just try . . I don't know what metaphor to use here—you cross the bridge when you come to it? No-o. You throw ten balls in the air and try to catch three? No-o. You throw ten pieces of silverware in the air and hope that the knives stick? Well, never mind. . . Now can you ask me an easier question?"

"Who intimidates you? Anybody?"

"I can re*mem*ber being intimidated. I was *very* scared when Buckley first came on; now I think of him as a friend. Let's see, who'd intimidate me now? I think I'd be scared only if I were foolish enough to get on the air and try to appear knowledgeable in some field that I know next to nothing about with somebody who really knew his business. Unfortunately, on this kind of show, you have to *pose* as an expert. I have to know enough to know what questions to ask. Sometimes that puts me on pretty thin ice. One of the traps of this job is to pre*tend* you know more than you do. You say, 'Oh, yes, *Witt*genstein.' I did that to Erhard. I said, 'What would Wittgenstein say about that?' Thank *God* he didn't ask me what I knew about Wittgenstein. If he had, I would have asked him if he'd seen any good movies lately."

"Some people were under the impression that ·Brando intimidated you."

"Yeah. He did a funny thing. He walked into my office and picked things up and turned letters over on my desk and peeked into my medicine cabinet. I told him to cut it out. . . . He and I talked about that show and how each of us was disappointed. He felt that I'd let him down, and I felt that he'd let me down. I can't begin to analyze it; it's almost as complex as he is. If I could rewrite the scenario, I'd say, 'But you *are* Marlon Brando, and one of these days you're going to have to admit that and understand that people want to hear you talk about acting, not about Indians.' I was afraid to say on the air that he had agreed to talk about anything at all during the first half and about Indians on the second half. He didn't play according to the rules, and I was afraid to call him on it. Maybe the *real* truth is that I was so blinded by his presence that I thought it was going sort of nicely, just because Brando was *there;* I guess that isn't enough. But how do you judge a show like that? In one sense it was a total success because somebody who saw it wrote out a seventy-five-thousand-dollar check for the Indians. For those who watched it and didn't give a *shit* about Indians and just wanted to see Brando or watch me confront or embarrass him, it was a failure. Then, of course, there are people like you who *prob*ably give a shit about Indians but don't want to hear Brando talking about them. I'm assuming that's true; you wouldn't want to hear Laurence Olivier talk about Welsh coal miners, would you? I thought not. . . ."

"During the Vietnam War, part of your appeal to students was that they believed you were on their side. Yet you don't sign your name to petitions, do you? You're not an overt advocate of causes."

"My personality would *tend* toward signing those things, but in a *bus*inesslike way I avoid it, simply because it destroys a little of—whatever—the 'objectivity' that you're supposed to have as a public figure in television. Maybe it's also my reluctance to be pigeonholed. I don't want anyone to say, 'Oh, he belongs to the National Rifle Association, and we know what *that* means'; or, conversely, 'He belongs to the Civil Liberties Union, and we know what *he* is.' In fact, I have belonged to both; does that surprise you? I once told Jerry Rubin on the air—partly to get a laugh—that politics bored my ass off. I was half-serious. He was saying that *every*body should be out fighting the good cause. My feeling was that there is *noth*ing *every*body should be doing. So I overstated my feelings. I just wanted to make a cranky little statement: *no*body should be required to do anything. . . . Actually, that's a fascist statement, too, isn't it? As bad as saying everybody should be doing something. My point was that even in times of what appears to be a clear moral imperative, like opposing the war, some people can be forgiven for just making bracelets or something. There *is* no universal imperative. If you live under Nazism or Fascism, I think personally that it's your duty to oppose it, but I wouldn't try to convince anyone *else* of that. . . . I graduated from Yale in 1958. It was a dull time. Fooling around with politics would simply have been seeking out something to do. I honestly couldn't keep straight in my mind whether the Right or the Left was the more conservative. I was interested in very little: I liked my studies; I loved being at Yale; I liked going to the theater. That's all spelled out in my book—some people think it's the worst part of the book, so you probably ought to read it."

"In your book there's a Salingeresque quote where you say that you thought, at Yale, that if you were ever to become famous, you'd ring strange people's doorbells and say, 'Hello. I'm famous Dick Cavett.' Do you ever get the urge to do that now?"

"No. *No.* You are *con*stantly aware, in a way that I find depressing, of the effect it has on some people to meet you. Leaving aside how much of it is that they met *me*, Dick Cavett, or just a guy they see on TV a lot—if you're tired and bored and they ask for your autograph and they squeal *I met him I met him I met him* and then you get a note later saying, 'Thank you for being so nice to my son and my daughter, you can't imagine what it meant to them, they'll remember it all their lives' . . . Well, you think, *I* don't get such a kick out of being me at this moment, what on *earth* is it doing to them? Why can't *I* feel it? The other thing is, you think, Here I have this balm that I could be dispensing, almost like the magic touch; it's not going to do what Jesus did to the blind person, but you do sometimes get that feeling . . . which is probably corrupting. . . . Can we talk about something else?"

"You've been married a long time. . . ."

"This comes as news to me."

"Surely you must have noticed."

"I don't know *how* long, though."

"Fourteen years. . . . Am I about to ask you for your recipe for a happy marriage?"

"Uh—two cups of tolerance . . . God, this could become sickening. There must be an icky answer to that that would involve measuring devices or something. Why don't you make one up? . . . Well, you assume that the marriage is happy, of course, in your question. Or don't you? It turns out that it *is*, but a lot of people who've been married as long as I have should have gotten out of it in the first two weeks. Longevity isn't a *true* indicator. However, I happen not to be a masochist. . . . Maybe it's that we amuse each other just enough so that any problems that come up are obviated. Maybe humor is our saving grace; I'm really not sure. I've never tried to imagine being married to anybody else, though I don't believe there's that one person you're destined to meet by fate, or any of that crap. There may be some sense, though, in which each of us was tolerable only to the other person. . . . Of course, getting married is a ri*dicu*lously unnatural thing to do—to bind yourself to one person who must by definition be largely a mystery to you, as any other human being is—but to decide that, even with all the unknowns, you're going to spend the rest of your life together. . . . How long has it been since you've read the marriage vows in The Book of Common Prayer? God, that language! And they're trying to change that glorious language for 'modern' language. Appalling. There are so few masterpieces left. I'm *mad* about this. What can we do about it? What's the rationale behind tampering with that language? To make religion more accessible to the masses? But religion shouldn't be accessible. It's something that is at its core unchanging . . . and if you can fit in with it, fine, and if you can't, too bad. . . ."

"Do you like rituals?"

"Yeah. I've come to realize that the very things in earlier life I found tiresome about rituals are the things that make them important. The familiarity of ritual is so comforting. But how the *prac*tice of ritual works its way inward to provide you with a glimpse of the divine or the eternal—that's a little bit beyond me. Marriage and ritual. Yes; I do think marriage has the virtue of repeated patterns and familiarity, and maybe we do need those rhythms. It brings to mind the Yeats line from *A Letter to His Daughter,* which I'm about to woefully misquote: 'May she live in a household where all is custom and ceremony.'

Sometimes when you live in the nerve-jangling absurdity of television you find yourself having just the *sim*plest envy of the guy who lives out in Mesa, Arizona, and makes a bracelet every day, and then when he's through with his bracelet he gets on his horse and rides back home and has his dinner at the same time every day and goes to bed at the same time every night, and the pattern is repeated and repeated."

"How long does it take you to realize that you've hopelessly romanticized the guy with the bracelets?"

"Not long. But there *are* people who live a good life like that and know it's good and don't complain about it. Maybe I'd be bored with it, but something a *little* closer to that would be desirable. It would be nice to have more pattern. . . . I'm very susceptible to nature. Oh, look at this picture—the whole thing I was going to describe."

Cavett shows me a black-and-white photo. I see a bleak, dry landscape for which I could never feel any affection. Cavett is standing in the foreground, wearing a cowboy hat and boots.

"It's the Sandoz country in Nebraska. I don't know if you can get any feeling from it. It's so beautiful. I'm happy every second I'm in it—grass, gently rolling hills, unearthly quiet. The whole area is soaked in Indian history. I wish you could see the colors—yellow, green. These are fruit trees; it's late autumn and they're turning brown. And all this sand is covered with long grass. When I drive there there's nothing quite like it; it's like entering Shangri-la. The day I left there—I had to leave at six in the morning, such a beautiful time in the prairies and plains—I had to get back for something dumb, and I thought, This is *stupid.* What the hell, a year from now I won't remember what it was I had to be back for. And in fact I *don't have any idea why I left. Damn it!* I can remember thinking, Why don't I just stay here and sit by the river all day; it will be paradise. I might even have had an *in*sight if I'd stayed, which is probably exactly why I didn't stay. . . . And to think that when I was a kid, all I wanted was to get to the city. Perverse! After a while, you miss the very things you believed you loathed. As soon as you find the exit, you want to find the way back in. That's not a very profound insight about human nature, is it? Thank God you're not laying the burden of profundity on both of us. . . . Cities still excite me, but I've had enough exposure to the claustrophobic, nerve-wracking, ghastly side of them. I wonder what would come into my head if I didn't have any distractions. Can you imagine Thoreau working in this medium? Television has built-in problems that make it impossible for it ever to be a promised land—it's technical and financial and artistic and un*imag*inably big. Sometimes I give a *sec*ond's thought to whether addiction to TV—or even any length of exposure to it—may be *lit*erally destructive of some kind of mental process. I'm thinking of a time when I was alone in someone else's house. It was a beautiful morning and I liked the feel of it, and I was un*will*ingly thinking a lot of interesting thoughts, and then I switched the TV on, just for maybe ten minutes or so. There wasn't anything memorable or dramatic or offensive on, but just the fact that it *was* on changed something in me. It was as if receptors had been turned off, or maybe receptors were turned *on* and *orig*inators were turned off. I couldn't get the feeling back. Maybe it's some undiscovered thing about the waves in the room or electronics or something. I asked Marshall McLuhan about that once; I said television deadened something in me, and he said, 'Yes, isn't that curious'; and that's *all* he said. Boy, is it hard to get enlightenment!

I often think of that survival program—you know, the one where they put you in the wilderness and on the last two days you just sit on a ledge, and there you are alone for two days and two nights. Everybody who's done it says it was the most profound experience he ever had. It's much more intriguing than anything I've heard coming out of est or yoga or TM. Some people report hallucinating. But maybe sitting in a chair for two days would do it, too. I wonder, if I had stayed alone in Sandoz country for a whole day, would I have had the screaming meemies? I've thought about trying to re-create that experience; I'm afraid I'd be too self-conscious. How could you help wondering, has 'it' started yet? What am I doing here? But I think, really, at its worst it would be nice. Have you ever been alone? What was it like?"

I told him what it was like. He said, "I don't want to stop talking now; I'm really pleasuring myself now. . . . Ask me another question."

"What's magic about magic?"

"I don't know. I just know that one of the great joys of my life is when I can go over to Slydini's apartment—Slydini is the legendary magician I've had on my show—and learn something from him and watch him perform. My nervous system and psyche are never more aroused than when I can do the miracle of the six disappearing coins, which he's taught me. I get a kind of pulse beat and nervous anxiety and palpitation that I don't get from *any*thing anymore. It isn't that I en*joy* it that much; it's the danger of it, I think. It's all tied up in the desire to make it work and *fool* the people and do it well. Not-to-get-caught. This is beginning to sound like *Crime and Punishment.* Guilt? Maybe it *is* that; maybe it reflects something deep in the psyche—you have a secret and you don't want it out, but you are risking exposing it. And there's that tre*men*dous sense of congratulation when the person you're doing it for says, 'Good *God,* how did you *do* that?' . . . You want me to think about all the metaphors you use when you do magic? 'Look, my hands are clean . . . I'm not hiding anything from you.' All of that could be used for guilt and innocence, couldn't it? Or religion. Miracles. How do you change something into something else? Care to see my transubstantiation trick? Here's one: pick a sin, any sin. You *do* ask strange questions."

"We have only five minutes left to talk. . . . Are you ever going to have kids?"

"How would I know? Do you mean in the next five minutes? Do I have to decide now?"

"Are you going to answer my question? Are you ever going to have babies?"

"If you'd like me to. I'd be glad to. I'd be happy to. If I've offended anybody by not having them, I'd certainly be glad to rectify it. . . . Ask me another question."

"Would you actually call this an interview?"

"I don't know *what* I'd call it, but it had some authenticity, didn't it? 'You can tell I'm not a wisecracker, can't you, honey?' . . . Oh, well . . . ask me one more question."

"What interests you most of all in the world?"

"I can't single the thing out. I envy those who can. I envy obsessive people who are doing what they're doing because they have to be doing it."

"What three things interest you?"

"The history of the West, and magic, and obituary columns. That wasn't a very good choice, was it? A lot of things bore me. More things interest me. I guess that's lucky, or—I forget what else it is."

IV.

Panaceas

est:
THE INVASION
OF THE MIND-STEALERS
(1976)

It's both silly and sinister. It's as if the Wizard of Oz had set up business in Dachau and invited victims to pay $250 a marked head for the privilege of being stripped naked and dynamited. Or, it's like being on a tour of a minefield with an insane guide who, speaking in tongues, leads his passive charges unerringly to exactly those mines that will explode in their beseeching faces. It is like being born again at the hands of a witch doctor who, during the bloodied Hallelujah-birthing, wears leering masks: in his several manifestations, he appears to be a small-town Booster, Houdini, Billy Graham, the Marquis de Sade; finally, to his grateful creatures, he appears in the likeness of God. It's like having the top of your head blown off and being rewarded with a prescription for aspirin.

(The metaphors shift and change, because the experience, like one's worst nightmare, is both muddy and electrifying; it is like being imprisoned in sticky black cotton candy and being obliged to draw sustenance from that appalling shroud.)

Over seventy-five thousand people—most of whom are seemingly no more cranky or crazy than you or I—have in fact shelled out $250 for the Erhard Seminars Training. Est, which has been touted by its graduates as the sixty-hour intensive training that will change your life (or, in est-eze, "transform your ability to experience living"), was founded, as everybody now knows, by Werner Erhard, a forty-one-year-old Gucci-

197

Pucci-Bally California-style guru who "got it" while driving along the California freeway, and promptly packaged "it," and is, as a consequence, awfully rich.

What is "it"? You may well ask. "It," so far as one can figure out, is a synonym for enlightenment—or, as one est graduate put it, "the ability to experience the world without the benefit of human understanding." (And I used to think "it" was something Clara Bow had.) Werner, as his devotees familiarly and reverentially call him, speaks in riddles. (Perhaps that's one reason he changed his name from the decidedly prosaic and unsphinxlike Jack Rosenberg. The other reason is that he was running away from his first wife and kids.) Anyway, it's no good asking Werner what "it" is: you have to take the training to find out.

The wonder is that so many people should want to. Why should thousands—among whom are Cloris Leachman, Joanne Woodward, Valerie Harper, and John Denver—pay to enter what is essentially a larger version of Patty Hearst's closet? I took the est training to find out.

Most of what I knew about the est technique I'd gleaned from *Mary Hartman, Mary Hartman,* which had satirized this Big Daddy of the "consciousness movement." Then I ran into my old friend Nancy, who had, since I'd seen her last, taken the training and avowedly gotten "it." Like many of the Human Potential Movement camp-followers est attracts, Nancy is a kind of barometer for what's happening on the psychic-panacea market. The last time we'd met, she was muttering *om* on her way to a Rolf massage after a lunch of soybeans and curds that she'd shared with her astrologer who'd confirmed her feeling that she'd been a Mongolian horseman in a previous incarnation. Now she was on her way to an est graduate seminar. She greeted me with this remarkable sentence: "I haven't been able to find the energy to clean my cellar, and at the sharing at the seminar I'll be assisted into my space to look at the barrier that stands between me and my spring cleaning and I'll disappear the barrier." I had no idea what she was talking about. Was Nancy satirizing Mary Hartman? "You've probably never experienced your experience," Nancy said. "I have no idea what you're talking about," I said. "You feel empty," she said, "right? Your life doesn't work. You don't like yourself." "Nonsense," I said. "*Good,*" Nancy said. "You're anxious and tense for sure. You probably have a dark-brown headache the size of a walnut between your eyes." "Well," I said, "I'm certainly anxious and tense. My father is very ill." "*Fabulous,*" Nancy said. "What is, is. Come to the seminar. It'll blow your mind."

I did; and it didn't. I ought to say right now that I was expelled from est—after twenty-four hours that didn't change my life. More about that later. For now, suffice it to say that whatever "it" is, it isn't worth what one has to go through to get it. I'm convinced that no good end can possibly result from est's scary (*evil,* is what I really want to say) means.

Monday, April 12, 9:30 A.M., the ballroom of a hotel on Central Park West. Est graduates convene to hear a lecture called *Be Here Now.* Everyone is issued a first-name tag, yellow for graduates, white for guests.

After being received with applause and grins by est graduates in a reception so warm it suggests we've all done something terribly clever, eight guests (all women) are quickly shunted off to a small room where we meet Jonathan, an est staffer who will answer our questions and encourage us to plunk down a $30 deposit against the training fee. Jonathan looks hand-pressed, deodorized, and sexless—not, as a matter of fact, un-like John Denver.

Guest: "I'm unemployed, and what I want to know is, why does est cost so much?"

Jonathan: "Because it does. . . . I had no money and no job

when I signed up for the training—and a week after I registered, I had a job. Est makes it possible for you to know that you have control over your life. *You cause your own experience.*"

Is Jonathan talking about control? or about magic? The minute one commits oneself to est, he implies, terrific things happen. He tells us about a fat man who began to lose weight as soon as he'd signed the est registration form . . . "without trying to."

"After my training," Jonathan says, "I took responsibility for my life. I cleared up the most rotten thing I'd ever done: when I was in prep school, I lost a manuscript for the senior yearbook. After my training, I wrote a letter of apology to my headmaster." Jonathan beams.

That's his nasty secret? The world is blowing up and he's worried about a prep-school essay? As if reading my thoughts, the preppie says, "You can't change the world. The way things are is the way things are. Life is what it is. There is no now and no then. There is no Marxism and no capitalism. Mass protests don't *work*—shouting and sulking don't work. Your life doesn't *work.* Werner's life works. Werner is the Source, the Synthesizer; it's Werner's intention to transform the world. By signing up for the training, *you* are transforming the world—without trying."

Guest: "But what will I learn if I take the training?"

Jonathan: "You will know what you already know."

Guest: "I'm really angry because you just don't seem to be answering the question."

Jonathan: "Good. It's not bad to be angry. It's just being angry. You're making moral judgments out of your belief system. Belief systems are what you get stuck in to prove you're right. And that's not bad either."

Guest: "Is *anything* bad?"

Jonathan: "No. And nothing's not bad, either."

Guest: "But what will I get from the est training?"

Jonathan: "You'll get what you get."

Jonathan explains that the training consists of *data* from the trainer, *processes*, and *sharing* the experience of the processes. He takes us through a sample process:

"Uncross your arms and legs, take everything off your lap, relax, and close your eyes. Thank you. . . . Recall a time when you were really happy with someone and notice what that experience was like for you. Great. . . . Now recall a time when someone was really happy with you. Notice how your body felt. Fabulous. . . . Now bring a stranger into the picture and notice what happens to the experience. How do you feel now? Good. . . . Now notice if there is any tension in your body. See if you have tension in the area of your forehead between your eyes. Is it the size of a pea? Is it the size of a walnut? Good. . . . Look at the tension and see if it's okay with you to release it. Great. . . . Now get a sense of the space you would like to be in with yourself. When you feel good about that space, smile and open your eyes into that space. Great."

"What I experienced," a woman said, "is that I have no friends. I have never been happy." "Thank you for sharing," Jonathan said.

"You will experience in the est training that you are powerful, and that people are really loving. Do you know that nobody has ever been mugged after leaving an est session, even at two in the morning?"

"Did somebody alert the muggers?" I asked.

"You might want to look at whether, if you're mugged, you want to be mugged," the preppie said.

"That sounds to me like, 'If she was raped, she was asking for it,' " I said. "Thank you for sharing," Jonathan said.

Jonathan attempts to shame his audience into paying $250, to manipulate vacillating (and unemployed) guests.

"Barbara signed up for the training. Isn't anyone else as brave and courageous as she is?"

"I'm not brave. I'm apprehensive. I think you ought to tell people that I'm here because I'm writing an article."

"*Good.* Fear is good. When you get on an airplane, you're frightened, but you know you're going to get there."

"No, I don't. That's why I'm frightened."

"What you don't get," Jonathan said, "is that people who go through their barriers die with smiles on their faces. Even if you crashed and splattered on a rock in the Grand Canyon, you'd have gotten there."

In the taxi coming home, I say to Nancy, "Doesn't it strike you that all this self-absorption is dangerous? Shouldn't you think about the social implications of all of this? Does a napalmed baby 'cause his own experience'? If, as Jonathan suggests, there is no evil, then we're not obliged to resist evil. Think of Hitler, for goodness' sake."

"Good," Nancy said. "You're resisting. What you resist, you 'get.' "

What I was getting was a headache the size of a watermelon.

Friday, April 16, 2 P.M., est Manhattan office. Everyone to whom I speak is brusque, purposeful; heads turn with bright, birdlike motions, revealing clear, determined eyes. Est staffers, when they speak to each other, pitch their voices just above conversational level, so that people sitting in the lobby can hear their conversations, which are, as we used to say in Sunday school, "edifying and uplifting." Everything is done for effect; the proselytizing has begun.

The young woman who greets me ("Hi! I'm Diane. How may I assist you?") refers me to an office worker who will process my application form ("Hi! I'm Suzie. How may I assist you?"). I am alarmed by a clause in the form that reads: "I understand that the material of the training, including, but not limited to, the names of the participants and their remarks, is private and confidential, and I agree to keep all such material private and confidential." I tell Suzie that I want to call my agent and my editor before I sign what looks to be a very dicey —and possibly illegal—disclaimer. Unfortunately, it is lunchtime, and Good Friday to boot, so neither person is likely to be in.

"If you call them with the intention of finding them in," Suzie says, a Delphic smile lighting her face, "you will find that they will be in." Can she be suggesting that I can *cause* them to be in? That my thoughts are a magic carpet that will transport them from East Hampton to midtown Manhattan? I would find that kind of power abhorrent.

"What if I woke up tomorrow morning with the intention of making the sun stand still?"

"It is Werner's destiny," Suzie replies cryptically, "to make the physical universe work."

When I return from a fruitless visit to a phone booth, Suzie says, "You didn't call with the intention of finding them in, did you? And they were out." It is impossible to assail her est-enlightened smile with logic.

During the week before I was scheduled to take the est training, I talked to a lot of my friends about the cloud-cuckoo-land encounters I'd had with est staffers. Many were loath to believe that anybody in real life talked and behaved as I said est-ers had; they implied I must be exaggerating. In the next breath, however, they expressed the fear that est would somehow "get" to me. (The media-hype—193 articles were written about est in 1975—had, I'm afraid, gotten to *them*. I felt as if I were being viewed as a candidate for the Mind-Stealers.) I knew that, on one level, est could and would get to me: the rules of the training were that no one could leave the room (even to go to the bathroom) for four-hour stretches; I considered that senseless deprivation an invitation to cystitis and claustrophobia. I figured that keeping my eyes closed for a sixty-minute process might very well precipitate a massive anxiety attack. (Who isn't afraid of the unfriendly dark?) I was afraid, most of all, that I would be bored into somnolence by mystical clichés and dreary encounter-group platitudes.

My friends said, "Look at all the skeptics who go into est and come out claiming that it's worked for them. Why should you be any different?" Why, indeed? Intelligence, I admit, is no safeguard if one is determined to leap into belief. My armor against est, I thought to myself (and it's hard, even with one's friends, to say things like this aloud—it's often perceived as a lack of humility), is that, while my life is far from perfect, I like myself. I can't in honesty say, as I heard people say in the pretraining, "I have never loved anybody, touched anybody, been loved; I am nothing; I am empty." The fact that est "works" (supposing it does have benevolent long-range effects) doesn't make it, as a social philosophy, good or true. Behavior modification worked for Hitler Youth, too—it gave their lives purpose, and they smiled a lot; that didn't make the behavior modifiers any less reprehensible. I was fully prepared to have a couple of insights during the training. So what? I've had insights on Amtrak parlor cars. If you sit long enough in one place, you have an insight. And what was all this relentless railing against belief systems I'd heard from est-ers? Why bother to empty people of their concepts, beliefs, judgments, and evaluations unless you planned to replace one system of beliefs with another? If I wanted a new belief system, I'd choose to believe in God—He's been in business longer than Werner, and He has better music. To say nothing of the fact that I'm a snob—and est, with its gobbledygook, supersalesmanship, and peach-faced gurus in bodysuits, struck me as ineffably tacky.

Monday, April 26, 7 P.M., the ballroom of a midtown hotel.
The training begins. We are calculatedly divided into Us
(250 of us) and Them. We exhibit various signs of nervous
anticipation; they greet us with stern, unsmiling visages, impervious to pleasantries or chagrin. We are ordered, in loud,
declamatory tones, to leave all watches and timepieces in an
anteroom. (Phooey. I slip my watch into my bra.) We are
then ordered to sit on hard-backed, dainty chairs, arranged so
that flesh—there is no more than a quarter of an inch between me and the people on either side of me—touches un-
familiar flesh. Est staffers are posted at the sealed doors. It is
uncomfortably hot.

Marvin, an unprepossessing young man who has total control of his facial muscles, which never once arrange themselves
into a semblance of a smile, takes his place on the podium and
drones out a series of rules that he calls agreements: no alcohol
and no medication other than that specifically prescribed by
doctors is to be taken by trainees for two weeks ("Is that
clear?"); no snacking during the training sessions; no milk is to
be drunk during the breaks ("Is that clear?"); nobody may leave
the room to go to the bathroom; no notes may be taken; est
staffers may tape-record the proceedings, trainees may not ("Is
that clear?"). The hour-long recitation is so boring, so repeti-
tive, so infantilizing—"When you can't hear, raise your hand
and say, 'I can't hear.' Is that clear?"—it amounts to an assault.

Trainee: "I'm going to the dentist on Wednesday to have
a tooth pulled. Can I take Novocain?"

Marvin: "The trainer will explain body pain on Tuesday. In
the meantime, be where you are."

Trainee: "Is it all right for me to relate to my husband during
the training?"

Marvin (after a long pause in which irony has no part):
"Yes."

Up through the center aisle bounds a pretty, athletic man,

something disturbingly concave about his mouth, sexless: "I'm Landon, and you're all assholes."

Landon is our trainer. His voice alternately oily and icy, he bludgeons, anticipating our objections: "You think Marvin is a Nazi, don't you, assholes? You think we're the antichrist. You're being *reasonable*. Where has reason gotten you? It's gotten you nowhere, and you're nothing. If you weren't nothing, why would you be here? Spending good money to be called assholes. If you assholes keep your agreements with me, your life will work. If you don't, it won't. A lot of what's wrong in this country is that people don't follow rules. The rules do not have to be explained. They're just rules. Is that clear? They are not reasonable. The training is not reasonable. Is that clear?"

Landon literally unsettles us: he shifts us around so that nobody winds up in the chair he or she had chosen. People look as if the chairs had been pulled out from under them, as indeed they have.

Trainee: "Why are no blacks taking the training?"

Landon: "*You* hate *niggers*, you asshole!"

(This technique, that of putting the questioner on the defensive and placing everything in the trainer's frame of reference, is consistently and brilliantly used by Landon to blunt all adversary questions . . . and to make the questioner feel like an ass.)

For hours, stopping only to answer questions with riddles or with contempt, Landon, with gathering momentum, sneers at and assaults logic, intellectual curiosity, reason, independence, belief systems, and "concepts"—all of which, according to him, keep our lives from "working." He draws complicated charts to illustrate his theses: none of us has "experienced our experience," and we are therefore doomed to repeat our experience forever and ever, like rats going through the same moldy tunnels for the same piece of stale cheese; catatonics are smarter than we are—at least they don't pretend to know anything; in order to be "truly knowing," we have first to be empty, to *accept*—to accept Landon, and est; if we're not here to accept, why are we here at all? Landon, a steamroller, knocks down everybody's props—including belief in God: "God is a *concept.* God is bullshit."

Trainee: "How can you say I haven't experienced my experience? My mother just died. . . ." She is racked with bitter sobs.

Landon: "Your *mother* didn't die, you asshole. *You* died . . . it's killing *you.*"

Trainee (currying favor): "My son died two years ago, and I felt fine."

Landon: "Very good. Did you feel a sense of completion? What is, is. You experienced that experience, so you're not stuck with it anymore."

This denial of grief is obscene, the ultimate in nihilism. Est refuses to confront the fact of mortality by denying that death exists (death is a "concept"). Landon says, "People choose their deaths. *You cause your own experience.*" Again, he is talking about control, but he really means magic: if people can be sold on the idea that they cause their own deaths, they can go through life armored with the invincible belief that no accident can ever befall them, that they need never fear the terrible black horseman who can ride through our lives, taking us surprised and unaware. I am reminded of what Nancy said when a friend died grotesquely: a flower pot (I wish this didn't sound funny—but life, contrary to est, is full of funny-terrible accidents) fell on her head as she was strolling down Fifth Avenue. Nancy said, "She must really have wanted to die."

Trainee: "What do you mean, we cause our own experience? If a drunk comes up and punches me in the nose, am I responsible? If a bus runs me over, am I responsible?"

Landon: "Yes. . . . *You* think of life as a punch in the nose, you asshole, you *look* as if you've been run over by a bus." Landon creates a world in which there are victims, but no victimizers.

The corollary to one's causing one's own experience is that one may never *help* anyone else. *Help* is a dirty word. "Why do you think Latin Americans hate us?" Landon asks triumphantly. "Because," he says, dangerously simplifying complex political and economic issues, "we *help* them! Nobody can help anybody. We can *assist* people to find their own space." (Werner has been quoted as saying, "There are only two things in this world, semantics and nothing." Language is being restructured in this room. People are being given a new vocabulary, and a new belief system—Werner's.)

A trainee shouts: "Stop, you're killing me! I've studied philosophy for twenty years, and you're stripping it all away! You're leaving me with nothing!"

How to explain the hysteria of her response? It can't be attributed to Landon's "philosophy," which is an unimpressive mishmash of psychiatric truisms and Eastern conundrums. (Landon even manages to confuse *mysticism* with *superstition*, which ought to tell serious scholars of Eastern philosophy something.) It is his technique, derived, in part, from Gestalt, Mind Dynamics, Scientology (and from Fuller Brush Company sales techniques), that is dazzlingly effective, combined, as it is, with a high degree of physical discomfort, approaching exhaustion—it is now 12 A.M.—and the terrible neediness that brought people here in the first place, looking for instant salvation.

Landon: "*Good.* This lady is far ahead of the rest of you assholes. She knows she's dying in this room. What she doesn't know is that she'll be born again."

Shortly after midnight, we are given a twenty-five-minute bathroom break . . . but since nobody is wearing a watch, and since everybody has trouble following complicated verbal directions to crowded bathrooms, the exodus has all the earmarks of panic. What should have been a release is another degradation.

When we return, the feeling in the room has palpably changed. People are tired of resisting, there is a sense of capitulation, of will-less surrender. People have understood that their comfort—perhaps their survival—depends on their giving Landon what he demands. This is what boot camp must be like. It's almost restful to do what the man says. Landon said he would dynamite our souls and suck us out like oranges. . . . There is a kind of sublimated sexuality in this submission to a dominant force.

Trainee: "I have an ulcer, and . . ."

Landon: "Asshole, an ulcer is just a concept, can you *see* your ulcer, can you *feel* it?"

Trainee: ". . . and when you said I couldn't have milk during the break, I tried to understand why not. But I should have just accepted it. So I decided to believe what you said because you told me to, is that right? I accept."

Like born-again Christians at a revival meeting, the trainees offer the sorry evidence of their lives to Landon. It is selected evidence, because Landon is an unwholesome saint: his followers' suppurating sores are his imprimatur. Everybody wants to bell the leper, everybody wants to *be* the leper; they want Landon to lick their wounds with his sandpaper tongue.

"My baby died a crib death, and I didn't feel anything. Do I have a problem with feeling, or did I experience my experience?"

"All my life I thought I was happy, now I realize I was just a rat going down tunnels for rotten cheese. I'm empty. I'm nothing."

Landon is as emotionless as if his charges were reciting the multiplication tables; he makes no compassionate connection.

I feel desolate, as if I'm in a sci-fi movie—the kind where

seedpods from Mars take over minds and bodies, and one turns to familiar faces and sees only alien vacuous stares. I feel nausea rising in me. An image flashes through my mind—my grandmother's room, dark poverty-brown and airless, the sick-sweet smell of incense contending with the smell of death, and around my grandmother's bed churchy crones in black, wailing, while my grandfather's vivid curses echo from another room . . . that smell is in this room now; it stinks, in here, of defeat.

A voice saying real words breaks the spell. A young woman has risen to her feet. "How can you be so arrogant?" she demands of Landon. "Was *Mozart* an asshole? There must be people in this room who are kind and courageous. Is *everybody* a shit?"

Landon, who has set up a situation in which only weakness is rewarded, says, "Thank you for sharing. . . . Mozart was an asshole. Everybody in this room is an asshole, and you're the biggest asshole because you're a *right*-machine—you have to believe you're right."

A small, insignificant-looking man says, slowly and carefully, "I'm a compulsive gambler, and I need every bit of ego I have to fight my addiction. I have a delicate balance of mental health, and you're destroying my ego. I'm leaving."

As he walks out, head bowed, Landon—without deigning to address him directly—says, "Mental health? What does he know about mental health? *I'll* tell you how the mind works on Sunday. He's just putting up defenses and justifying himself —the way you are, you assholes."

Ten minutes later, the gambler reenters. He stands at attention while an est woman runs down the aisle to bring him a mike. (The est running-crouch is a cross between Namath's quarterback sprint and the White Rock nymph in bionic motion.) "I want to say that Marvin assisted me to come back, and I'm glad I'm here." The sustained applause that greets the prodigal's return is proof—if more were needed—that the group has solidified behind Landon. Anyone who challenges Landon now will have the group to contend with. It is a peculiarly dispiriting realization. If there are any protestors left here, they have been quarantined, isolated by the group's disapproval.

It is now 3 A.M. The temperature has dropped dramatically. It is uncomfortably cold. Landon takes us through a process. (The timing is exquisite—all mental and physical resources have been eroded, everyone is totally suggestible.) We close our eyes. From hidden loudspeakers comes the sound of surf. Landon's disembodied voice suggests that we are not tired, our aches and pains are disappearing, we are *relaaaaxed,* we will sleep well and wake refreshed, we are *relaaaaaxed.* Est people soundlessly prowl the aisles . . . I know they do, I peep. At Landon's cue, everyone surfaces from a hypnotic trance, as if from a communal wet dream.

Tuesday, April 27. I have asked Suzanne, the young woman who endeared herself to me by asking the Mozart question, to have dinner with me at the Oyster Bar. (I have oysters, white wine—thus breaking an est rule—and strawberries. Being good to oneself is the best revenge.) Suzanne, a network TV producer, is, on the face of it, an unlikely candidate for coercive persuasion. Her lover, an est convert, has paid her $250 tuition, and she is hanging in, she says, because she is fascinated by group dynamics. Well read in Eastern philosophy, she is appalled that Landon should "vulgarize mystical concepts—and charge all those poor people so much to be punished." She giggles: "I feel like a kid playing Simon Says, don't you?

You won't let them get to you, will you? They won't be able to get to you? I don't think they can get to me. . . . I'm so tired. I had two hours' sleep last night, I'm really flakey, I'm frightened."

April 27, 7 P.M., the ballroom of a midtown hotel. My body aches. I feel as if I'd been beaten with a rubber hose. All around me people are standing up to testify that they have slept well, they are refreshed, they have never had so little sleep and so much energy. . . . Well, of course! Their nerve ends are exposed, they're experiencing the illusory clarity and high that comes with total physical exhaustion, and, I suspect, they are acting out of posthypnotic suggestion. . . . The woman sitting next to me is rocking herself back and forth, crying. A man behind me says he has never felt better in his life, he doesn't know what's happening to him, he's gay and a jealous lover, and could he please have a bag to vomit in.

Landon says, "Everybody is perfect *and* has barriers to perfection [there are no *buts* in est-land, no on-the-other-hands, no complexities or shades of gray]; what you try to change persists; if you just *observe* a problem, you 'disappear' it; if you try to *understand* a problem, you get the booby prize." The killings at Kent State and at Attica, he says, and revolutions everywhere, are a result of assholes trying to change things, examples of the futility of struggle; *he* never gets upset when he reads the news—what is, is.

(Is Rockefeller financing est? Is the CIA financing est? Hardly likely, but: if you can get a well-drilled army of good soldiers to believe that all struggles to bring about change are puerile and counterproductive, what a wonderful way to maintain the status quo, to prepare people for withdrawal, to encourage narcissism in the midst of social unrest. Werner demands that all est staffers give up their "own intentions, purposes, desires, and objectives in life" in order to serve him. Will est be used to create a Werner-world where each man is an island, where intellectual vitality and political action are perceived as moral defects? Is Werner creating a whole school of social dropouts who will obey his will? Werner, his disciples rumor, may some day wish to be President.)

Panacea time. Landon takes us through a process to teach us how to "disappear" physical pain: "Close your eyes and go into your space. Good. Locate a space in your right ankle. Good. Locate a space in your left ankle. Good. Locate your pain. Is it the size of an orange? Is it round? Is it square? Is it triangular? Good. What color is it? Good. Now look at the pain. Observe it. Experience it. Re-create it. Good. The pain you have re-created will enter the space of the pain you are observing and will disappear it. Good. Relax. Open your eyes."

(Nancy says that since she's taken the training she no longer has migraines. Actually, what she says is, "I go *through* my migraines and *experience* them, so I don't experience them as pain." . . It sounds to me as if she still has migraines.)

All over the room people are testifying that their aches and pains have been "disappeared." Without even the laying on of hands. . . . Well, why not? As long as they don't claim to cure cancer. . . .

The Cancer Lady Speaks: "I have cancer. And a heart condition. And my family and friends live in Philadelphia, but my husband made me move to New York, and I'm terrified of New York, all the buildings close around me, I'm all alone here, and my doctors said my husband was killing me. . . . Why is he killing me?"

"Your husband isn't killing *you*, you're killing *him. You* caused your experience—you caused pieces of yourself to be cut out—so you could kill him, so you could prove you were right and he was wrong. Cancer," Landon says, "is a concept." A concept for which she is responsible. A concept that can be "disappeared."

We are to go through a "truth process." Everyone is to get in touch with an unwanted "item" in his or her experience, in order to "disappear" it.

"What is your item?"

"Guilt?"

"Guilt is a concept. Pick an item, any item."

"Sadness? I'm sad because my mother . . ."

"Your item is sadness. Don't assign a cause to that item. Your life is like a vegetable stew . . . reach in and grab one item . . . and remember, peas don't cause *carrots.*"

Item: Sadness.

Item: Fear.

Item: Despair.

We close our eyes. The recorded surf pounds again. "You are on a beach. . . . Experience what it was like to be on that beach. Good. Experience what comes up for you. Is it a person? Good. Experience that person. Now look at how you are feeling. . . ."

During the process, I play these (unauthorized) games: I imagine a passage of Job written in est-eze (item: despair); and I understand that the reduction of all human emotions to single-word "items" makes art—and emotion itself—impossible. . . . I think of people I would like to have sitting around me: novelist Muriel Spark, for her iconoclastic intelligence, her irony, her absolute faith in an absolute God; Ralph Nader and a whole bunch of his Raiders; my Marxist friend Sol Yurick (part of what is going on in this room is a denial of cause and effect, which is a denial of history); a Jesuit; Woody Allen; and anybody at all who will make a convincing case for human reciprocity—who will convince people that people do hurt one another, help one another, drive one another crazy, and make one another happy. . . . I try to imagine what would happen if anyone introduced the following things into this room: somebody with a gun. A Beethoven quartet. Somebody having a heart attack. A crying baby. . . . I cast my eyes down, but do not close them, anxiety nibbling at my nerves. . . . Landon, his voice now soothing and syrupy (creepy, is what it is), chants:

"You are powerful. And you have the power to project your consciousness anywhere in the universe, and into the space [the mind?] of any other person. Relaaax. Open your eyes and come out of your space." The process has lasted one hour. It is now 3 A.M.

Wednesday, April 28, 7 P.M., the ballroom of the midtown hotel. Landon has drawn complicated charts on two blackboards—circles, squares, and arrows that purport to illustrate how est can "transform your ability to experience living so that the situations you have been trying to change, or have been putting up with, clear up just in the process of life itself."

Before the formal session begins, I copy the charts and the struggle-free recipe for Happy Living. Marvin appears at my shoulder: "Is there anything in your space that prevents you from keeping your agreement not to take notes?"

"Are you telling me you don't want me to take notes? I won't take notes."

"I'll take the book you're writing in."

"No, you can't have the book."

Marvin orders me to the back of the room, where he hands me a pencil. "Erase the notes," he says.

"You do it. You're the one who wants the notes erased."

Grim, Marvin hands my book and the eraser to an est woman, whose ability to erase for the cause is second only to that of Rose Mary Woods's.

"Now take that book and put it over there in the cloak room."

"Do you want my fillings, too?"

"No, just your book. . . . Now I want to know what there is in your space that is a barrier keeping you from obeying the agreements. Is it your intention to keep the agreements?"

"I've said I wouldn't take notes, and I've said I would put my book away."

Marvin has to be satisfied with my oblique answers. It's clear, however, that what he expected was for me to dither about "spaces" and "agreements" and "barriers," for me to question, not him, but myself. He's counted on my being on the defensive. A look of pure fury contorts his face and is just as quickly erased as he orders me roughly back to my seat.

Tonight people are "sharing" what they "got" in the "truth process." These are some of the words one doesn't hear in their mouths: courage, loyalty, goodness, economics, hope, joy. When love is mentioned, it is only in a negative context: *"I got that I had never loved anybody"; "I got that I am afraid to love men"; "I got that what I thought was love was bullshit."* Landon is well pleased.

Thursday, April 29, back at the ballroom. The Gambler/ Prodigal speaks again: "I can't go through another process. It's too painful. Too much terrible stuff comes up. I've had two heart attacks, and my doctor says that it's bad for my heart for me to go through this."

Landon: "Your *heart*? You don't even know where your heart *is*, asshole. Can you *feel* it? The only way to know something is experientially. Are you experiencing a heart attack right now? You're walking out of this room because of a bullshit concept. You're leaving because of your bullshit doctor. You don't know your heart from your asshole."

The Gambler stays.

Suzanne, my dinner partner, is in a rage: "How dare you!" she shouts. "How can you manipulate vulnerable people like this?"

A woman turns to shush her: "We're here because we want to be here. We're not vulnerable, we're assholes."

Landon says, "Suzanne, you might want to look at your arrogance. You just have to be right, don't you? You have to win. You don't care about these people, you just care about winning. Arrogant. Asshole. Suzanne is an arrogant asshole."

Everybody applauds.

Suzanne, teary and trembling, pleads with me to say something in her support. I don't want to blow my journalistic cool, but Suzanne's stricken face is hard to deny.

"Did the people in Hiroshima cause their own experience?" I ask. "If they had 'observed' the bomb, would they have 'disappeared' it?"

Landon says, "Let Werner and me worry about the world. I'll tell you what caused Hiroshima on Sunday. And you know what? You're not really concerned with Hiroshima at all, you're angry. You're so angry you can't see   anger is your item, asshole."

He's right, of course, to this extent: wild horses wouldn't have dragged anything personal out of me at that moment; I had an almost fetishistic horror of revealing anything of my personal life to Landon. I find that I am shaking with anger, I can barely stand, hardly contain it. I think of what Simone Weil said about the Warsaw uprising—"indignation is the fiercest form of love"—and I try to tell Landon that, in this situation, anger is entirely appropriate. "But your anger is hurting you, asshole, it's not hurting me. Your anger is killing *you*." I do in fact feel murderous.

During the break, the Cancer Lady says, "Don't worry about Hiroshima, honey, he'll explain it to you on Sunday "

And if, on Sunday, he told them that the niggers and the kikes caused Hiroshima? He won't, of course; but if he did, what are they not prepared to accept?

After the break, we go into a process designed to take us into our sadness, fear, and pain and, by "looking at it," to exorcise it. It is 2 A.M., and uncomfortably cold. We are instructed to lie prone on the floor. Landon preps us for hypnosis: people will shout, vomit, and scream during this process, he says, and under no circumstances may anyone come to the aid of another —everyone's alone on this roller-coaster ride. This is payoff time. (And everyone who's paid $250 is eager to be complicit in his own victimization.)

The surf again. The beach again. Landon's voice: "Remember a time when you were sad. Good. Remember a time when you were terrified."

I hear the most awful wails I have ever heard in my life. Like a hundred Arab women keening. Over and over and over again. People pound the carpet with their fists, drum the floor with their heels, writhe. Voices scream, *no! no! no!* People are infatuated with their own suffering, their faces closed to what is going on around them, absorbed in the violent satisfactions of their fantasies.

I can't keep my eyes closed. There's no way I'm going to put my sanity to this test, no way I'm going to put my welfare in Landon's fleshy white manicured hands. Too much violence is being done in this room. How can anyone learn anything good from the brutal indifference that is being inculcated here? Demons could appear to drink the blood of virgins—Werner could appear to drink the blood of virgins—and this crowd would still be on their beaches, experiencing their experience.

A woman lying near me stiffens; her arms, then her legs, shoot up in the air, her head twists uncontrollably. Est staffers gather round, nod and smile at one another, make cabalistic signs over her body—apparently she is not dying. Landon sees that I see. He comes over to me: *"Shut your eyes."* "I can't." "You're not going to shut your eyes?" "I can't." "Get out."

Navigating over people's heads, stepping over people's bodies, I make my way through this writhing obstacle course, to the door, and the safety of the world.

It is 3 A.M. Acting on an impulse I don't understand, I telephone my children from a phone booth in the lobby. An extravagant call to match an extravagant mood: it is noon in Bombay, where they are visiting their father. *"Mommy?"* As soon as their voices leap over the transatlantic cable I know why I've called them. Their safe, sane voices, happy and alive with warm curiosity and affection, call me back beautifully to the world.

The streets are deserted, the air is rain-fresh; I've never been so happy to be going home.

Suzanne called me after she finished her training to tell me what I'd missed. Landon had taken the group through a "fear process"—he'd sent them into their space to "experience" being mugged, raped, strangled, knifed. They were choking on their fears, Suzanne said, and then, when it seemed that they would die of it, Landon said, "Assholes, don't you know that the person next to you is afraid of *you?* Doctors are afraid of you—that's why they write in Latin; cops are afraid of you—that's why they have guns. *You are powerful.* Now *you* go out and give someone *else* an ulcer. There is nobody in the universe more powerful than you."

Wonderful. Nothing like mystifying the sources of temporal power.

Next, the group got the est word about love: "Love is bullshit. When you're hot, you're hot; when you're not, you're not." That's a slogan to *live* by? "Well," Suzanne said, "it's certainly a slogan to fuck by."

On the final Sunday, the group had learned what "it" was: "What is, is. What ain't, ain't." Talk of a dying fall. It all seemed sadly anticlimactic.

I told Suzanne that I'd been pretty scared. "Oh, no," she said, "I can't bear that they got to you. It's so *silly.*" I took that to mean that they hadn't gotten to her. Then she said, "I did get that I was arrogant . . . that I always wanted to win, that I had to be right. . . ."

"The impression I got was that you wanted to be good," I said.

". . . and I got that Landon loved me," she said.

So I thought Suzanne was lost to the est world of endless graduate-seminar fixes, garbage-language, beach-spaces, disappearing fruit-shaped headaches, and Werner-love. Then she called me again: She felt "spacey," she said. She hadn't been able to sleep. "Nothing matters. I feel like a machine, I feel hollow. I feel like what Landon said I was—a mechanical asshole. I try to remember what I was like before the training, but I feel like a collection of empty spaces. In my head, I'm always back on that beach."

It's not the River Jordan, it isn't even Malibu. That beach is a cold and lonely place. I wonder how many est graduates have been stranded there, and who will help them back to the real world of struggle and pain and love.

THE HELANDERS
AND THE MOONIES:
A FAMILY STORY

(October, 1979)

This is a story about families and about a Family. It is the story of a young woman's apparently hopeless alienation from her anguished and bewildered parents and of her tested and determined allegiance to a cult some observers consider bizarre, others regard as silly, and still others believe to be dangerous and pernicious. The story of twenty-two-year-old Wendy Joy Helander—for four years a member of Sun Myung Moon's Unification Church—and of her parents, Carolyn and Elton Helander—who have been financially and emotionally devastated by their efforts to rescue their youngest daughter from what they deem to be a life of involuntary servitude—is more than an exotic variation on the Generation Gap. It is an American melodrama, an American tragedy, and an American conundrum. A story of deformed lives, lives twisted out of shape by obsessions and desires foreign to most of us, it is not an isolated happening but a story that could unfold within any "normal" family It is, in the wake of Jonestown, a story that raises a host of urgent and vexing questions—questions that none of us can pretend are irrelevant to our own lives, however ordered, stable, and sane our own lives appear to be.

First, the questions—to which there are no easy answers. Then, the story, which, heartbreaking and complex, one is hard-pressed to tell simply and cleanly: There are so many voices shouting for equal time in this drama that the questions *What is truth?* and *What is good?* seem made for the story—and the story, with all its ramifications, seems designed to defeat the questions.

The questions: Is radical and passionate commitment to a cult—a Family that supplants one's own—and to a charismatic religious leader pathological? Can one distinguish objectively among such phenomena as conversion, coercive persuasion, and "brainwashing"? Does the Unification Church present a clear and present danger to the health and welfare of the citizenry? If, in fact, Rev. Moon's cult can be proved harmful to its adherents, is the remedy—"kidnapping" and "deprogramming"—as bad as the illness? (Is "kidnapping" the operative word? Is "rescue" the operative word?) Is the Unification Church a political group masquerading as a religious group? Can the church lay claim to protection under the First Amendment, which guarantees freedom to exercise one's religious beliefs, abhorrent though they may be to the majority? Why are young people drawn to cults that have the effect of separating them from their parents? And—the questions that cut closest to the bone—who is susceptible? And is there any way to end the suffering of all those involved?

> *My dream is to organize a Christian political party including the Protestant denominations and Catholics and all the religious sects.*
>
> *When [the world] is against us then they are going to get the punishment. . . . Every people or every organization that goes against the Unification Church will gradually come down and die. Many people will die—those who go against our movement.*

> *The world is my goal and target.*

These are the words of Rev. Sun Myung Moon, the head of the Unification Church, referred to by his young followers—an army of clean-cut crusaders—as their True Parent, the self-proclaimed incarnation of God. Moon, and his ascetic American adherents—"Moonies," of whom there are an estimated thirty thousand—have received enormous media exposure over the past five years. Attention has focused on their fund-raising activities: seven thousand "core members" hawk flowers, candy, and candles at an estimated four-hundred-percent markup; fund-raisers, according to ex-Moonies, are required to fill a quota of $100 a day, no matter how many hours of work this requires, and no matter what ruses they are obliged to use to sell their wares.

In 1978, the Fraser Committee of the U.S. House of Representatives concluded that there were strong ties between the Unification Church and the repressive South Korean government: "While pursuing its own goals, the Moon Organization promoted the interests of the ROK [Republic of Korea] Government, and at times did so in cooperation with, or at the direction of, ROK agencies and officials. . . . A Moon Organization business . . . in Korea . . . is involved in the production of M-16 rifles, antiaircraft guns, and other weapons. . . . The Moon Organization used church and other tax-exempt components in support of its political and economic activities. Although many of the goals and activities of the Moon Organization were legitimate and lawful, there was evidence that it had systematically violated United States tax, immigration, banking, currency, and Foreign Agents Registration Act laws, as well as state and local laws relating to charity fraud, and that these violations were related to the Organization's overall goals of gaining temporal power. . . . The Moon Organization's ulterior motives behind even its most benign activities tended to negate its positive contributions."

The notion of a "religious" group acting as an agent for a foreign power is disturbing. But what has most spectacularly disturbed concerned observers comes, literally, much closer to home than the production of M-16's. It is one thing for a Moonie coyly to suggest that we are living in the Last Days and that Moon is the new Messiah—the "Lord of the Second Advent"; parents of Moon's troops could conceivably live with that idea, however uncomfortable it might make them. Even Moon's pathological anti-Communism, his claim—on the face of it absurd—that "American-type democracy" is "a good nursery for the growth of Communism," might be overlooked by some, as might even his anti-Semitism. Most people would probably find it funny to read, in a Moonie publication, that "in the ideal world centered upon God, everyone will speak only Korean." But nobody is laughing.

The reason nobody is laughing is that Moon has captured the imaginations—if not the minds and bodies—of so many young people. For parents of Moonie children, the heart of the matter is that their families have been torn asunder by their children's unquestioning loyalty to Sun Myung Moon.

What follows is the story of one such family. It is a terrible story.

Up until the time of her eighteenth birthday in 1974, Wendy Helander—blond and pretty—gave every appearance of being a reasonably contented young woman, reasonably in tune with the values of her middle-class family. With her brothers and sister (Joel, an emergency medical technician, and Forrest and Holly, both students) Wendy lived in unostentatious comfort in the Yankee shore village of Guilford, Connecticut. A good, rounded student, a cheerleader who apparently loved to play the piano and flute, to ski, swim, cook, sew, pot, weave, and to help her mother with household chores, Wendy was never involved with dope and was very much against permissive sex. She dated very little. She appears also to have been almost entirely apolitical, more like a fifties child than a sixties child—though, as we shall see, the seventies, with its emphasis on spiritual (or pseudo-spiritual) searching, have made their mark on her.

Wendy had had minor difficulties with her mother and father—typical growing pains, one might have thought. She wanted to finish high school in three and a half years; her parents, Elton and Carolyn Helander, wishing her to keep pace with her peers, encouraged her to complete the course in the allotted four years, and Wendy acquiesced. There was a slight tremor in the household when strong-willed Wendy announced her decision to spend a summer in France after her junior year as a mother's helper; her parents reluctantly agreed. Always a health-food enthusiast, Wendy became a vegetarian in France, and adopted a macrobiotic diet. Like many children of the seventies, she equated diet with spirituality: macrobiotics led her to an involvement in Eastern religion; she found a mentor and dabbled in Zen Buddhism. After high school graduation—which she seems to have endured begrudgingly—Wendy wanted to go to a "macrobiotics school" in Boston and to live in a commune that stressed macrobiotics and acupuncture. Her conventional parents protested; Wendy was, after all, only seventeen.

Shortly before her eighteenth birthday, Wendy enrolled at the University of New Hampshire. Around Thanksgiving, according to her parents, "she abruptly disappeared. We later learned that she had been invited and strongly urged to go on what she thought was a friendly weekend camping trip." Wendy had been approached by Moon's campus recruiters, and agreed to spend a weekend in Maine. After that "camping" (or indoctrination) weekend, Wendy, without informing her parents, moved out of her college dorm to live in a Unification commune. In early December, she became a member of the Unification Church, dropping out of the university without taking her final exams. During the Christmas holidays, she returned home for a few days. "She cried so much of the time," Carolyn Helander says, "and she kept saying she was so happy with her new 'Family.'" She also gave away many of her cherished possessions.

At Wendy's request, Elton and Carolyn attended a three-day church workshop on the weekend of January 10. What they saw there, they say, left them "in a state of utter shock. Not only did we find complete suppression of thought, but we observed one young man leaving the lecture hall only to be chased after by five leaders and bodily dragged back into the room." What they observed, and what they had read about the Moonies, convinced the Helanders that their daughter's situation required a dire remedy. On January 25 they visited Wendy and offered to take her to lunch. The "lunch" lasted for over a month: Wendy was driven to a house in Connecticut, where intensive efforts were made to convince her to leave the church. She was then moved to a house in New Jersey, where the process of deprogramming continued. After a while, she returned to her parents' home, where she enjoyed freedom of action.

During this time, say the senior Helanders, they were "terribly harassed and threatened by members of the Unification Church." Moonies telephoned them, they say, at strange hours; cult members wrote intimidating letters; Moonies' vans frequently cruised past their door. Also, during this time, Wendy signed an affidavit asking that authorities remove her from the Unification Church if she ever returned to it—the implication being that, having been subject to the Moonies' "mind-control," she might revert to her previous Moonie identity. In a notarized statement, she wrote, in part, "If in any event the Unification 'Church' or any other cult or sect psychologically kidnaps me back, I am requesting immediate action by the authorities to come and physically remove me from the cult, as, regardless of what I may say or do, I will not be acting of my own free will."

On February 25, 1975, exactly a month after her parents had "rescued" her, Wendy—who had the use of the family car—left home and returned to the Unification Church. The car was found abandoned by a roadside two miles away from her home.

Following Wendy's departure, the Helanders took her affidavit to the Washington, D.C., Superior Court, which issued a writ of habeas corpus; the Unification Church refused to produce Wendy in court, arguing that to do so would traumatize her. Furthermore, Wendy's attorney argued, Wendy had not been brainwashed and was not under the control of the church. The judge accepted as evidence a tape recording of Wendy's voice, in which she said that she was acting of her own free will and wished to remain in the church. Five ex-Moonies testified that their minds had been "overpowered" by the cult, and that they had been powerless to free themselves from the influence of the church without the intervention of parents and deprogrammers. This testimony notwithstanding, the judge dismissed the case for lack of evidence. The Helanders had suffered the first of many defeats.

Six weeks after the trial, Wendy phoned her parents and invited them to visit her at the cult's 250-acre estate in Barrytown, New York. Elton and Carolyn say that this visit convinced them that their daughter was in grave danger: "Our daughter—the girl we raised and loved—was not our daughter anymore." Believing that Wendy was in psychological bondage —and having heard the testimony of many ex-Moonies who spoke of physical and mental abuse at the hands of cult leaders —they determined to rescue their daughter again. On November 23, 1975, Carolyn and Elton, along with their daughter and their sons, went to the Moonies' Training Center in Barrytown and once again rescued ("captured," Wendy says) their daughter. For three months, the family traveled throughout seven states, convinced that cult members were searching for them.

During the course of their travels, a young man was observed staking out a house in Warwick, Rhode Island. Police were summoned by the householder, Albert Turner, the father of an ex-Moonie. The young man, David M. Byer, was arrested on charges of possessing Mace and a small shaft used in martial arts. Byer, a member of the Unification Church, told police that he believed Turner could lead him to Wendy. It was common, he said, for members of the church to search for "kidnapped" members. The case against him was dismissed on technicalities.

While Wendy regards her parents as "paranoid," it is certainly likely that Moonies were actively searching for her. She is regarded by the church as "a very important person, important because she is a symbol of our rights and our cause."

In February, 1976, with the help of another young man, Wendy fled from a "rehabilitation" house in Ohio and once again returned to the church. The Moonies attribute her escape to God's providence; the Helanders attribute it to the machinations of a Moonie "plant."

A flurry of lawsuits, charges, and countercharges followed, as a result of which the Helanders are $60,000 in debt.

Wendy Joy Helander sued the deprogrammers and Citizens Engaged in Reuniting Families, Inc. (CERF) for $9 million, charging them with wrongful imprisonment, violation of her civil rights, denial of equal protection of the law, and complaining of "physical injury, mental and emotional distress, and damage to her reputation." The suit also charged "the express and tacit connivance of police and other officials" in Wendy's "imprisonment." Wendy—whose attorney are Richard Ben-Veniste, a former Watergate prosecutor, and Jeremiah Gutman, who frequently acts in concert with the American Civil Liberties Union—named her parents as defendants; she brought suit against them for "a permanent injunction restraining . . . them from further interference with the exercise of her civil rights and liberties."*

For three years Carolyn and Elton Helander have had no contact with their daughter outside of courtrooms and legislatures. At a hearing in the Connecticut State Capitol in Hartford on March 7, 1978, Carolyn—a strong, solid, matronly-looking woman—testified with much emotion: "Not to see your child for the last three years other than in a court or the State Capitol is one of the most painful things a family can experience. . . . I would like to see some kind of legislation that can protect the family from being ripped apart." Wendy countered that "it is pathetic and sad" that people "try and blame all their problems on the Unification Church." Her parents, she said, "had no respect for me at all . . . I was treated like someone with no rights, like I was mentally retarded." When her worn and elderly father tentatively approached her, Wendy pushed him away. "Dad," she said, "just go home and follow Christ."

These are just the bare bones of the story, bits and pieces compiled from interviews with Wendy, her parents, and from court records and newspaper files.

Upon certain facts and dates all the Helanders agree. Their interpretation of the facts differs as night from day. In certain cases, the facts themselves are in dispute.

Wendy Helander claims to be happy.

Carolyn and Elton cannot understand why they have been singled out for so much suffering.

---

*The action brought against her parents was later settled when Wendy discontinued her claims against them in exchange for their agreement not to "attempt to interfere with the rights of the plaintiff to affiliate herself with any religious or other groups." The claim against CERF was also settled upon the stipulation that CERF would not "hold or detain or attempt to hold or detain the plaintiff against her will."

Wendy says the deprogramming was brutal and brutalizing.

Carolyn and Elton say the deprogramming was the only possible way to shock their daughter out of an identity imposed upon her by the demonic behavioral techniques of her masters.

Each side accuses the other of standing truth on its head.

It is possible that no one will ever know the exact truth of what happened on the afternoon of February 25, 1975, when Wendy "escaped" from home after her first deprogramming, leaving her parents' car abandoned on a roadside. According to her parents' poignant account, Wendy had been happily engaged, for several days, in redecorating her bedroom— stacking furniture in the middle of the room, puttying nail holes in the sheetrock wall, preparing to paper the wall. Carolyn says: "On the morning of the day that she disappeared, she made a huge pot of barley soup and mixed some yeast bread. She asked me to watch the dough rise and the soup boil while she drove to town to buy paint to match the wall-paper she'd chosen." The soup boiled and the dough rose, and Wendy never returned. It is the Helanders' belief that Moonies were lying in wait for Wendy, while "fund-raising" in town, and that they bent her to their will. But Wendy says her escape had been carefully calculated: "I told my mother I was going to get some paint, but actually I planned to drive to a phone booth and call the Connecticut Church Center . . . I'd found the phone number in a pamphlet in my mother's stuff. When I reached the church members, they were just going out the door—I'd phoned them just in time. I prayed and prayed, maybe for twenty minutes, till a church member came and got me. We flew to Unification headquarters in Washington. Naturally my mother will never believe this story."

Which story is true? Is Wendy a victim of brainwashing, enticed back into the church? Or did she return voluntarily?

Whom does one believe? In this, as in so many other matters, does it come down to one's instinct as to who is more credible, more "sincere"? Fortunately for the reporter, there are some external reality tests—the testimony of ex-Moonies, of mental-health experts, of disinterested observers, and of congressional investigators. Most important, perhaps, there is the *Divine Principle*—Rev. Moon's theological writings, which make understandable much that would otherwise be inexplicable. I tested everything Wendy said, and everything Carolyn and Elton Helander said, against the other evidence available . . . and still, to some extent, I felt as if I were walking through a hall of trick mirrors.

"I am your brain," Moon has told his followers. "What I wish must be your wish."

I think Wendy Helander is a victim of coercive persuasion, and that the Moonies have indeed, reprehensibly, gained control of her mind. I think it is also possible that she is complicit in her victimization. And I find her—evasive and repressed though she appears to me—enormously likable. If she were my daughter, I would want to save her.

I spent the better part of three beautiful April days with Wendy at the Unification Church's World Mission Center, in what used to be the two-thousand-room New Yorker Hotel, on Thirty-fourth Street and Eighth Avenue in New York City.

She greeted me in the once elegant, cavernous hotel lobby after I had passed the scrutiny of security guards. Bikes, and paraphernalia for the Moonies' weekly World of Hope music-and-dance Festival, were placed incongruously under giant, graceless chandeliers. We walked past an escalator to the elevator bank.

That escalator figures in Moonie lore: the taxi driver who dropped me off at the hotel had heard it rumored that a disaffected Moonie had fallen—or been pushed—to his death on that now-stationary and gratuitous (and, in the dim light, oddly sinister) escalator. Wendy's eyes narrowed when I asked her about this. In the careful, measured tones she used throughout our conversation, she told me that a Moonie had once fallen down an elevator shaft at the hotel while maintaining it—an accident, she said.

The elevator carried Wendy and me to a huge, mirrored penthouse suite. We talked in a sterile room, both cold and stuffy, from which we could see, spread out like a city of dreams, the towers of lower Manhattan, golden on this spring day, and the Hudson River, shining in the early afternoon sunlight. As I readied my tape recorder, Wendy said, "Don't play my voice to my mother. It'll make her sick. It'll make me sick." She smiled, a smile that had little to do with her words. A security guard, gun in his holster, walked in (the door remained open throughout our interviews), opened the closet, and ran his hands over my coat. "Yours?" he asked. "Yes." Scenes from Late Night movies flashed before me: two-way mirrors? I thought it was not impossible that we were being observed.

Wendy slipped in and out, catering to my desire for coffee and pleasing me with offerings: sour balls, Hershey Kisses, Fig Newtons, crystalized papaya.

She wore a cherry-red woolen dress a little too tight for her, and low-heeled, matronly shoes. (Her body, lithe in all the photographs Carolyn and Elton showed me, is beginning to thicken.) Her slip, torn, hung beneath her hem; she plucked at it continuously, seemingly unconscious of what she was doing. The Moonies choose their clothing from a collective source (individualism is discouraged even in small things), and the bright red looked incongruous on Wendy, whose scrubbed face had the look of someone who eats too much starch. She looked—how can I say this?—both set and matronly, and young and lost. It was as if I were looking at two Wendys, one image superimposing itself on another in rapid succession.

She had no conversation that did not relate expressly to her life in the church. She tried to please me, and, I think, also to manipulate me, by short-circuiting questions that displeased or alarmed her. She spoke as if from a memorized text: no small talk, no humor. I did not for a moment doubt the sincerity of her belief.

She talked freely about her parents' attempt to deprogram her; indeed, her sense of worth seemed to derive from her sense of having been persecuted—"like Jesus." She shied away nervously from questions about her indoctrination into the church, about the specifics of the three-, seven- , and twenty-one-day workshops she'd attended before making her commitment.

"Have I offended you in some way?" I asked. "I feel that you're anxious when I ask you about the workshops."

"Well, I know that what you're trying to detect is whether or not I've been brainwashed. . . ." She looked tearful: "I really *want* to tell you my experience. I've been searching all my life to hear the Divine Principle . . . it was like music to my ears, and I wanted to hear more, and . . . I *asked* if I could join, it wasn't as if anybody asked me if I wanted to join; *I* asked. I didn't know if they'd have room for me. . . ."

Her voice trailed off into vagueness when she was asked about Moon's personal wealth and his political and commercial interests; she neatly sidestepped all questions relating to the Moon organization's industrial wealth and its purported lobbying on behalf of the Republic of South Korea, taking refuge in bromides and patriotic platitudes: "God has chosen America," she said, not quite to the point, smiling sweetly.

Her grasp of Moon's convoluted theology seemed rather dim, convincing me that it was context, not content, that mattered to her: Harmony-unity-higher purpose-beautiful feelings-love-joy-peace, she recited; a litany that rendered doctrinal specifics irrelevant.

When we walked to a restaurant—a fancy restaurant, at her request, one that her lawyers had taken her to—she seemed supremely unaware of her surroundings, disassociated from her environment. We walked down squalid Eighth Avenue, and she talked about the Kingdom of Heaven. At the Spanish restaurant where we lunched, she wolfed down ice cream like a happy child having an unaccustomed treat.

What Wendy wanted most to talk about was her family— and her Family. Ironically and paradoxically, the sanctity of the family is the cornerstone of Moon's theology. Until I read the *Divine Principle,* I had difficulty understanding the way in which Wendy spoke of her parents—the animus, bitterness, hostility, and resentment that warred with pat expressions of love and gratitude and respect for her parents. It made me feel crazy, until I realized I was hearing two messages—her own feelings (hidden, perhaps, even to her), and her Master's words. Moonies are not permitted to feel resentment. So how to believe the authenticity of Wendy's "love" for her parents —particularly when she speaks of them with scorn?

Moon says: "If one of my disciples denounces his parents, he is not really my disciple. A good disciple will gain the respect of his parents. . . . When they come into our movement . . . for the first time they see something and somebody they can trust and love."

He has also been quoted as saying, "You must start over again your new life, from that point denying your past families, friends, neighbors, and relatives."

Perhaps this accounts for Wendy's own stunningly contradictory remarks.

Wendy: "I want to say, first of all, that I'm so thankful for the upbringing, the morality, the love, they gave me; I'm so thankful. I'm really grateful to my mother for encouraging me and having confidence in me. . . . I love her very much. I'm really so grateful. It's ironic that everything they've taught me has brought me to where I am. And that's why I'm so grateful."

"Junk," "trash," "garbage," "hogwash," Wendy said when I told her her mother's version of what brought her to where she was now.

But: "My mother, yes, she trusted me."

Later: "They don't trust my thinking, my feelings, my words. They think I've been *hypnotized*—all this junk, this scientific garble and junk they talk."

Still later: "They blame everything on the church, but mistrust started in my childhood."

But: "I was far from being alienated from my parents before this deprogramming began."

"They'll tell you their sob story, how I never come home. . . . See, my mother's very emotional. Just because I'm not crying when I tell you this story doesn't mean I'm a cold, emotionless person."

"I had to wait till I was eighteen in order to do anything on my own. . . . My own parents—wrecking everything."

"I got along better with my parents than my brothers and sister did."

"I never really got to know my parents. . . . We never communicated. We never did. We went on vacations together, but she was always sick, we'd always be taking care of *her*. I felt bad that she was sick so much. . . . My father? The only thing we ever did together was eat dinner."

"The only thing they care about is what the neighbors will think."

"I want to unify my family. I want to have God as head of my family."

"They were so crass."

"I was born by them, I was raised by them, I was taught by

them, and I'll always be grateful to them for everything. My whole upbringing. I'll always be thankful to them."

"My mother tries to get pity upon herself and convince people it's all so terribly sad, what's happened; they're trying to paint a picture like I was some little insane child who had gone retarded or something."

"I'm always praying for my parents because I know how much they are suffering. I love them."

"My mother has the feeling that I was really out of the church, but that somehow my mind just kind of slipped back. . . . Because if I'm being controlled that takes all the responsibility off of them. They can have a scapegoat, they can tell everybody, Well, our relationship was so beautiful, we were getting along fine—and then suddenly the Unification Church whisked her away. . . ."

"I can't say to them . . . I want to say to them, 'How well did you ever really know me?' "

In exchange for a family she describes as status-conscious, as both uncommunicative and overprotective, as deceived by deprogrammers and the media ("My parents are very righteous people who are scared and guilty"), and in exchange for siblings who quarreled, what does Wendy think she has gained? A Family that is not self-centered, not materialistic, a Family that shares "a message of hope," and a mandate to "save America." Her ambivalence toward her natural family was matched by her enormous, unqualified devotion to Sun Myung Moon: "Now —here—no other person, no other group can claim . . . so many people from all over the world . . . just a beautiful experience . . . so wonderful."

During the entire time I spent with Wendy, she never once inquired into the welfare of her own family, with whom she knew I'd spent hours on the phone. She never once asked about her brothers, her sister, or her parents—who spend virtually all their time consumed with *her* welfare. She spoke of them as if they were abstractions—almost as if they were dead.

Wendy's account of her "conversion," or indoctrination, into the Unification Church is sketchy. She was approached, on campus, by a group of "idealistic young people" who invited her to dinner. She met at dinner one Dr. Bergman, who lectured on science and health. Encouraged by his "philosophy," she went to a three-day workshop, a seven-day workshop, a twenty-one-day workshop, where "we had sports . . . we sang. . . . We studied *Divine Principle.* It was like summer camp. We shared together. We had discussion groups together. . . . It all seemed very natural to me; it was very natural to be with the people, they were all so sincere. Everything was so beautiful. I really felt the purity of these people. God showed me my life."

When I asked Wendy for specifics, she said, "You can't analyze it. You can't say what happened this day and what happened the next day and what happened this minute and what were you thinking of at the time." Is this an impairment of memory? "No; it's a whole act of God."

Other people have not been so reluctant to analyze the means of approach and the indoctrination methods employed by Moonies.

All ex-Moonies agree that the approach is duplicitous. Moonies never identify themselves as Moonies until the potential convert has been subjected to "love-bombings," or the blandishments of the communards in a Moonie center. They tailor their approach to the victim. Sometimes they describe themselves as an "international peace group," other times they pose as members of a neighborhood community health project. In my own urban neighborhood, where Moonies endeared themselves to merchants by building and setting up tree planters—for a "contribution"—and where they are now active in a local block association, they set up a storefront "nutritional, diet, and health center"; nothing in their literature indicated to the passersby that the center had anything to do with the Unification Church.

The case of Steve Hassan, a twenty-five-year-old ex-Moonie who is a part-time deprogrammer, is typical. Nineteen, a student at Queens College in New York City, he was approached by people calling themselves members of an "International One-World Campaign." Steve was led to believe that it was some kind of international students' coalition—which appealed to his "idealistic, perfectionist, Utopianist" temperament; no mention was made of religion, Moon, the Unification Church, or of Christianity. Steve is Jewish. (While Christ figures in Moonie theology, mainline churches regard the cult as heretical.) Hassan accepted an invitation to visit a commune; he was not impressed with the conversation there, but he, like Wendy, *was* impressed with the "love" shown within the interracial group, and with the sympathy they showered upon him. He accepted an invitation to a three-day workshop.

The Moonies' approach to potential recruits finds its justification in their theology. Evil has deceived goodness into evil, the theory goes; so goodness must deceive evil into goodness in order for God's will to be accomplished. As Hassan notes, this is an invitation to deceive based on the premise that God needs to steal Satan's children back. Moonies are encouraged to practice "Heavenly Deception." (This may account for my feeling that Wendy was both sincere *and* trying to con me.)

Much controversy swirls around conversion of recruits: Is it accomplished through "brainwashing"? Scientists argue endlessly about what constitutes brainwashing, if indeed brainwashing can be said to exist at all. (What is an "unwashed" brain?) But it is not disputed that behavior can be modified and dramatically altered by coercive persuasion. Among the characteristics of coercive persuasion are: isolating the victim in a controlled environment and limiting all forms of communication with the outside world; infantilizing and humiliating the victim; inspiring guilt; convincing him that his only hope for salvation lies in the approval of the group; inducing sleep deprivation along with a change of diet.

Chris Edwards is only one of scores of ex-Moonies who believe that all these techniques are employed by the Unification Church. In his book *Crazy for God* * Edwards describes the way a Moonie workshop group is designed to bewilder, and finally absorb, a newcomer: "Family members squeezed the hands of bewildered guests, pumped the hands up and down, and jumped in rhythm to screams of 'Choo-choo-choo, choo-choo-choo, choo-choo-choo. Yay, Yay—Pow!' " Newcomers were assigned groups and scurried around "like children inside a circle. . . . 'These are the Last Days, yes, these are the Last Days,' the Family chanted. . . . The men stood up and the women promptly sat down. Then the men plopped down and the women popped up. . . . The group ran through an entire repertoire of songs, each one sillier than the next. These were interspersed with religious songs proclaiming some sort of new Messiah." Edwards found this behavior ludicrous, but he held on because of his deep longing for community. Shouting and clapping, he felt his sense of involvement growing; he felt "a desire to merge into this family, this group, this game, to become part of this vibrant, loving circle." Part skeptic, he also saw these carryings-on as childlike innocence; he believed his obligation was to disavow the rational part of his nature, which had not brought him happiness, and to trust and to obey. Besides games—including Simon Says and "hokey-pokey"—there were skits, playlets illustrating themes of despair and hope. Guests were "tickled, mocked, poked, or otherwise treated as . . . naughty little children by . . . supervisor[s]."

*Prentice-Hall, 1979

Many complied with their supervisors' commands "out of sheer embarrassment."

It wasn't all fun and games. Satan was very real to them. Moonies claim actually to see demons (Moon, on the other hand, claims to speak to angels). When Moonies fall asleep during lectures, fellow Moonies rap them on the forehead with their knuckles to get rid of "sleepy spirits." They sleep in sleeping bags on the ground in order to shake off the "sleepy spirits" quickly in the morning.

Edwards was not left alone for a moment—not even to go to the bathroom; his sleeping and eating habits were regulated and controlled. His watch was taken away from him, so he had no sense of time. The role of the Moonies "was to tease me with their love, dishing it out and withdrawing it as they saw fit. My role was not to question but to be their child, dependent on them for affection. The kiddie games, the raucous singing, the silly laughter, were all part of a scenario geared to help me assume my new identity." Soon he experienced "an ecstatic merger into the mass, the pleasure that accompanies loss of ego." He was committed to the group before he understood the theology of the group. By the time he learned the doctrine, it was too late for him to reject it. He accepted Moon as the new Messiah. Because he had learned to believe that everything around him was evil, he imagined that his doubts were caused by Satan. When his hand, hurt in arduous physical labor, became inflamed and septic, he was able to accept the doctrine that he was paying "indemnity" for his sins, just as he was able to accept the idea that Moon would soon be the most powerful man in America, and that he—Edwards—could change the world. The Moonies had loved him to death, controlled him to death. He had been fed with despair, and zapped with hope—the only hope, the Family. He had become part of a "classless universe of giggling children," holding Satan at bay by obeying the rules— the rules all the silly games had prepared him to accept. Edwards concludes that Moonies "destroy all your other roles, your identity as an individual, and they only allow the child to break through." The "child" is obedient to the Father.

Bolstered by similar accounts from other ex-Moonies, Carolyn and Elton Helander have no doubt that their daughter went through a dehumanizing process much like Chris Edwards's. They believe absolutely that Wendy has surrendered her former identity, and that she is a victim of brainwashing.

The third time I saw Wendy Helander, she showed me a room she said was hers in the World Mission Center at the New Yorker Hotel. It was cramped and narrow; one dirty window had an oblique view of the Hudson. There were seven unpacked cartons and eight dead cactus plants. On the cover of the single bed were two stuffed monkeys, entwined.

In the living room of the Helander house there is a framed needlework motto: Loving Is Giving. The rambling house has the accidental nature of a house made for happy, spontaneous living. My eye swept over chintz, overstuffed armchairs, piano sheet music, family photos, bird prints. There are bird feeders all over the green lawn; we saw a blue jay and a robin. The asparagus plants were ripening.

Joel, the Helanders' oldest son, made a brief appearance before he received a call to serve on ambulance duty—he is twenty-seven, and he still lives at home, writing a history of his shore community. Somewhat dry and pedantic, he is also friendly and courteous. Forrest, the younger son, who is working in town until he enters college, came in excitedly—he had seen a deer in the woods. Open and cheerful, he is also shy; he asked gruffly and sadly about Wendy. Their sister Holly was working in Boston. The pleasant house was informed by Wendy's absence.

From the moment she met me, Carolyn Helander, a mass

of nervous energy, bombarded me with questions about
Wendy: "How does she look? Does she seem healthy? happy?
What did she have for lunch? Did she talk about us? Do you
think they're holding her there physically?" The Helanders are
starved for information about their daughter. Wendy writes,
perfunctorily and not more than every few months, to her
parents, who write to her every week; they cannot be sure she
receives their letters. She simply assures them of her happiness,
and she never answers their questions or responds to anything
they say, nor does she acknowledge the gifts they send. It is as
if her past were dead. (Wendy had anticipated her parents'
charge that her leaders instructed her as to when to write and
what to say. Maybe, she said, sometimes somebody will suggest
—just a tiny suggestion—what they should write . . . "and then
parents go and make a whole big deal about it.")

The cruelest charge Wendy had leveled against her mother,
who is a deaconess at the local First Congregational Church
(Elton Helander, a mechanical engineer with his own small
business, is a deacon and church treasurer), is that Carolyn
Helander had "found a cause" and was getting "juice" from
the family drama: "She didn't have too much confidence and
she wasn't popular or anything. I think in a way now this is her
'reign.' This is her time—people come to her and ask her for
help." Indeed, Carolyn, a former elementary-school teacher,
does spend much of her time working with a network of parents in similar straits. But her shocked and unhappy response
to her daughter's accusation was, "She thought I *needed* this?
Oh, I've had so many other things I've wanted to do with my
life—*no*. Yes, I talk a lot. We can't afford to be quiet—for the
sake of the others. Elton suffers more than I do, I think,
because he's a quiet man."

Wendy had presented a picture of a strong domineering
woman, and of an undemonstrative father given to bouts of
temper. Carolyn says she could not have endured this ordeal

without the quiet strength of her husband. Having talked to this gentle sixty-two-year-old man with strong convictions, I am inclined to believe Carolyn; and I do not believe that she is feasting on her troubles.

Wendy spoke very little of her father—and then only to accuse him of "hugging" her unexpectedly and inappropriately before the deprogrammings. She seemed to feel deprived of paternal affection. Her animus toward her mother was far more pronounced; she was also more directly connected to her mother, if the amount of accusatory talk she leveled at Carolyn is any indication.

Neither Carolyn nor Elton Helander was defensive about their parenting: all children have problems, they said, and so did Wendy—normal problems, as far as they could see. They both felt that lines of communication had been open among them, though, as Carolyn pointed out, "Every child is a mystery to her parents to some degree." With the sad, immemorial cry of all parents for whom something has gone hopelessly awry, they said, "We did the best we knew how."

For Wendy, their best was not good enough. To their daughter's heated accusation that Carolyn had once confessed to having religious doubts, Carolyn replied, "Of course I sometimes doubt, and I shared my doubts with Wendy; why not? Doesn't *everybody* doubt?" "Everybody" may doubt (the saints did); Moonies do not. They live in a world of rigid certainties, they have answers to all questions—a world view that interprets all of history for them, that gives them a sure hope for the future. Wendy's chief grievance against her parents seems to be that they did not provide her with a cohesive world view, a narrow simplicity.

According to Moonie doctrine, America is "the foundation of God's blessing prepared for the Lord of the Second Advent. . . The nation in which our Lord comes must be the front line of both God and Satan . . . where . . . life and death and good and evil confront one another. . . . Where our Lord comes is where the two powers of democracy and Communism confront one another; it is the focal point of both God's love and Satan's hate . . . the 38th parallel in the Korean peninsula. . Korea will be the center of world salvation."

Wendy claims to have had prescience of this long before she became a Moonie. When her parents took her to Plymouth Rock, she says, she had a beautiful "spiritual" experience. (She was fourteen.) When missionaries at her Congregational church showed slides of their activities in Korea, she had a beautiful, "spiritual" experience. (She was in Sunday School.) Is this hindsight? Elton and Carolyn shake their heads in puzzlement when they hear these stories.

Wendy's claim that her parents were overprotective evokes a bewildered reaction: "Did she tell you she went to France twice? Once when she was sixteen? That we allowed it? Oh, yes, and she wrote reams of letters to us then, she wasn't alienated from us then. . . . She told you we wouldn't let her come home from work alone? Didn't she tell you she worked at Howard Johnson till three in the morning and that would have meant coming home alone on dark country roads? Of *course* we drove her home. . . . They have turned her against us."

I don't know if Wendy's parents—Yankee conservatives— are the parents I would have chosen for myself, but I do think the Moonies have managed to magnify minor grievances so that Wendy can justify her separation from her parents. This is more than a young woman's understandable wish for independence (which could have been satisfied by Wendy's attendance at the University of New Hampshire); Wendy, after all, sued her parents . . . for deprogramming.

It is about the deprogrammings that Wendy and her parents most violently disagree—both as to facts and as to motives.

This is a summary of Wendy's horrifying account of her deprogrammings: Her parents came to Barrytown, ostensibly to take her to lunch. "When my dad met me, he gave me this kind of false hug. He never hugged me before. He gave me this kind of false hug, and he said, 'Oh, Mom's in the car and she's sick.' I got into the car and we drove to a small supermarket; there was another car waiting there—my brother was in it and two of my uncles and my cousin. I thought, Why are they all waiting in this parking lot? I didn't want to be suspicious of them. When I asked my dad where we were going, he said, 'Didn't Mom tell you that we were going to talk to some people?' She hadn't. They drove me to a house where I met Ted Patrick. [Patrick is a deprogrammer who claims to have deprogrammed over a thousand cult-involved kids; he was one of the defendants in Wendy's $9 million lawsuit.] I was in a state of shock.

"Patrick said, 'You've been held under mind control and I'm here to bring you back to your normal state.' First he spoke kind of softly, then he started shouting, 'You've been a prostitute for Moon and you've been worshiping Satan and snakes, and you've been acting as a tool of the Devil. Look at your parents, you're destroying your parents. You've left your family, dadadadadada.' All these people were standing around me, looking at me like I had no mind, as if I was some kind of mysterious creature who'd been zapped by some outer-space monster. Patrick was yelling at me and ridiculing me and shouting Bible verses like *Honor thy Father and thy Mother*. He told my mother not to look at me because I was a 'zombie, nothing but a hypnotized zombie.' They guarded the door, and Patrick said they'd keep me there for as long as it would take for me to give up my faith. I was really crying, because I realized how he was doing damage to my parents, making them feel guilty.

"During this time I realized the value of Reverend Moon

like I never had before. I really felt protected by God. I felt very calm, and I knew I wouldn't panic. I used silence as a weapon—my mother had taught me how to do that. I wanted to pacify them, to get them off my back."

At this point, on the second day of the first deprogramming, Wendy signed her affidavit asking for release from the Unification Church if she were ever to return. Her parents evidently believed the deprogramming had "taken." "But if you look at the circumstances I was under," Wendy says, "that paper is illegal; I signed it under duress, as a victim of kidnapping. I begged my mother not to ask me to sign it.

"If you are deprogrammed and decide to go back to the church, they call that 'floating' [some psychiatrists do say Moonies float back and forth between identities], so if I'd sing church songs, hymns, they'd say, 'No, don't do that—mind control will slip back in.' It was horrible."

Wendy's account of her second deprogramming shows it to have been even more bizarre than her first, and is more condemnatory of her parents:

"Their love is like an uncertain, unnatural love—like my father never used to hug me, never at all. He came and put his arms around me, kind of shaking, and . . . it was just all very strange. They came for a picnic lunch, and we decided to go for a walk. A car stopped behind us on an isolated road, and two men got out, and, together with my mother and father and my sister, they pushed me in the car. I was screaming and they were pushing. I heard my mother say, 'Stop her mouth, stop her mouth, she's making too much noise!' My brother stuffed a net in my mouth. I didn't know it was my brother—my younger brother—because his face was painted black and he had a fake moustache on, and this old beat-up hat. . . . When we got out of the car, I started screaming again and they gagged me again; they carried me in by the arms and legs to the basement of a house where the deprogramming began. All my parents could say was, 'It's for your own good. You'll understand some day.'

"I was thinking, What must Jesus have gone through? He was seized and mocked and totally humiliated. What was his attitude, how could he overcome? So I tried to be like him— I didn't want to be angry, I just wanted to endure.

"The deprogrammers said, 'Look at your father, he looks so terrible and drawn-out, how could you do such a thing to him, you're killing him slowly, how can you be so awful?' They really use the guilt thing on you. They try to turn you against Reverend Moon; they tell you he's just money hungry and you're a prostitute for him. . . . They babble on, the same old junk, like maybe twenty hours a day, maybe thirty hours at a time.

"They brought me to the apartment of a psychiatrist where people were smoking dope.

"I just cried. If I let them know I was praying—if I shut my eyes or something—they'd say that praying or singing hymns would keep my mind in Reverend Moon's control.

"They used filthy, just absolutely filthy, words.

"They took away all my clothes, because they said my old clothes would make me 'float.' They didn't even let me sleep on the floor. I like to sleep on the floor, I always did; and in the church centers we do because it's easier, you know, and you can fit more people in." (You can also shake the "sleepy spirits" off quickly.)

"They kept me up like thirty or thirty-five hours. They dripped water on my nose to keep me awake. They brought in a big kitchen knife and said, 'Wendy, you're killing yourself slowly, why don't you just get it over with?' Like they were taunting me. My parents didn't know this was going on. And if I told them, they wouldn't believe me. They can't believe me, they think I'm making it up.

"They asked me every five minutes, 'What are you thinking

now? Do you feel any hatred toward the Unification Church? What's going through your mind now? Do you feel you've been deceived by your church?' And finally they told me I would have to go through 'intense rehabilitation.' I thought, Oh my gosh, this is it, you guys accuse the Unification Church of watching people and following people and brainwashing people? I pinned it right back on them.

"And in the rehabilitation center they try to take your spirit away from you and break your virginity.

"Well, my relationship with Jesus was even deepened so that I could understand that *He* had to suffer what *I* suffered."

I asked the Helanders to comment on some of Wendy's charges.

"Oh, heavens, yes," Carolyn said, "Ted Patrick did swear, he used awful words. I wouldn't have approved if I knew he was going to say those things. But on the other hand he had to use shock treatment. Wendy isn't used to that kind of language, and he wanted to shock her into thinking, get her mad, get her angry, bring her out of it.

"Ted Patrick isn't a mercenary, as far as we're concerned. We paid him fourteen hundred dollars, out of which he paid for a round-trip ticket to California. People don't understand that the majority of deprogrammers are ex-cult members who don't want other people to suffer. We paid kids who helped us because you can't expect them to give their time without ever earning a penny. It isn't as if the deprogrammers come to parents looking for business; *we* go to *them.*"

Why all the cloak-and-dagger stuff?

"Well, we were very green then, and Ted Patrick suggested that we take a backup car along, in case Wendy got violent; some do get violent—some try to jump out of the car. It was security. But as we look back on it now, there was no earthly reason we needed all those people in two cars: Wendy was so exhausted from fund-raising, she couldn't have jumped out if she wanted to. . . . Did she tell you that we told her before the first deprogramming that we wanted her to talk to someone outside the cult? Did she tell you that she agreed? She *didn't* tell you?

"You know, everything that *they* are guilty of, they turn around and accuse *us* of. Now they're saying *we* brainwashed the kid!"

(If so much were not at stake, it would be of academic interest, and even a little amusing, to see how each side routinely accuses the other of the same things.)

The Helanders—who were not entirely forthcoming, litigation having convinced them of the merits of caution—deny that Wendy was deprived of sleep. "She did stay up late, but it's not true that she didn't sleep for thirty or thirty-five hours," Elton says. "We were always close enough to her to know if she was being brutalized—and she wasn't." Did deprogrammers drip water on Wendy's nose to keep her awake? "Well, who knows," Carolyn says wearily, "I mean, that's fairly benign. I don't know that they did that, but what if they had? I felt the former members knew best how to relate to Wendy; I was there, in the same house, though not necessarily in the same room with her, all the time, and I am satisfied that she was not abused. We couldn't conspire to abuse a daughter we love." Her parents also deny that Wendy was brought to the apartment of a psychiatrist where dope was used: "We did take her, at her own request, to a psychiatrist in a state hospital in Vermont. There was no apartment, and there was certainly no dope; we don't approve of drugs." Deeply hurt, they ferociously denied the suggestion that sexual intimacy among cult members was encouraged as part of the rehabilitation program. "Sex," Carolyn says, "is used as part of mind control in the cults. There they are again, accusing us exactly of what destructive cults are guilty of. When a boy defects from a cult, a girl is sent to lure him back; when a girl leaves, a boy tries to entice her back." With equal fervor they denied that she was gagged: "A former member tells us that they make up stories, and each one tries to top the other because the more horrible the story the more heroic they become in the eyes of other cult members."

Wendy had said that her parents were "scared and guilty" during the deprogramming. Yes, Elton said, they were "scared"—frightened because of what had become of her and what she would have to undergo to assume her "former identity." Guilty? No. "What's the alternative to deprogramming?" Elton asked. "There is none." Carolyn agreed that the remedy was appropriate to the malady. "The real professionals are the kids who have experienced it. And I have yet to see any kid come out of a cult and say he had *not* been brainwashed. Their minds have been raped. . . .

"Why doesn't Wendy have any contact with her family? She hasn't called us in three years. We can't 'kidnap' her over the telephone.

"We loved her so much, we can't love her more."

As if to prove their love (I didn't require any convincing), the Helanders showed me pictures of Wendy baking a cake during her deprogramming: "Does she *look* abused?" And they showed me a picture of Elton, trying hard to maintain a semblance of normalcy, in a red Santa Claus suit, carrying on a family tradition . . . although the family would probably never be the same again. The family photo album came out. I saw dozens of snapshots of a silken-haired, buoyant-looking Wendy (whose hair is chopped short now, presumably as protection against vanity). Carolyn, as if to reassure herself that, although she didn't even know where her daughter was living, she still had something of her left, showed me a beautiful quilt Wendy had made (and which, according to Elton, she had clung to during a deprogramming). I saw material Wendy had batiked, clothes she had designed (it was hard for me to believe that those subtle batiks had been executed by the monomaniacal ideologue I'd met in the New Yorker Hotel); a music box Elton and Carolyn had given Wendy as a birthday present; term papers and poems, bound in plastic. Wendy in her junior year of high school writes about Sin and Isolation, Good and Evil, in the novels of Hawthorne—her work is intellectually rigorous, nothing like the mushy-minded platitudes she uttered at the hotel. The poems, lyrical, are about loneliness, magic, and transformations. They are written in a fine calligraphic hand; now—in notes to me—her handwriting is rounded, babyish, unformed. Are there clues here to what Wendy has become? I cannot find any.

Before I leave, Carolyn and Elton give me a small package for Wendy: a rain scarf, a letter from an aunt, a box of stationery—the envelopes stamped, ready for letters that will probably never come. They do not expect to hear from Wendy that she has received it; nor do they.

I am entirely convinced of the passionate sincerity of Carolyn and Elton Helander, and of their devotion to their daughter, and of the selflessness of their attempts to rescue her. But they did not entirely persuade me of the appropriateness of deprogramming (although I know that scores, if not hundreds, of ex-cult members are grateful for having been deprogrammed); nor did they entirely succeed in convincing me that all of Wendy's charges were inaccurate.

Almost no theologian is willing to come out in favor of deprogramming, although the Unification Church has been denounced by leaders of all major religious groups, including the American Jewish Committee, the National Council of Churches, and the Roman Catholic Church. The New York

City Council of Churches rejected the church's request for membership, in part because of Moon's assuming the role of Messiah. James LaBar, Director of Communications of the Roman Catholic Archdiocese of New York, denounced the Unification Church on four grounds: close allegiance to a person rather than to God; an inordinate preoccupation with the acquisition of money, which is used not for the poor or charity but for the enrichment of the leader; deceptive practices in recruitment; and deprivation of freedom within the group. Rabbi Marc H. Tannenbaum asks: "Why are Reverend Moon and his political backers resorting to the Nazi model of exploiting anti-Semitism for ideological purposes?" The minister of Wendy's own First Congregational Church in Guilford called the cult "demonic," because it "undercut the ethic of suffering love, the room for diversity in the midst of unity."

But many theologians, as well as scientists and lawyers, find deprogramming techniques repugnant, and contrary to constitutional guarantees.

The Governing Board of the National Council of Churches argues that "religious liberty . . . is grossly violated by forcible abduction and protracted efforts to change a person's religious commitments by duress. Kidnapping for ransom is heinous indeed, but kidnapping to compel religious deconversion is equally criminal."

Even one of Moon's most outspoken critics, activist Rabbi Maurice Davis of White Plains, New York, acknowledges that deprogramming can be just as brutal as the alleged brainwashing. "And if it doesn't work," he tells parents, "you may lose your child."

Ira Glasser of the American Civil Liberties Union argues that if cult members can be deprogrammed, the religious liberties of all of us are put in jeopardy: a daughter who enters a convent, a son of a secular family who returns to Orthodox Judaism, may be next.

But Moonies have been duplicitously recruited, and brainwashed, their parents protest!

Richard Delgado, Professor of Law at UCLA, is convinced that some remedy must be available to parents: "If someone ropes you in and brings you to a doctor who prescribes something that he doesn't tell you is poison or may kill you, the doctor has to be stopped!" Delgado, however, prefers remedies "less harsh, less risky" than confrontational deprogramming. He suggests a preventive remedy—a law that would require all proselytizers to identify themselves, a kind of "truth in advertising" applied to salesmen of cults. Because Delgado feels there is no "informed consent" on the part of the new Moonie recruit, he would like it to be legally incumbent upon the proselytizer to explain to a potential convert where a summary of beliefs and practices can be found—and to do so immediately. If groups have been found to have violated public confidence by deception and manipulation, converts should be released, he believes, "into the world, for a short period of time for advice, perspective, sleep, talk. If after the cooling-off period they want to go back, okay. If all else fails," he adds, "then deprogramming, in certain cases, may be the last recourse." He would first have parents exhaust all other legal remedies. They might, for example, apply to the courts for a conservatorship order, issued when a judge has rendered an impartial decision that the person in question is "mentally incapacitated, gravely disabled, compromised."

Jeremiah Gutman, one of Wendy's attorneys, dismisses Delgado's suggestions as unconstitutional and unworkable. "If a young woman joins a cult," he says, "no matter how she got there, she *is* there, and she has a right to be there. She has a right to be manipulated if she lends herself to manipulation. Parents who deprogram their children are really saying, Come back to normal social life *as defined by us.*" It is his contention that in most cases the parents are "materialistic, hedonistic, and capitalistic"—and that that is precisely what the young people are rebelling against.

This harsh indictment of parents is matched in fervor by ex-Moonies, who make the strongest case for deprogramming: "Moon is actually training an army; the members are trained to kill and die for Moon." "Behind all those smiling young faces are mindless automatons . . . in an induced psychotic state. . . . Parents who love their children cannot bear to see them completely change behavior patterns . . . completely devoid of spontaneity."

Ex-Moonie Steve Hassan was deprogrammed by four ex-Moonies—one of whom he had converted; he is "grateful to all of them. The purpose of deprogramming," he says, "is not to tell you how to think or what to believe, but to evaluate theological information contradicting Moon. A good deprogrammer—there are some charlatans, of course—also documents the political corruption of the Unification Church and its involvement with the Korean CIA. Deprogramming gives Moonies time away from the group and the emotional support they need to reenter the world—a world that has been made to look evil. Moon ordered everybody to see *The Exorcist:* God made this movie, he said, to show you that if you leave, the evil world will get you and you will be demon-possessed as this girl was." Hassan insists that he was not physically abused by deprogrammers: "*I* abused *them*. In all the deprogrammings I've been part of, it's the Moonies who assault or abuse. . . . If you've made attempts to have a daughter come home and listen rationally and she refuses, what else is there but deprogramming?"

He says his deprogramming saved his life.

Dr. John G. Clark, Assistant Professor of Psychiatry, Harvard Medical School and Massachusetts General Hospital, agrees that the "thought-reformed" state induced by Moonies on "naïve, uninformed subjects" can be reversed "in a large number of cases, [bringing] a fairly rapid return to the old organization of the mind, a 'repersonalization,' and . . . with it the old language skills and memories, original personal relationship patterns and, of course, the old problems." Dr. Clark, who has seen kids brought in by parents when they were wavering and has seen them in hospitals, physically or mentally ill, cannot legally recommend deprogramming, although he believes Moonies do develop a "second personality in forced conversion." Nevertheless, he sees deprogramming as "a benign process on balance because the intent is different from that of brainwashing—the intent is to reunite the individual with his or her own mind; the intent is not to control, but to set free."

Clark enters a chilling caveat for Moonies who stay within the organization for a protracted period of time: the longer they remain, he says, the more their ability to establish real intimacy and to think rationally is impaired—the thought-reform process may be irreversible.

This is what the Helanders are so dreadfully afraid of.

Closely aligned to the problems of deprogramming are problems surrounding the First Amendment, which, designed to ensure freedom of religious belief, is "choking us," according to Carolyn Helander.

When the findings of the Fraser congressional subcommittee were released in 1978, the Helanders and other Moonie parents believed that at last they were seeing light at the end of the tunnel. The Fraser findings, while somewhat ambiguous, tended toward the conclusion that Moon's ultimate goal was temporal power. It is easy to conclude, from a reading of the report, that the Unification Church is a political movement masquerading as a religion. On the other hand, it is also possible to read the report in such a way as to conclude that the cult is a genuine religious movement that shrewdly makes use of politics and commerce to accomplish religious goals.

If the church is a political entity, it cannot lay claim to First Amendment protection.

Attorney Jeremiah Gutman argues that, while the report's findings were indeed condemnatory, "Even if you are rich and have an industrial empire you're entitled to First Amendment protection. If you're an *agent* of another government you forfeit your rights to exercise freedom of religion; but if you act, as the Unification Church does, in a way that is *mutually beneficial* with a foreign government, you do not forfeit First Amendment rights. If there is a specific violation of a specific law, then the courts or the government agency involved should prosecute for that specific violation: private individuals have no right to take unto themselves police functions. The courts have consistently ruled that if there is a less drastic alternative to cutting off religious freedom, it must be used. The courts have ruled against groups who refuse to inoculate their adherents, groups that practice polygamy or that refuse blood transfusions for minors—because in those cases public morality was offended. But it is ridiculous to 'outlaw' a cult on the grounds that it is a cult: Christianity was a cult; the cult of the Madonna resulted in the beatification of Mary."

The Helanders regard all of this as so much nonsense: "If there is a murder in a church, are you not going to investigate because it's a religion?" They cannot understand why "this hands-off approach should be condoned just because the Moonies claim to be a legitimate religion."

Robert Boettcher, Staff Director for the Fraser Committee, emphatically states that "First Amendment protection doesn't apply to the Unification Church, because there have been violations of law. The Committee recommended that the Executive Branch set up an interagency investigative task force composed of the IRS, the Justice Department, the SEC, the

Treasury Department, and Immigration and Naturalization. No such force has been formed. Federal agencies feel inhibited when churches are involved. There is also the possibility that since the Korean CIA was the creature of our own CIA, there is some reluctance on that score." Boettcher does feel that there is "a slowly growing investigatory mood." According to his sources, the Justice Department is planning to look hard at the findings of the Committee. The SEC is taking another look at the church's investments. And the Immigration and Naturalization Service is pressing for alien Moonies to leave the country. New York City has denied tax exemption for certain Unification Church properties.

None of this gets the Helanders their daughter back.

Meanwhile, as lawyers and legislators quarrel, there is Wendy. Idealistic, as many Moonies are, rejoicing in her singularity, living in her "ideal community," claiming to feel "new hope, new life," living a totally controlled and regulated life, "preparing for the Second Coming," singing and doing calisthenics and celebrating her "childlike innocence" under totalitarian leadership, fund-raising, street "witnessing," recruiting on campuses, working with her lawyers—and, I suspect, taking pleasure from the status her $9 million lawsuit afforded her—a stranger to her parents . . . claiming, "I am more myself than I ever was."

Why Wendy?

When Wendy was seventeen, she put an ad in *The Mother Earth News: I'm a girl of seventeen who's graduating in June and looking for a summer job in the country in exchange for a little money to use in continuing my education. . . . I will do almost anything to get close to nature and to good healthy people. A vegetarian that respects the natural laws of the universe, I'm disillusioned by the amount of spiritual illness in the present world.*

Many young people who join cults have in common a desire for things to be better—"to be right," as Wendy says; they share a disillusionment with things as they are. Unhappiness with the status quo—a hunger for the transcendental—is not in itself pathological. On the contrary, it might be argued that there is a human need for community that is unsatisfied in a fragmented, materialistic, secular society.

In his classic work *The Varieties of Religious Experience* William James said that he believed both "healthy" souls and "sick" souls were drawn to religion. Dr. John Clark says that "while a great many converts" he has studied "suffered emotional troubles during their earlier years and have led disordered lives, another large group, about 40%, had never demonstrated any signs of mental illness. Some came from disturbed families; others did not."

Moon, playing on the increased longing for certainty in troubled times, has been able to attract to his closed community intelligent young men and women, many the children of lapsed Catholics and nonpracticing Jews, most middle- to upper-middle class.

While it would please most of us if we could believe that only people with a pathological need to succumb to absolute authority were vulnerable to the ploys of charismatic leaders, it is possible that it is the best and the brightest of our young people who are drawn into cults. Moonies may be casualties of an apathetic, self-centered generation, finding themselves in times of despair and frustration susceptible to promises of deliverance. If a void exists in spiritual life, the demonic may fill the void.

Wendy Helander says she had been looking into that void all her life—until the *Divine Principle* found her.

What this suggests to me is that any youngster who is not deeply rooted in a religious belief that he has made his own rather than accepted blindly as part of his parents' cultural equipment, or any youngster who is not committed to a satisfying ideological or humanitarian cause, or not lovingly involved in a community—religious or secular—with a defined purpose, may be susceptible to the Moonies—if he is approached at a time of personal dislocation, depression, disorientation, or despair.

The pastor of the Helanders' church says: "The Helanders' torment could be ours. It could be mine."

It would be absurd to act on the premise that anyone who seeks spiritual meaning is crazy, and that the Moonies are just a little crazier. Just as there are "sick souls" and "healthy souls," there are sick religions and healthy religions. If we deny the validity of all absolutes, we leave the field open to mischievous charlatans and psychopaths—like Jim Jones, and, some would say, like Sun Myung Moon. We ought instead to recognize that longing for the transcendental is a reality of the human condition, and not one to be scorned. We have to stop being embarrassed by religion before we can begin to come to grips with the cults.

But for those already lost to the cults, it may be too late. What of the Helanders' anguish? Have they exhausted their remedies? They carry on valiantly, writing to Wendy, talking, always talking, about their daughter—and perhaps their busyness helps to keep despair at bay. They look for hope everywhere. They grasp at straws. After telling their story to one reporter, Elton Helander said, "Maybe you'll be able to do what the courts cannot do." That is so sad. They cannot allow themselves to believe that Wendy is lost to them.

On Monday, May 14, the Unification Church's newspaper, *News World*, announced that Sun Myung Moon had "matched and engaged" 1410 of his followers.

Wendy Helander was one of the couples engaged on Mother's Day at the New Yorker Hotel.

After the "matching"— or the "blessing"— couples (few of

whom have any prior knowledge of each other) wait until it pleases Moon for them to be married—a period usually lasting for two years. (Moon married 1800 couples in a mass ceremony in Seoul in 1975; he has announced that another mass marriage will be held in 1981.) The marriage ceremony is regarded as a combination of "baptism, taking of holy orders, and matrimony." After they are wed, couples may not engage in sexual intercourse for forty days, and then they are not infrequently separately assigned to serve in different locations. Ex-Moonies say that children that result from these arranged marriages are placed in communal child-care centers. Romantic love is regarded by the church as decadent.

In April, when I first spoke to Wendy, she told me she was not "ready" for marriage, that she was "preparing herself for growth to perfection." But what if you should fall in love? I asked. She would not fall in love, she answered. Moon apparently controlled even the most private parts of her heart. In any case, she said, Moon did not permit his disciples to become engaged until they were twenty-four; Wendy was only twenty-two. Moon relaxed his rule in Wendy's case—why is anybody's guess.

When I spoke with Wendy in mid-May, over the telephone, she was bubbly—but cautious. She had been matched, she said, with a young man who was studying "naturopathic medicine" in New York. She would say no more about him.

Did she feel "ready" now?

Of course. Moon had told her she was ready.

Would she tell her parents?

"I'm not really sure how to tell them. They don't like the idea of 'the blessing.' But I think," she added quaintly, "my 'fancy' will win their hearts."

A month later I spoke to Carolyn and Elton Helander. Wendy had not seen fit to tell them about her engagement; they'd read about it in the newspaper—a humiliation, and a heartbreak.

"Oh, Barbara," Carolyn said, "think how you would feel if it was *your* daughter. . . . Did Wendy tell you whether she'd gotten the rain scarf we sent her?"

Another month passed. In mid-July, at eleven thirty P.M., Wendy telephoned her parents. A surprised Carolyn was so grateful to hear her daughter's voice that when she reported to me, she was both tearful and euphoric: "She didn't sound like herself. It was Wendy, but it wasn't *our* Wendy." Wendy had called to say that she was already married. Moon had relaxed yet another rule for her—in order, Carolyn and Elton surmise, to preclude any further move on the part of the Helanders to get the courts to return their daughter to them. Wendy, proclaiming her great happiness, told her parents she was married to a Moonie named Frank Fastiggi. She wants her parents to meet him "some day." "What day?" Carolyn pressed. "I'm so joyful," Wendy answered. Wendy and Frank are not living together. Nothing has changed for the Helanders.

The night Carolyn called me with her news I prayed for my daughter—and for Wendy Helander.

THE OTHER HUSTLE:

Breaktime:
Living Without Work
in a Nine-to-Five World
by Bernard Lefkowitz*

(August, 1979)

This is a book about people who have chosen, for a variety of reasons—chief among which is self-indulgence masquerading as idealism—not to work, written by a reporter whose intelligence is spongelike rather than analytical. *Breaktime* is painful, sad, troubling, and confusing. I am not sure that Bernard Lefkowitz—who does not pretend to be a sociologist, a philosopher, or a moralist—knows exactly how troubling the implications of his study are; nor, for that matter, am I convinced that he understands that he has inadvertently raised a host of vexing questions about the quality of life, private and public, in America. What is clear, I am afraid, is that Mr. Lefkowitz has written a cynical book in the belief that he has written an optimistic one. He has also written a messy, disjointed book. Little wonder: people who don't work make people who do work nervous—even those people who, like Mr. Lefkowitz, express more than a little sympathy for men and women who disdain the "rat race" and choose not to hustle for a paycheck.

The reason for our nervousness lies, I think, not so much in the fact that we feel nonworkers threaten the cherished American work ethic (it is hardly a secret, after all, that many jobs are dehumanizing, dead-ended, and, in a word, perfectly awful); the reason is that employable, middle-class people who

*Hawthorn Books, 1979

wheel and deal and manipulate in order to live on unemployment insurance, on welfare and food stamps—or on the earnings of their often embittered spouses—work just as hard at not working as they would at working, and with very little to show for it except a smug self-righteousness entirely inappropriate to their circumstances. The people Mr. Lefkowitz encountered in the course of his work as a journalist and a consultant to the Ford Foundation left the marketplace so as not to hustle; they are now engaged in a different—but equally debilitating—hustle. And there are few things so unedifying as the spectacle of parasitical, self-deluding people who celebrate the chains they forge for themselves in the name of "freedom," "self-fulfillment," and "personal growth."

Mr. Lefkowitz makes me nervous because he is unwilling to make distinctions between jobs and careers, or work (in the sense of vocation) and labor for pay. Nor does his book adequately address itself to the role of technology in disinheriting Americans from significant, satisfying work. (I am trying to avoid the term "meaningful work," because the people he interviewed use that catch phrase to explain or justify their peculiar brands of chicanery almost as often as they blather on about "finding themselves.") If Mr. Lefkowitz is right when he says that forty percent of the unemployed choose not to work, we are dealing with a profound and widespread malaise. Mr. Lefkowitz is interested almost exclusively in personal solutions to what is surely an affliction of the body politic—and the personal solutions don't (if you'll excuse the play on words) work.

In the words of Kahlil Gibran (whom I never thought I'd catch myself quoting; but there you are, this book has made me irritable), "Work is love made visible. And if you cannot work with love but only with distaste, it is better that you should leave your work . . . and take alms of those who work with joy." Thomas Carlyle said, "All work . . . is noble; . . . work is alone

noble." The Benedictines say, "To work is to pray." Most of
the one hundred people Mr. Lefkowitz interviewed are engaged in taking alms. Put less kindly, they are ripping off
taxpayers (justifying their doing so on the ground that corporations and the government have ripped *them* off). Far from
regarding work as noble, they define work as a botheration, as
little more than a distraction from leisure or ease. They don't,
God knows, pray, though many of them are engaged in a search
for some vague, ectoplasmic, "laid-back" "spirituality," which
they are hard-pressed to define. For almost all of them, "work
is like any other convenient shelter. You stay as long as it's
comfortable. When things begin to break down, when the
paint starts to peel, when roaches invade the kitchen, you
move." And because they regard work, family, and children as
a package, they move on as soon as the novelty of marriage
fades, as soon as the children threaten to become burdensome.
(In this subculture loyalty, responsibility, discipline, and commitment—so quaint, so old-fashioned, so bourgeois and confining—count for very little; what counts is "commitment to
oneself," whatever that may mean.) With few exceptions these
people are boring and duplicitous, and I wish they'd conduct
their search for "personal development" in discreet and dignified silence.

Case histories: Martha Gorham (Mr. Lefkowitz does not use
real names) is "a teacher, school administrator, actress, organ-
izer for Hadassah, suburbanite wife, and mother." She also
whines a lot. The Hadassah bureaucracy got her down: "It
wasn't fulfilling . . . I'm an idealist." "Her children left her no
choice but to split because they [had] become a burden." She
had an extramarital affair, and a "wise doctor absolved" her,
and she went on her "merry way." Good-bye husband, nine-
and eleven-year-old kids (leaving them was "heavy"); hello est,
Esalen, a communal residence in Boulder where nobody "lays
trips" on her, and group sex—"I'd been repressed in that area.

. . . It's just what feels good to me now." She found a group that instructs people in the science of eating without working; they helped her to understand that it was okay to steal from the government, okay to lie. Maybe some day she'll go back to work—she'd "like a color TV."

Charles Braithwaite is a black journalist who covered important stories—civil-rights demonstrations, riots in Harlem and Newark. Nevertheless, he says (the exact nature of his grievance is unclear), "I never felt the relationship between my ideas and my work," or between his "emotional life and the white organizations he served." He engineered his dismissal so that he could collect unemployment insurance. When he left his job, he left his wife and children; now he can have picnics in the park, "unencumbered." He no longer writes: "The writing is in my mind, in my eyes." Uh-huh. Not working, he says, "gives me an opportunity to be generous" to neighbors, friends, strangers. But not to his children; he does not help his own kids. Mr. Lefkowitz says: "Such triumphs should be celebrated." He is looking for "the perfect job." In the meantime, food stamps and, according to Mr. Lefkowitz, "fresh reserves of kindness, generosity, and empathy."

Arthur Schwartz is a tenured professor in the Middle West. "After 25 years in the academic world, Schwartz felt he had been knifed, double-crossed by a callous administration that didn't give a damn about the students or dedicated teachers. . . . 'I represented a threat to the school's apathy and superficiality.' " His not seeking work, however, has in reality nothing to do with "idealism": "I'm breaking out of my role, the husband, the provider. My wife'd want me to take any job, security is so important to her. By not doing that, I'm separating myself from her. I'm declaring my independence." Unable to tell his wife directly that he wants a divorce, what he is in fact declaring is his cowardice. He hopes to wear her down by attrition. He lives on unemployment insurance.

Without wives and mistresses—and mothers and fathers— the nonworking men in this book could not pursue the happiness (read *idleness*) to which they believe they are entitled. For the most part, it is women who support the men who refuse to be "competitive"; a case in point is the man, "retired," who used to be a contract hitter for organized-crime families. He regards the woman with whom he lives as "a bank account. I'll never have to do anything again. She'll take care of me."

That's the trouble, of course. There are several men and women in this book for whom one is able to feel some genuine sympathy: disaffected and disillusioned for good reason, they found their work lives intolerable. But, in almost every instance, they purchased their happiness at the expense of others. The victims became victimizers. Nasty. And, according to Mr. Lefkowitz, a form of hustle that is increasingly sanctioned by the community at large—few reproach those who manage to get away with it.

I agree with sociologist Peter Berger, whom Mr. Lefkowitz quotes: "To be human and to work appear as inextricably intertwined notions. To work means to modify the world as it is found. . . . To work is to mime creation itself."

Of course, I am obliged to suspect my own motives in writing in this vein. I am one of the world's lucky ones: I love my work. As a reality test, I called my father, a printer who worked, as the saying goes, all his life, and who now lives on Social Security, unable to pay his medical bills, his union pension fund gone bust—the very plight the work dropouts rail against. "Daddy, if you had it to do all over again . . ." "Remember the chicken livers?" he answered. "Your grandfather [an immigrant carpenter from Calabria] brought you chicken livers from the kitchen of the hospital he worked in when he first came to America. To the day he died, he believed that those chicken livers saved you from scarlet fever. How's that for a fringe benefit? . . . Sure I'm broke; but you had roller skates when you were a kid. And I'll never forget the noise of the presses and the smell of the ink . . . and besides, I like to play poker with the guys at the union hall. They all remember old Dom. They love me." Yes. Sometimes I watch my old father lovingly touch the printed page with his fingers, as if to extract the meaning of his life from this tactile pleasure. And I am confirmed in my belief in the sanctity of work, a necessary discipline and—with good faith and good luck—a source of community and a joy.

Naturally one must concede that most jobs are so rigidly structured and claustrophobic, so devoid of any reward except the financial, as to drive people to wild extremes to escape from what they have come to perceive as servitude. Life plays dirty tricks on good people, and only the strong survive. (Mr. Lefkowitz does give one splendid example of a dispossessed black farmer, Betty Tallgood, who turned her enforced leisure to noble use, helping to form farming cooperatives in the Mississippi Delta.) It would be presumptuous to talk about the nobility and joy of work in the context of textile sweatshops, to the miners dying of black lung, to the woman with five kids who works in the dime store. These are the ones who merit compassion, the ones for whom public solutions must be found. But Mr. Lefkowitz is not writing about them. It is the spoiled brats who compel his attention. And that is a shame, and an affront to working people.

"JESUS WEPT":
Billy Graham: a Parable
of the American Righteousness
by Marshall Frady*

(July, 1979)

This is a flawed and fascinating book, flawed not so much because of the florid language to which critics have alluded—the southern rococo overembellishment that sometimes makes one feel as if one were about to be buried under decaying magnolia blossoms—but because of the idolatry that lies at the heart of Frady's study of Graham, the terminal infatuation of the biographer with his subject. Here lies an irony: Frady acknowledges not only his initial "huge liking for and empathy with Graham [and] . . . the greatest enthusiasms about everything around him," but the obligation of a biographer to later "withdraw into a detachment, a remove almost of impersonality." Of course Frady is correct when he suggests that in order to solicit information about a subject one must be enthralled by that subject. Interviewers who claim they get their stuff by "seducing" their interviewees have it backwards; in writing profiles, it is the interviewer who must allow himself to be seduced . . . until, and only until, the ruthless act of writing begins. At that point, if one allows one's judgment to be perverted by one's affection, the subject will be perversely romanticized. That is what has happened here.

Frady persists in seeing Billy Graham as "wholly guileless and winsomely self-effacing," as possessed of "simple huge

*Little, Brown and Company, 1979

goodwill," as "commanding, splendid," "thin and clean and shining," "arresting," a "luminous young divine," an "imperishable country boy innocent," "tall and lordly and luminous," a "blond, valorous prince out of a Nordic fairy tale" governed by "righteous sensitivities" and "childlike unblinking goodness," as "Adam first stepped forth out of the soft flare of his own Creation, striding bright and silvery-eyed [*silvery-* eyed?] in the Garden. . . ." This is the language of love, applied to a man who—on Frady's own meticulously documented evidence—is shallow, banal, insensitive, megalomaniacal, a dissembler who "has succeeded in acquainting himself with everything while finally understanding nothing." Frady cannot resist coming to that conclusion; his honesty propels him to it. On the other hand, he cannot resist being drawn to Graham, either. So his book has a peculiarly elegaic quality as well as a schizophrenic one. The language is tortured because Frady's intelligence is at war with his emotions: the facts damn Graham; the language exalts him.

A Parable of the American Righteousness, this biography is subtitled; and throughout the book—which, let us say at once, has been exhaustively and honorably researched and which abounds in nicely rendered detail—there are troubling confusions that resonate around that word *righteous.* Wading through the treacly prose, the reader anxiously looks for reassurance that Frady knows absolutely the difference between niceness and goodness, between innocence and willful ignorance, between the need (Graham's) for approval and the desire (Graham's) for worldly power. Graham has sprinkled stardust in Frady's eyes. There is something soft at the core here: brilliant though Frady's insights often are, he cannot quite get Graham in sharp focus; nor, however much he strains, can he make a clean and clear parallel between America's "righteousness" and America's prophet, Billy Graham. The nature of both eludes him; bedazzled, his vision falters. The giveaway is that Frady is reduced, in the end, to calling Graham a tragic hero. No. To call Graham tragic is to relieve him of responsibility for his acts (or, more to the point, his nonaction); it is to imply that an impersonal fate decreed a rise, a fall. If we regard someone as tragic, we are able to regard blemishes with an excess of tenderness, or, at least, to see them as indignities visited upon him by others. No. Billy Graham is not Billy Budd, a "child-man" to whom "double meanings and insinuations [were] quite foreign"; Richard Nixon, in his "wantonness of atrocity," is not Graham's Claggert; Graham is not, Budd-like, "unsuspecting and helpless." Frady invokes Melville to describe Graham's "fresh and simple goodness," but that helplessness and that goodness look more—on Frady's own evidence—like a determined pragmatism, a desire to ingratiate that is so refined as to amount to cunning, a pragmatism that stems from a lust to be Caesar's buddy, to share in Caesar's power. This is so abundantly clear that Frady (the son of a Southern Baptist preacher) skitters away, finally, from a task he has set himself: "to measure and play everything against the nature and implications of Jesus' own ministry and message." The reader must do his job for him—infer, extrapolate. Frady will not, or cannot, sacrifice his original vision of Graham even in the interest of truth. . . . How terribly difficult this book must have been for him to write!

It is true, as Frady says, that Graham has existed in our minds "largely as a cliché, a kind of animated mannikin." (To watch one of Graham's TV Crusades does nothing to eradicate this image.) And Frady succeeds admirably—in spite of the flowery language of love that insinuates itself between the reader and Frady's subject and threatens to muffle all definition—in allowing Graham's "faithful and his critics as well as those simply curious about him" to "know the man as they'd never known him before."

Billy Graham likes to talk about the "acres of hard red clay where my father eked out a bare subsistence." In fact, Graham's father was a prosperous, abstemious young farmer, over whom, says Frady, "disembodied charges of sheer guilt . . . hung so muggily in the general religious weathers." His free-floating guilt was dispelled when, at eighteen, as he rode in a buggy, "the light from heaven broke over my soul, and a great burden just rolled off my heart." After that, so orderly and respectable did Frank Graham become, he wore a tie and hat even when he was manning his tractor. The elder Graham's piety was, however, not accompanied by anything resembling an aroused social conscience: according to a former neighbor, "Those poor tenants who worked on his place, he hardly paid them anything at all, it was really shameful." He was manipulative and less than scrupulous in his business dealings, and everything he touched turned to profit; meanwhile, he continued to worry about the state of his soul. Billy Graham did not cry at his father's funeral. He remembers the beatings he received at his hands.

"He was always sweating, always sweaty," Graham says about his father; but his mother—"she was very much a lady." A lady, according to Frady, with "a certain chaste vanilla freshness" about her (oh, yes; Frady can make language work for him), a lady who took a Bible with her on her honeymoon and who spends her declining years watching TV, especially the Waltons. "That's just the way we used to be," she says. Frady says she was "a kind of winter madonna of the nice, the pure." He also says she beat her son with a hickory stick.

(And, in case you're wondering—yes, of course Billy Graham "spanked" his own five kids. But not without a recitation of their transgressions and a scriptural reading first and a prayer afterward. Never in heat or in anger. Always in the spirit of rectitude, probity, respectability. Silvery-eyed.)

With his genteel mother—who believed above all in the seemly, the pleasant, the nice—and his business-shrewd father, and with an uncle who had lurid, pop-religious, sentimental apocalyptic fantasies, Sabbath-keeping Billy Graham grew up "a glad and easy country princeling, his own world simple and bright and blithe . . . as if he had about him . . . some quality of an aboriginal moralness beyond all catechisms and hymn-books." Well, perhaps not quite so simple, so moral, so blithe as Frady would like to believe: Graham is remembered by neighbors as a prissy tattletale who initiated mischief and didn't take responsibility for it. This "young Gabriel" drove his father's car hell-bent-for-leather at night. When racing companions had a near accident, "he just immediately turned around, never even stopped to talk or check on us." Meanwhile, in high school, the boy who, according to his biographer, "had acquired the arresting look almost of some young country archangel," had trouble keeping up his grades. Frady (poor thing, he just can't help himself) says it was "as if all cerebration, all intellection and abstraction beyond the immediate and spontaneously experienced, were simply alien to him—almost as if he were one of those accidental pure specimens the Elizabethans called, in that ultimate and mystic sense of the word, a Natural." Graham's high school principal says, rather more to the point, "There was never any actual question of his graduating. His daddy happened to be chairman of the school board."

Indeed, Graham may not have loved his father, but he knew when to use him (he learned very early the uses of temporal power). Once he commanded an irate garage mechanic not to take the name of the Lord in vain. When the workman threatened to shut the priggish teenager up with force, Billy Graham countered, "I'll tell my daddy if you do that. My daddy's Mr. Frank Graham and he brings all his Deere trucks in here." Like his father, Graham honored—as he was later to celebrate—established law and order: "Long as there's a white barbershop in Charlotte," he said, "I'll never have my hair cut at a nigger barbershop. Never."

When he was seventeen, Billy Graham came under the influence of one Mordecai Ham, a choleric preacher who ranted against "International Jewry." At one of Ham's revival meetings, Graham was "saved." Questioned about Ham's anti-Semitism years later, Graham said, "I'm sure there was some while Ham was in Charlotte, but I never noticed it. . . . I just got caught up in the services." What the external manifestations of his "decision for Christ" were it's difficult to say. It's doubtful whether it even provided a moment's orgasmic release from the ordinary: Graham couldn't forswear dancing or drinking because he was already an abstainer (although he did "kiss girls until his mouth was chapped"). His curiously unemotional experience of Christ simply made him determined to be "nicer," more pleasant. It did not lead him to any profound insights as to the ways in which politics and morality intersect, or partake of one another. In his beginning was his end: civil rights, Vietnam, and finally Watergate—his mind never ranged over the rugged terrain where the worldly and the sacred meet; there has never been for him that flash point of disinterested moral indignation that is the fiercest form of Christian love.

He determined to become a preacher almost the way a provincial Spaniard determines to become a bullfighter. It was a way, sanctioned, out of his small town and into a larger world. (For a while he had wanted to be a baseball player.) That determination lost him his first girl friend, Pauline, a worldly, pretty young woman upon whom Graham showered gifts of Evening in Paris. As Frady writes perceptively, "This confoundment—the impossible inconsonance between her own spirit and the 'salvation' he had in mind, seems to have told him nothing, indicated nothing to him of what that salvation might actually mean, or that it might hold something less than universal validity."

In a more romantic vein, Frady—who says Pauline now remembers nostalgically the "sweetness" of her dates with Graham in the backseat of his father's Plymouth—writes about powerful lost women who

> seem to behold in [Graham] the palpable image of what they somehow missed in their own men through their lives: that lost bright man-angel of their sweet American maid-enhoods back in that brief nebula of time when they were good and pure and undamaged, their whole life a soft pastel shimmering of possibilities, and they knew and be-lieved in a potential of love as they never would again.

As one who is impervious to Graham's charms, I am inclined to believe that this is a fancy way of saying that Graham's "innocence" consisted, then, of sexual gaucherie. (Graham himself says he "never engaged in sexual immorality. For some reason God kept me clean." Besides, he adds, he was "just shy.") If his "innocence" then was in fact nothing more than sexual passivity, later, I believe, it took the form of passivity in the face of evil, a deadly blandness, a complicity with wrongdo-ing, an inability to feel remorse . . . which is, of course, one definition of sin.

After a short stint as a Fuller Brush salesman ("Sincerity is the biggest part of selling anything . . . including salvation," Graham was later to say, in the time-honored tradition of American entrepreneurial preachers), he went to the Florida Bible Institute near Tampa, where he distinguished himself by wearing "radiant bow ties, pinstripe suits of primary colors, suede shoes in maroon and rust and purple." There the desire to preach suddenly deserted him. The man who was later to call St. Paul "an ardent sports fan" and to insist upon the virility of Christ—"a real he-man, a real man who had a strong jaw and strong shoulders"—saw preachers as revoltingly "weak"; he thought there were more "masculine" ways of living. At this time Graham fell in love with a girl named Emily, about whom he says (in a line worthy of Woody Allen): "She was a deeply spiritual girl, beautiful, brunette, highly dedicated." Frady, piling it on, says she "seemed the utter fulfillment of all his heart's glad and simple poetries." But Emily—"eyes sweetly spangling in a face with the clear glow of a candlelit chapel madonna"—rejected him, "indicating that he seemed a bit spiritually frivolous to her."

What happened next seems almost too good—by which I mean too stagey—to be true: Graham had what Frady (whose editor must have been asleep) calls an "eighteenth-hole catharsis of heart": "On the eighteenth green of the golf course . . . Graham experienced at last his true-climactic Gethsemane . . . 'All right, Lord! . . . If I'm never to get Emily, I'm gonna follow you. . . . You can have all of me from now on.' "

Soon after that epiphany, Billy Graham became a member of a posse tracking down "two Christians" suspected of sexual offenses. The sight of a naked man skulking in a closet did for Graham what the Depression, segregation, the poverty of tenant farmers, did not: "That incident . . . constituted the first trauma visited on the simplicities of his vision of goodness . . . his instant reflex was to contract more fixedly into the certitudes of his simplicity."

Salacious certitudes, one might add. Even Frady acknowledges that when Graham speaks of the sins of the flesh, "there seems to be a certain extra smack and vibrancy in his enunciation, a higher vigor in his movements." The flesh, for him, was intrinsically evil; he took four or five baths or showers daily: "It gets the poison out." When he achieved fame, he said: "I determined I would never walk alone with my secretary, never have lunch or ride alone in a car with her. . . ." For a while he was obsessed with the notion that a beautiful "demon-possessed woman" would be the agent of his destruction. Upon his first visit to England, Graham told reporters that London parks were unfit to walk in: "I was so embarrassed, I took my wife out of them." Pressed for details, he blurted, "We saw two couples in the midst of the sex act in broad daylight."

He was repulsed by sex and fascinated by it; he was magnetized by power.

At Wheaton College, "a doctrinaire evangelical conservatory" south of Chicago, Graham met Ruth Bell, and "fell in love with her at first sight." She looked, he says, like his mother; she even sounded like her. She was the daughter of Presbyterian missionaries, reared in China. One of the family's favorite pastimes was to put on "in full costume and blackface with mandolins and guitars their own minstrel shows." Decorous, insular—"quarantined," Frady says—she might have been brought up in Iowa. Their attraction was "spiritual," their courtship antiseptic; three years after they declared themselves, they exchanged "their first full kiss." In 1943, when Billy Graham was twenty-four, two years after the kiss and after several doctrinal debates threatened to disturb their peace, they were married. Graham spent his wedding night on the floor—"I don't mean right away, of course."

Graham began broadcasting locally; as a member of an evangelistic movement in America and Canada called Youth for Christ he spent seventy-five percent of his time away from Ruth, who moved in with her parents. With the birth of the second of their five children in 1946, Ruth and Billy Graham established joint residence. He was still home no more than two or three months of the year. Ruth flourished, Frady says, in isolation. She grew more handsome. "You get used to it," Ruth Graham says. "You keep busy. The best thing for any of us is keeping busy."

Is it morbid of me to find that statement chilling? I've heard it before: from overseas wives, on army bases, from wives whose husbands were roving diplomats, soldiers, mercenaries, and, yes, ministers . . . from women who coped and smiled and smiled and smiled—and sometimes cracked. I want to know more about Ruth Graham, a woman of silences, a woman who is said to have no moods, who—always ready with coffee and sympathy—never raises her voice in anger. One senses in her strength that is constrained, energy fiercely reined in; do I only imagine a slight hint of mockery in her voice when she addresses her husband? I wish Frady had been more interested in her. She had wanted, once, to be a missionary in Tibet. Does she ever regret her chosen domesticity, her satellite life? After her children were grown, for a brief while she took to riding motorcycles, hang-gliding, being towed by speedboats. She loved speed and motion. She spends her evenings now watching television. If she has regrets, to whom does she confess them?

By 1946 Graham, moving perkily through devastated Europe in sherbet-colored suits, had attracted the attention of William Randolph Hearst. By 1949 the AP, UPI, INS, *Time, Newsweek,* and *Life* were covering his Los Angeles Crusade. (And—God bless America—"before Graham finally left town, he was offered a screen test by Cecil B. DeMille.") An indomitable cold warrior, he soon counted Henry Luce, Sam Rayburn, and John Foster Dulles among his friends; Generalissimo and Madame Chiang Kai-shek were among his heroes. He appeared on the Bob Hope Show, *The Jack Benny Show, The Jackie Gleason Show,* with Steve Allen and with John Cameron Swayze. He won the Horatio Alger Award. When he came to New York—"Sodom"—in 1957, his New York executive committee included the president of Mutual Life of New York; Ogden Reid of the *Herald Tribune;* the president of Chase Manhattan; Captain Eddie Rickenbacker; William Randolph

Hearst, Jr. The finances for his Crusade were supervised by Howard E. Isham, vice president and treasurer of U.S. Steel. He had the support of the Vanderbilts, the Goulds, the Whitneys—as Dwight Moody before him had received the support of J. P. Morgan, and as Billy Sunday had received the support of John D. Rockefeller. And why not? Graham, friend of the military establishment, complicit in McCarthyism, was not above describing Paradise as a place with "no union dues, no labor leaders, no snakes." He accepted a $75,000 contribution from Russell Maguire, whose broker's license the SEC had revoked for flagrant violations. (But Graham was innocent/ignorant of this, and of Maguire's anti-Semitism.)

The 1950s were the halcyon years, lived in the glow of his association with Eisenhower—an association that, to Graham, who once said, "Boy, I sure hope they have a golf course up there," must have prefigured heaven. Truman had given him rather short shrift, and with JFK he had no more than a superficially amiable relationship. But for Eisenhower, Johnson, and of course for Nixon (for whom he served as "Pastor-without-Portfolio"), he acted both as religious court-jester, unquestioning and uncritical of authority, and as guru and comforter, assuring his elected leaders of their probity and righteousness.

Frady asks Graham if he was ever conscious of being used by those in power. Graham: "Well, I usually *thought* I could tell. . . ." But the question is silly; Frady might as well have asked if the right hand uses the left. They were all—including Graham, despite his protestations of political neutrality—powerful, and they all routinely used one another, exchanged blandishments, stroked one another's egos. (Bill Moyers is wonderful on this subject: he makes Graham and Johnson sound almost like Butch Cassidy and the Sundance Kid.) This is implicit in one of Frady's good anecdotes:

At the dedication of a $2 million Esso Standard building in Charlotte on the old pastures of the Graham farmland, Esso President William Naden proposed . . . "What a great combination it would be to have Billy Graham associated with Esso Standard Oil." Of course in a sense he already had been for some time.

Quite. By this time, Graham, with his vast constituency, was in his own way as much a power as any elected official. As he said when it was suggested that he run for office, "Why should I demote myself to be a Senator?"

Frady manages, with a blitz of words, to imply that Graham's relationship to power was like that of a poor hungry gangly country boy with his nose pressed against the bakery window; he is thus able to excuse—and even in some measure to find endearing—Graham's inordinate yearning for "the various appointments of earthly importance." He says that, starting with Eisenhower, Graham "entered a tragic equation." Graham is likened, by Frady, to Christ being tempted on the mountaintop by Satan. The analogy is false. Christ was not a social climber. (Graham: "I'm appealing to a higher-type social strata.") Christ did not seek to ingratiate himself with the Scribes and the Pharisees and with Pontius Pilate; his identification was with the lowly. When he rejected the principalities and the dominions of this world, he knew exactly the value of what he was refusing.

For Graham, there was no "tragedy"—only a logical progression that led in the end to Watergate, to his living almost as a prisoner in a pretty chintz-and-antique-filled house (paid for by the president of Sun Oil), surrounded by an eight-foot-high electrified fence surmounted by a sign: "Vicious Dogs . . . Trespassers Will Be Eaten."

If Frady's analyses of and digressions into the nature of good and evil are sometimes fuzzy, his anecdotes are marvelously—

terribly—revealing. Do read this book. Read what Graham has had to say about Vietnam—"We have all had our My Lais in one way or another . . . a thoughtless word . . . a selfish deed. . . . I've always been careful not to take any real position on the war"; about civil rights—"Only when Christ comes again will little white children of Alabama walk hand in hand with little black children"; about Watergate—"And all those people around [Nixon], Haldeman, Ehrlichman, Dwight Chapin— they seemed to be people who were so clean, so upstanding. . . . I think it was sleeping pills. Sleeping pills and demons." To read this is to agree with Frady that "evil is simply the advance of emptiness—an advance that, like cancer, has the appearance of a robust, bristling vitality. But its effect is a progressive, discreet etherizing of the true nerves of experience and meaning."

Bomb the Cambodians, Cardinal Spellman advised President Johnson. "Bomb them! Just bomb them." I am a Catholic; and I find that monstrous. But I find equally monstrous the coarseness of mind that allows Billy Graham to say, "We also had the problem of rats. The only difference between then and now is we didn't call upon the government to kill them. We killed our own!" (That's bad enough; what's worse is that, in spite of those expressed sentiments, expedience led Graham to lend verbal support to Lyndon Johnson's poverty program.) I find Graham's parochialism breathtakingly offensive (Dodsworth would have known better; Henry James would have been appalled): when our global TV prophet came back from India, he was moved to say, "Wouldn't it be a wonderful thing if we gave to India a beautiful new train, or Mr. Nehru a white air-conditioned Cadillac?" (His only recorded comment on Benares is that it had a superb amplifying system.) Is that monstrous or amusing (or possibly both dangerous *and* funny)? And what manner of man hears—on a golf course—that another man's brains have been blown out of his beautiful head and moralizes, "It was a terrible thing, but we must have a terrible shock sometimes to rouse us out of our spiritual neglect and apathy"? (He was talking about John F. Kennedy.)

It is this man: a man who "just drives himself nuts worrying all the time about whether he's got too much"—but divests himself of nothing. A man who has suffered from hernias, retina clots, pleurisies, ulcerative colitis, jaw abscesses, insomnia, urinary infections. . . . "Something is always breaking out somewhere," he says. He has had polyps and tumors on his forehead: "I was actually growing horns—polyps or whatever they were—these horns out of my mouth, out of my forehead." "I have the feeling that Satan's constantly laying land mines for me. . . . I'm sure I'm a prime target. . . . They've got this electronic equipment now. . . . I even watch what I say to my wife in our own bedroom now," he says.

Why do I think of Howard Hughes?

One of us—Frady or me—is deluded (or perhaps it is just that Frady is charitable and I am not). Graham's "own arrival at a peace" after Watergate, Frady says, was "his lifetime's most heroic triumph over despair." I do not believe that a dishonorable accommodation can be called "peace."

Will Campbell—scruffy, tobacco-chewing minister-activist of the Committee of Southern Churchmen—says: "Jesus judges us by what we do to the children, the prisoners, the whores, the addicts, the scared and bewildered, the poor, the hungry—to 'the least of them.' "

Billy Graham—voted in 1970 one of the ten best-dressed men in the world—says: "I've never known a moment of despair."

The Gospel according to St. John says: "Jesus wept."

Final Things

THE PROFOUND
HYPOCHONDRIAC

(May, 1977)

I come from a family that does not go gently into death.

My maternal grandfather—a feisty ninety-four-year-old—spent the day before he died hoarsely but vividly cursing at his forty-five-year-old female companion because she'd had the impertinence to pick tomatoes from the plants he permitted only his own gnarled, arthritic hands to touch. Borne to the hospital, he swore loudly, and in two languages, that he was unready and unwilling to die. Grandpa died with his shiny-black Sunday suit on, sitting up in a hospital chair. He said, embellishing his pronouncements with rude Italian gestures, that the angel of death was not going to catch him lying down —and neither were the nurses. His last words were (as he feebly shook his cane in the general direction of heaven), "I spit on death."

He shook a stick at death; my paternal grandmother might be said to have grinned defiantly at it: toward the end of her long life, she rose early in order to place her false teeth on the bathroom sink, deriving some satisfaction from the fact that the sight of them vexed her healthy daughters almost as much as the knowledge of her own increasing frailty vexed her.

My seventy-four-year-old father was recovering from two heart attacks and an embolism when a physician told him that he wanted to do an exploratory operation in his stomach. "You're not Columbus and I'm not a continent," my father said; "nobody's doing any exploring around here." Then he signed himself out of the hospital and hitchhiked three miles, in his pajamas, to his house in Brooklyn. He now adamantly insists that he never had a heart attack, cardiovascular testimony notwithstanding: indigestion, he says it was; "What do doctors know?" And he has a surefire remedy for the pains in his stomach: he eats a pound of raw hot peppers every day for lunch and washes them down with whiskey.

I admire these hardy souls who defy death, either by pretending it doesn't exist or by trying to outwit it or by executing gestures, spiteful or magnificent, to prove that they are equal to that ferocious force. I thought, however, before I sat down to write what was to have been a funny piece about hypochondria, that I, having resigned myself to my own mortality, was not of their company. I am a hypochondriac (although hysteria perhaps more aptly describes my physical alarms in the night . and in the morning and in the afternoon). Had you asked me a day before I wrote this article whether I was afraid of death, I would have answered, "No; but I am afraid of dying" (a fine, but real, distinction). But I've now remembered my own first encounter with death, and I'm beginning to wonder if my hypochondria isn't my own perverse way of whistling past the graveyard.

This is my first memory of death:

On my fifth birthday, I wore a dress of yellow watered silk, and I sat on the sun porch waiting for my aunt Lu to take me to the circus. But Aunt Lu had a dizzy spell, and in a fading, sliding voice she asked me to get her the spirits of ammonia we kept ready for medical emergencies, so I did; and she applied the evil-smelling stuff to her lawn handkerchief, breathed it in, consoled me . : . and six months later she was dead. She was twenty-four and very pretty when her rheumatic heart killed her; and they laid her out in a dress cut from the same bolt of cloth my watered-silk dress had come from, and put her slim body in a mahogany coffin surrounded by hothouse flowers in the living room of my grandmother's house. Consigned to an upper bedroom, to which the scent of flowers and burning candles and the sounds of wailing rose, feverishly exciting me, I was not permitted to enter the room of mourning. This well-intentioned device to preserve my peace served only to excite me beyond endurance; so on the night of the second day of ritual mourning, I crept down to the darkened living room—where even the massive formal furniture, stripped for the first time in my memory of its muslin dustcovers, looked strange and menacing—and forced myself to gaze at my lifeless, pretty, uninhabited aunt. I became violently ill; and I vowed never to die.

That awful experience may have been where my hypochondria originated; certainly ever since then I've been infatuated with my internal organs. And while I vowed never to die, I never vowed to shut up: I tell everybody who asks (and everybody who doesn't) how I feel.

I operate, I think, on the theory that if I broadcast my symptoms loudly and at length, making light of them, they'll have the grace to slink away. In this, I am the mirror image of my relatives, who seem to act on the premise that if once you *label* something, it becomes real; and if you pretend it doesn't exist, it will go away. "It's a sin to be sick" is a common, and very *fraught*, Italian expression.

It isn't funny.

But the way we deal with physical symptoms frequently has all the elements of farce. (I'm sure Aunt Lu—who understood that all comedy springs from the tragedy of the human condition—would understand that I am not being frivolous about her death.)

By this time, you may be wondering why I haven't been to a shrink about my hypochondria. I tried that. But unfortunately I'm phobic, too: my shrink's elevator was once out of order, and I was obliged to bump down nine flights of stairs, clinging to the banisters, on my rear end. (I'm afraid of steps.) I had a brilliant insight on the way down: my analyst was the last person in the world I'd ask for a helping hand. Anyway, I think I have my hypochondria psyched out. It all has to do with guilt.

Take *Dr. Fishbein's Handy Home Medical Advisor. Dr. Fishbein's Handy Home Medical Advisor* was the Gideon Bible of all the families I baby-sat for when I was a kid. I read it (the way young boys used to look at pictures in *National Geographic*) because it contained anatomical references I was unable to find anywhere else.

The first thing I learned from Dr. Fishbein was that I had gonorrhea. I was eleven years old at the time. Gonorrhea, it said there, was characterized by a bone spur on the heel. My frightened and uneducated eye saw a bone spur on each of my heels (and I didn't dare wear sandals until I was seventeen). Now, my heels are, as heels go, perfectly within the range of the normal—not beautiful, perhaps, but perfectly functional. The thing is, just before I gleaned this tidbit from Dr. Fishbein's *HHMA,* I'd had a spot of sexual experimentation with my friend Rosie. Not much, mind you, not even enough to make me qualify as a Kinsey statistic. But if you could get *you know what* from toilet seats, why (or so my eleven-year-old logic took me) couldn't you get it from soul-kissing Rosie on the back steps of her apartment building? And, to top it off, my chatty family chiropractor happened to mention to me, while he was popping my spine, that if he were to find a patient with VD, he'd have no recourse but to report her to the board of health. (I don't know why he offered me this gratuitous information, but he also fancied grapes and garlic as a cancer cure, so I guess it would be fair to say that his behavior and advice occasionally partook of the bizarre.) For six months I lived in terror, waiting for the board of health's white truck to come and cart me off to wherever it was they deposited vene-really diseased eleven-year-olds. And every time my mother went to visit the chiropractor, I hid out in the attic room.

Hypochondria and hysteria are strange and awful ailments. They strike like a thief in the night (and result in insomnia ... true hypochondriacs/hysterics don't count sheep, we count twinges, and spend restless hours locating and interpreting our pain). Very strange: I spent four years in India, a hypochon-driac's heaven (or hell); but with all the exotic illnesses avail-able to me there, I never once produced the symptoms of a single one.

The closest I've come to understanding this hiatus in my hypochondriacal life is that I was pregnant a lot of the time—and when I'm pregnant I feel invulnerable. I was also busy tending to the very real sicknesses of small babies, so I didn't have the time or the inclination to listen to what my internal organs were doing. (And I do mean *listen:* I spend an inordi-nate amount of time in bed, rolling around to see what foreign noises my body produces; I *thump* myself a lot, hoping—fearing—that the resultant noises will reveal something; and whenever I wheeze or cough or sneeze, I immediately duplicate the wheeze or cough or sneeze to hear what it has to tell me.)

Anyway, I was as fit as a fiddle in India; and when real emergencies—like a threatened miscarriage—arose, I dealt with them calmly and with aplomb, never doubting that my body or my doctors would see me through. (I think it's only fair to say that I love being pregnant, and I love menstruating. If you want to get psychological about it—I don't—you might say that I feel guilt-free when my body is doing what a woman's body is uniquely equipped to do.)

It wasn't until I returned from the land of cobras, pythons, typhoid, typhus, et al.—and left a marriage I had sleepwalked through (numbing both body and soul and repressing good as well as bad emotions and feelings)—that I renewed my nega-

tive interest in my body. My brain was like a tuning fork: it
picked up symptoms even Dr. Fishbein had never heard of.

When I read (entirely by mistake) an article in *Reader's
Digest* explaining "Your Body's Early Warning Signals," I had
every symptom for every killer disease (even prostate cancer,
until I realized that that one was biologically impossible). A
bursitis-like pain in one shoulder, according to this scary piece,
may presage lung cancer. I developed a bursitis-like pain in my
left shoulder. Pain in the chest was, of course, mentioned as
one of the symptoms of lung cancer. My chest cavity was one
massive pain. "A significant enlargement of the area around
the nails, called clubbing," was, I read, another symptom of
lung cancer. My fingernails became as great a cause of concern
to me as my heels had once been.

I also had the misfortune to read that a small percentage of
people who snore may be suffering from something called
apnea, a breath stoppage that can lead to high blood pressure
and heart disease. People who have apnea make sudden explosive noises—as if punctuating little zzzz's with one huge Z—
in their sleep. Ninety percent of those afflicted with apnea are
male—but I'm always convinced that I'm part of the freak ten
percent—just as I'm always convinced that it will be *my* head
on which somebody's air conditioner will decide to fall. (Unlike
Aristotle, I choose to believe in the improbable possible rather
than the possible improbable.) I snore. How am I to know that
I don't make explosive noises as well? Maybe lovers have been
too kind to tell me? (I asked my kids to make periodic bed
checks on me; they quite rightly refused to be partners to such
cuckoo goings-on.)

The point is that, like a first-year medical student, whatever
I read or hear about, I "get." For which reason I assiduously
avoid listening to doctor-gurus on television. I want Dr. Frank
Field to talk about the weather (and preferably about the
weather in Honolulu, where it can't hurt me), and not about

early-warning heart-attack symptoms, which I can acquire all by myself without his earnest advice.

I have a heart attack every night at approximately seven thirty. Now, my intellect tells me that one cannot have a heart attack every night at seven thirty and still be ambulatory. But what my intellect asserts, my viscera refute. Somebody once told me that aching molars were signs of an impending heart attack. (I wish people would keep information like this to themselves.) I happen to have two missing molars because when I was a kid I went to a poor people's $2-a-week alcoholic dentist (which is another story), so I tell myself that I can't be having an ache in a tooth that doesn't exist. But I immediately remind myself that amputees often feel pain in missing limbs —and I'm right back where I started.

No matter how often this scenario is repeated, each time I have a non-heart-attack heart attack, I tell myself, okay, last night it *was* gas—*this* time it's the real thing.

I call hospital emergency rooms; I hang up.

I frequently have heart attacks at dinner parties. I carry on as if nothing were happening—hyperventilating in between courses—because I want people to think of me as a woman who died gracefully and with dignity. It's only after the event that I tell jokes about it.

It isn't funny.

Why does my heart ache? Is it because I'm heartsick? Why do I have a lump in the back of my throat? Is it because of the tears I'm too controlled to shed? In classical hysteria, there is a conversion of psychic pain to body pain. When you're love-sore, you're body-sore. When poets talk of broken hearts, they are speaking of real physical pain located in the combat area —the wounded, assaulted heart, the citadel of affection. (And do I have that bursitis-like pain in my shoulder because I hold my arm scrunched up close against my body, tense, as if anticipating, or warding off, attack?)

Sometimes I wonder if I'm not a hypochondriac but a hysteric. When I was twenty-two, I broke away from a harsh, confining fundamentalist religion. My body did the work my will alone was not equal to. I physically could not walk up steps to ring doorbells in order to proselytize; and when I did make it to somebody's front door, nothing came out when I opened my mouth to speak—hysterical paralysis.

Philip Roth's right arm goes numb—I have it on good authority—whenever he sits down to type: hysteria. I have a friend who eloquently denies, as she lies swathed in cotton flannel and surrounded by hot-water bottles, that she is either a hypochondriac or a hysteric. She simply develops a head cold every time she has to board a plane to meet her lover: hysteria.

Another friend of mine—who visits a doctor at least four times a month—has invented another category for herself: she is pleased to call herself neither a hypochondriac nor a hysteric but "an alarmist." This same friend refutes my contention that I'm a hypochondriac. "You work and you socialize," she says. "You may have palpitations, but you function. True hypochondriacs escape anxiety-producing situations by feigning illness or creating symptoms in order to withdraw and retreat from their obligations. They use sickness as an attention-getter. You can command attention without forcing people to cater to your symptoms, so you're not a hypochondriac."

"What am I then?"

"A nut."

She bolsters her argument by pointing out that I almost never go to a doctor. She's right: I avoid doctors' offices the way lapsed Catholics avoid confessionals. (And I don't feel my breasts for lumps—because I'm afraid I'll find some; and I close my eyes to what my mother was good enough to call "beauty marks"—because if moles are changing shape or color on my person, I don't want to know about it. . . . *Don't* do what I do; it's *dumb.*) And she's wrong: the reason I don't go to doctors is precisely because I am so hypochondriacal I'm afraid they'll confirm my darkest fears. Also I'm afraid they'll yell at me.

Because—and this is the heart of the matter—why shouldn't they? The truth is, I think I deserve to have heart attacks and cancer. (I told you this was all about guilt.) I smoke; I eat too much. So (this is unconscious logic, but I know, in my lucid moments, that it's at the root of things), why shouldn't I be punished with a heart attack and/or cancer? It's as simple as cause and effect, reaping what one sows, the punishment fits the crime. I ought to have sufficient discipline to stop abusing my body; I don't. I make excuses for myself: "I live under pressure . . . the world is crazy . . . we're all a bit dippy . . . if it doesn't show one way it shows another . . . we all forge our own necessary homeostatic relationships with our environment. . . ." But I'm not convinced by my own excuses. I equate discipline with goodness, lack of discipline with serious wrongdoing; hence, I am a Bad Person; hence the nightly "heart attacks."

It gets more complicated: there is pain that springs, not from guilt, but from grief.

When my father was very ill, I reproduced his symptoms in my own body. I felt his pain. My father once reported that he had "water on the heart": since he so much distrusts doctors, he tends to make a verbal hash of their diagnoses, which he seldom gives more than half an ear to—for which I can hardly blame him, given the fact that doctors seem to love obscurity as much as they dislike the idea of socialized medicine. Anyway, that night I actually *heard* liquid sloshing around in my chest when I rolled around in bed. . . . .(I am perfectly capable of acquiring diseases that don't exist.) I knew what I was doing (on one level I knew); but, while I wasn't consciously inviting pain, it paid me hourly visits nonetheless.

And sometimes I have consciously invited it. When my children had painful accidents, I used a formula familiar, I'm

sure, to all mothers who have anguished over their children's
unbearable suffering, and to shamans and to faith healers: I
have a clear picture of myself sitting next to my son's hospital
bed, his broken-limbed body in traction, his face white with
fear and pain. . . . He is gripping my hand fiercely, as I tell him
to let the pain flow from him to me; I want to bear his affliction. Magic; hocus-pocus. Neither of us actually believes that
I can become a vessel for his suffering, but we are both comforted, nevertheless; we are bonded together by his pain, literally joined—his hand never releases its grip on mine. (And now
I am remembering something else. My son is a stoic: when he
fractured his thigh, he never cried, he never cried *out.* But, in
the months of his healing, he would wake up suddenly in the
night and cry, "Mommy, are my eyes bleeding? Mommy, my
eyes are bleeding." He drew a veil over the horror. The tears
he did not shed became, in his nightmares, a veil of blood. He
didn't want to see—to see is to know; he didn't want to remember. His body chose a bloody metaphor for an experience that
threatened his life's blood. . . . That is the kind of collusion
between body and mind that we call hysteria.) And I have a
clear picture of my daughter lying in an intensive-care unit: she
seems to be in a deep, drug-induced sleep; but whenever I
break my vigil and move away from her bedside, a subliminal
alarm flashes in her brain; she cries, her voice fuzzy with pain,
"Mommy, come back; come near." I touch her; and she
resumes her steady, regular breathing.

As for my own hypochondriacal pain, compounded of guilt
and grief, and—let's face it—narcissism, I'd rather be without
it.

Well, actually, I'm not so sure. I went to a hypnotist once
(in order to lose weight), and as soon as he began to intone
Now all the pain will leave your body, I jerked up out of my
semitrance. "No," I said.

"No?"

"What would I be without my pain? Who would I be without my pain?"

I understood then—and the realization was terrible—that pain had become so much a part of my identity (a beloved intimate) that I was afraid to let go of it, because I couldn't imagine who I would be without it.

THE FACTS OF LIFE AND DEATH:
The View in Winter:
Reflections on Old Age
by Ronald Blythe*

(October, 1979)

Senescence: the word itself, with its insistent, hissing, forbidding sibilants, is ugly. But one reads—and I write about—this book, this lovely book, with joy. It would be impossible to overpraise Ronald Blythe's most excellent, wise, and lyrical book—a book that deals with facts that are hard and terrible, and yet manages to achieve a beauty that nourishes and astounds.

The View in Winter owes its beauty to the luminosity of Mr. Blythe's prose, to the profundity of his insights, to his unobtrusive compassion (which calls attention to his subject, not to himself), and, most of all, to the way in which he must have listened—whole-souled and, miraculously, without the static of preconceptions—to the men and women from whom he has elicited fragments of autobiography, "flakes of colourful minutiae," that are lucid and entirely without artifice or contrivance and, at the same time, so densely textured and mysterious as to be novelistic. There is the stuff of a dozen novels here; there is the stuff of life here. *The View in Winter* is "about" the aged and the dying. In fact—and it is to this that it owes its moral splendor—it is about life. Mr. Blythe listens; he sees. What he sees is that "they" are we; we are they: *they,* the aged, are not *other.* We share their mortal predicament. It does not follow

*Harcourt Brace Jovanovich, 1979

—such is Mr. Blythe's genius—that to read this book is to be afflicted with dismay, disgust, or despair, or to be seduced into resigning oneself, with pious sentimentality, to the fact that we must die. In the midst of life we are in death, our ancestors said. As Mr. Blythe points out, "to them it was a fact; to us it is a metaphor." What Mr. Blythe's book tells us—gorgeously, exhilaratingly—is that in the midst of death we are in life. That he conveys this message without sermonizing is a matter of no small wonder. *The View in Winter* is one of those books that have the power to alter one's moral universe. No one can read this book without looking at old people in a different way—more importantly, no one can read this book and no longer *look* at old people—for, as Mr. Blythe says, our crime has been to fear contagion from the elderly: "Some shutter falls across our vision to distance them from us—some adult version of 'Don't stare, it's rude,' which in this case means 'Don't look, it's myself, it's all of us.' " Afraid to see our future in theirs, we are "unable to love the old." However dutiful we are, we choose not to see them as "whole people." If circumstances oblige us to deal with the elderly, we are likely to do so with "angry patience."

In the process of looking at old people—"whose last fate . . . is to be toyed with by time . . . mutilated and mocked by it"—we must take a new look at our own lives because, like it or not, we are looking into a mirror. If Mr. Blythe has readers worthy of him, they will look; and they will allow themselves to be jarred loose from many of the doctrinaire notions—notions about sex, religion, and class, as well as about age—that they have held dear. What a dazzling accomplishment!

Ronald Blythe—highly acclaimed for his portrait of a rural Suffolk village, *Akenfield*—listens here, with that finely tuned internal apparatus of his that renders tape recorders redundant, to the voices of the aged in rural England and in Wales. Their voices are diverse, idiosyncratic: we hear aristocrats, former gamekeepers and housemaids for royalty, retired schoolmasters, miners and farmers, priests and empire builders and socialists, old veterans of World War I ("The Beloved Holocaust") for whom the Great War, with its imbecility and its comradeship, remains the moral pivot of their experience, in part because "they find themselves talking of something still sacred to themselves, but almost impossible to convey to their children." ("It is strange to think we are now very near the day when everyone who fought on the Western Front will be dead.")

These people do not dissemble about the present; they "drop the curtain." When time is short, one no longer troubles to speak in platitudes becoming to one's station. "A few/ drop/the masque by which the world . . . had known them and/confess/to what they really were. These masques were primarily those of orthodoxy hiding the married homosexual, the church-going unbeliever, and the heretic in the political party. More of a conspiratorial than a cowardly attitude was revealed in the reasons for wearing masques. All the world being a stage, it appears that there are far more people who get their dramatic kicks by operating its conventions than is suspected. The old, too, revealed conversions to a host of well-nigh forgotten causes and loyalty towards vanished concepts. . . . ('Ah,' said the eighty-year-old Henry Williamson gently, going through his snapshots, 'the S.S. . . .')."

In the course of listening and reporting, Mr. Blythe presents us with an unexcelled social history of the late nineteenth and early twentieth century: "Except for a few spiritual travellers . . . all movement in the talk is backward to youth and childhood. . . . They embark . . . for the beginning, where things still move fast and are bright and clearly defined." ("I was a bad boy and I'm glad ont!" says one seventy-nine-year-old: "Glad . . . Glad! . . . wholly merry in me day. . . . You couldn't exist then if you was too good. . . . It all comes back to me. . . . I'm a boy and I'm by that river, an' we're all there like we used to be. I can hear our talk as plain as plain. . . . I can smell that river and I can see us all so clear.")

Mr. Blythe also listens to children possessed of a devastating talent for honesty discuss their attitudes toward the aged, and he listens to those who care for old people—administrators of small nursing homes and public health visitors with a true vocation who are, blessedly, "unable to differentiate, so far as human contact is concerned, between the interesting things to be found in the personality of an octogenarian and in that of a man of any age." In his Introduction, and in the introductory remarks that preface each individual's "say," Mr. Blythe presents his analyses. It is to his very great credit that he never trims the evidence to fit a pet theory.

"Our earthly time allowance has rapidly shot up from an average of forty years to an average of seventy years plus within the experience of all the old people alive at present." Just as that is an almost impossible fact for our intelligence to grasp, it is one that our unruly emotions repudiate: "It secretly disturbs us to see old people talking and behaving as if they were in the midst of life. . . . One of the reasons why the old suffer is because those not old dislike the notion that the old are vital still. . . . The old have been made to feel that they have been sentenced to life and turned into a matter for public concern. . . . Such a situation can only alter when it becomes natural to say that the old *are* us—and to believe it. . . . This book listens to them talking."

Believe it! Mr. Blythe has helped me to believe it because he adamantly refuses to regard the aged as a lumpy, undifferentiated "class." (More concerned with underlying attitudes than with charting social programs—"the old do not want outreach, they want association"—he offers only one specific suggestion: because "the old become their own novelists when they fall into abstract street-watching," and because "to walk in the streets themselves puts them back into the story . . . what is clearly needed in every city centre, and particularly in vast new shops and public buildings, are many more seats.") He sees the elderly as unique and valuable human beings—as contrary, sexual, noble, spiritual, weary, exalted, messy, muddled, happy, accepting, denying, grouchy, pleasant . . . any adjective that can be applied to a man or woman in the prime of life can be applied to a man or woman of seventy, eighty, ninety, or one hundred. This ought not to come as a shock; nevertheless, it does. And I wish it were possible, in order to give justice to Mr. Blythe and to them, to quote them all.

I want to quote the seventy-seven-year-old chauffeur-mechanic whose lack of rancor is confounding, although in a refrain that echoes throughout this book, he says he's "Poor!" "People were dirt poor, dirt poor." "There you are," he says, "change, change, change" (another refrain of the aged). "The Lady went into the theatre, and then I'd find a place to park and sit in the motor. They never gave you anything. I used to find a bun and wait. They never thought anything about you at all. You were the servant. I tell myself I'm pleased those days are gone and then when I look back on them, I see that they were good days really. Life is very contradictory."

I want to quote the "handsome, urbane London bachelor" who says, "When I was a lad . . . we lived cheek by jowl with the nobility, and . . . my parents knew their station and accepted it. There wasn't the acrimony. There was this acceptance of class which made life interesting. Mind you, when one analyses it, one realizes that it was not quite right for one section of the community to have all this, and another to have nothing much. You can't argue that that's right. And I do regret the poverty when I was a boy—terrible, terrible poverty which wouldn't be understood now. [Again, a tragic refrain: "Nobody understands now," there is a "drying up of witness."]

Nevertheless, I regret the change in gracious living. . . . Unless you're a bloody idiot, if you've lived for eighty years you must know *something*! But for some reason you're not supposed to know what you know, or what the young know—not any more. But you do. That is why it hurts to be old."

Of course the poor—and the bachelor I have quoted above was reared in poverty—are often worse snobs than those with pretensions to gentility, as witness Walter, seventy-eight, who was brought up "in a world of such ghastly awful snobbery as you couldn't imagine today. . . . Mother being not *quite* mid-dle-class was a genius on class. . . . A movement, a vowel, the way a cake was taken off a plate . . . would suddenly reveal All, and her guest would be ticketed common. . . . Mother also believed that ladies had to give orders, and that to be an order-giver was really a great privilege given you by the Al-mighty, so you always had to remember this and Be Fair. . . . She gave orders all day long. To the servants, the children, to the tradespeople, and, before she went to sleep, to God. . . . Dear Mother, she worked hard to keep society unequal and they all loved her for it. And they knew they'd all helped her in their way."

Walter also says something interesting about sex, a subject in which the elderly man or woman finds it prudent to conceal any interest, lest he or she be considered "nasty," or "silly." He believes that a lot of old people who denigrate the young "are secretly enthralled" by them "but don't want people to see how much they attract them. . . . Using a framework of morals and manners is a way of talking openly about young bodies." (An-other old man, religious and robust, says casually, "bottom-pinching, you know. You have to watch that when you get old —bottom-pinching.") For bawdy old men and women, raucous and defiant, whose flesh has become absurd to them as well as to other people, Mr. Blythe appears to have admiration.

BARBARA GRIZZUTI HARRISON   *302*

(" 'There was a time when I could throw 'em over me shoulder.
. . . Now they're like two fried eggs! . . . Fancy my Ted
eighty-one! 'Ere, get him some whiskey. To warm him up.' ")
And why not?

"To be old today is to be contemptible." Part of the tragedy
of the old is that the middle-aged insist on believing that the
sexual passion of their elders is spent, whereas the truth is that
"old age is not an emancipation from desire for most of us."
It is terrible also to find one's intellectual passions mocked by
the passage of time: "It is a strange thing to be left behind by
later generations whose moral or material advance is due to the
heart-and-soul battles of one's youth. And stranger still to be
battling on when the cause has been won and forgotten.
Worse, to find that although the cause was a correct one
. . . it is now slotted into a general orthodoxy with no very great
addition to the sum of human happiness."

After we have heard the old men talk, we meet a Welsh
"town activist and wise woman, married [for seventy-three
years] to the local charmer. . . . The reforms they worked for
have long become a legislation which itself needs reforming."
They are sustained—in the Welsh mining village Mr. Blythe
describes so freshly—by the love they have for each other and
the memories they share of their passionate radicalism in the
black days of the coal-masters. They have become introverts;
remembering "those . . . happy, awful days, awful, awful, happy
days," they think of themselves as lovers. (What will happen
when one of them dies, one wonders? They are, after all, like
some two-headed animal; they are an endangered species. *They*
wonder. They know that to be old is to be in a stranger's world.)
We also meet a ninety-one-year-old Montessori teacher, who,
once part of an historic movement, has managed "without being defensive or reactionary . . . to stay one of the
'New Women of 1912.' " As Mr. Blythe says, the contact
with this woman, who at an early age discovered a truth

that exactly suited her personality, is "rather overwhelming."

Mr. Blythe understands the geography of the mind; he has also—as he so well demonstrated in *Akenfield*—a sure and true sense of physical landscape and the effect it has on the human spirit. As he talks of the old who grow old in the village, and of those who retire to the village to grow old, no nuance escapes him. He writes, exquisitely, about the sea-watchers on England's South Coast, their "unique calm." The ocean is "a powerful drug. It seems to extend life by exercising the intelligence outside of the factors which formed it. Those at the tail end of life are dragged into its pull and immersed in life's origins." The elderly at Eastbourne may be devitalized, but "the draining can be exquisite." And he writes of Cambridge, where "the old and the young appear to assert themselves with equal confidence and vigor." In this university town, old age is paraded almost as much as is youth—and the old are not freaks. (I am reminded of seeing at Oxford octogenarians whiz by on bikes, their academic gowns flying, while middle-aged shoppers labored along the High.)

Mr. Blythe brings his formidable intelligence and, most generous of listeners, his love, to an understanding of the young, too. Children talk, in one of the most wonderful sections of *The View in Winter*, and Mr. Blythe understands (what does he *not* understand?) that he is hearing one half of "one of the great dialogues of opposites." He sees linkings: just as "the cradle and the grave were once terribly adjacent," the very old and the very young are in some ways conspiratorial. Both groups must wail to prove, in a world governed by the middle-aged, that they matter: "Both have a terrible sense of being dictated to. . . . The young, who are great cravers, have a special sympathy with a final craving to have one's say. And that is the bond." The young are frankly affectionate ("I say that everybody who is alive fits in," a seventeen-year-old says); they are also frankly pitying and horrified ("My grandfather . . . thought of himself as being a boy of about twenty-two even when he was in his *seventies*. His seventies! I thought it was horrible . . . wrong. Horrible," another says.). Oh, I wish I could quote them all! Nothing I say in praise of Mr. Blythe can match his eloquence, and theirs—the poetry of dailiness that he celebrates.

Of course they think about dying: "The old woman awaiting death—or Meals on Wheels. When one is ninety, it becomes a merely academic matter which arrives first." Lady Thelma, ninety, thinks about her death, "naturally. You have to when you have a dog, don't you? I tell myself I'm thinking about death, but what I'm really thinking about is the dog. Death—dog, that's the way my mind goes now."

In stark contrast to those retired elderly who fall into purposelessness and out of consideration, in the final section of his book Mr. Blythe points to the aged members of the Anglican order of the Society of Saint John the Evangelist at Oxford, the Cowley Fathers. These modest old men are doubly blessed. They are secure in the knowledge that nothing can remove them from the community until they die; and they are part of a physically and intellectually active group that regards life as a natural entity, as a consequence of which their love and appreciation for the physical world is increased: "By constantly reminding themselves that the world to which they belong is not that of any one generation but the eternal world . . . they . . . make a positive effort to concern themselves with it for as long as they are part of it." When, in spite of all the familiar and beautiful disciplines, their spirits become parched and prayer dries up, they offer God what they have—"Nothing." Father Stephen, eighty-nine, says, "Be patient, be gentle, be *nothing*. Somebody said that the real message of old age was to give out love. So no more doing, but being." The founder of the order, Father Congreve, toward the end of his very long life, said—and these are words to cherish—"Memory sleeps, action sleeps, but love is awake. It does not think, or plan or labour to remember, but it loves; it is withdrawn from the surface of life to the centre."

Please do not think that in my vast admiration for this book I have quoted all the best bits. Treasures await you. It is rash to prophesy, but it does not take much imagination or courage to predict that *The View in Winter: Reflections on Old Age* will become another classic. I plan to keep it on my bookshelf next to Muriel Spark's *Memento Mori,* which is in some ways its fictional counterpart. I know that there will come a time when I will want and need and love it even more than I do now.

"It's all ages and ages ago, of course, years and years ago," says a ninety-two-year-old clergyman's widow: Life that was is life that is so long as there is anyone alive to remember it, and so long as those who remember it are honored.

ABOUT THE AUTHOR

BARBARA GRIZZUTI HARRISON was born in Brooklyn, New York. Besides *Visions of Glory*, she is the author of *Learning the Lie: Sexism in Schools* (1970) and numerous articles and reviews. She has lived in India, Libya, and Guatemala, and now resides in Brooklyn with her two children, where she is currently working on her first novel.

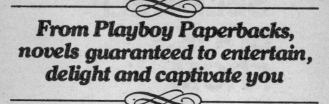

From Playboy Paperbacks,
novels guaranteed to entertain,
delight and captivate you